THE
NEW
PUBERTY

THE
NEW
PUBERTY

HOW TO NAVIGATE
EARLY DEVELOPMENT
IN TODAY'S GIRLS

LOUISE GREENSPAN, MD, AND
JULIANNA DEARDORFF, PhD
WITH KRISTIN LOBERG

RODALE.

Mention of specific companies, organizations, or authorities in this book does not imply endorsement by the author or publisher, nor does mention of specific companies, organizations, or authorities imply that they endorse this book, its author, or the publisher. Internet addresses and telephone numbers given in this book were accurate at the time it went to press.

© 2014 by Louise Greenspan, MD, and Julianna Deardorff, PhD

Rodale books may be purchased for business or promotional use or for special sales. For information, please write to:
Special Markets Department, Rodale Inc., 733 Third Avenue, New York, NY 10017

Printed in the United States of America

Rodale Inc. makes every effort to use acid-free ♾, recycled paper ♻.

Book interior design by Carol Angstadt

Library of Congress Cataloging-in-Publication Data is on file with the publisher.

ISBN 978-1-62336-342-0   trade hardcover

ISBN 978-1-62336-598-1   trade paperback

Distributed to the trade by Macmillan

2   4   6   8   10   9   7   5   3   1   hardcover

2   4   6   8   10   9   7   5   3   paperback

To the children we've worked with and treated through the years,
for teaching us what it's like to grow up today.

To the children we'll never meet,
for this is why we wrote the book.

And to our own children, EB, JB, RC, and AC,
for being a parent's greatest teacher.

CONTENTS

"Are you there God? It's me, Margaret. I just told my mother I want a bra. Please help me grow, God. You know where."

—Judy Blume, *Are You There God? It's Me, Margaret* (1970)

WELCOME TO THE NEW PUBERTY

Is She Entering Puberty Early?

ISABEL'S TRANSITION INTO PUBERTY WAS like that of millions of other girls, from a purely physical standpoint. After Isabel complained of discomfort in her left nipple, her mother noticed a bump under it that started to grow bigger. Within a few weeks, the same thing happened to her right nipple. The pediatrician noticed that Isabel's height had edged out of the average range since her last visit, and she was now taller than most of her peers. When the doctor examined Isabel's breasts, she confirmed that Isabel was developing breast tissue even though she had no pubic hair yet.

All of this would have reflected an ordinary start of puberty had it not been for one significant difference: Isabel wasn't a preteen with dreams of dancing with her current crush. She was just 7½ years old. When the doctor ordered a bone age x-ray, which would reveal how "old" Isabel was from a physiological standpoint, the results indicated that Isabel's bones were as biologically mature as those of a 9-year-old. (An image of the wrist and hand can determine if there's been long-term estrogen exposure, which causes early maturation.)

Further testing demonstrated that the hormones responsible for triggering her physical changes were coming from her pituitary gland, the initiator of puberty, which signals certain hormones to instigate the process. To rule out any rare anomalies like a brain tumor that could have sparked puberty, the doctor also ordered an MRI. Fortunately, it didn't reveal any abnormalities, so Isabel was deemed to be an otherwise healthy girl beginning puberty during the phase of her life when she was still playing house with her dolls.

Welcome to the new puberty.

If you've found yourself in panicky discussions with other parents or been reading media coverage about girls developing faster these days and entering puberty at an earlier age than previous generations, the reports are true. Indeed, a growing number of young girls are being catapulted into early physical development long before they are socially and emotionally ready for the change. According to the National Institutes of Health, puberty typically happens between ages 8 and 13 for girls, ending with sexual maturity and the ability to reproduce. Just a generation ago, less than 5 percent of girls started puberty before the age of 8; today, that percentage has more than doubled. In fact, our longitudinal study as part of the Breast Cancer and the Environment Research Program (BCERP), which assessed the onset of puberty in more than 1,200 girls who have been tracked since 2005 across three cities and was published in the medical journal *Pediatrics* in 2010, found that by age 7, more than 10 percent of Caucasian girls in America had started growing breasts, along with almost 25 percent of African American girls and 15 percent of Hispanic girls. And by age 8, those percentages had spiked to 18, 43, and 31, respectively. This begs the question: *What's going on?*

We'll answer that important question in this book. What hasn't changed is that puberty typically starts with breast development, then armpit and pubic hair, acne, a growth spurt, and, finally, menstruation. While it's easy to start wondering how environmental chemicals or dietary choices may be affecting our children's development, the new puberty reflects a much more complex set of circumstances than most people think. And it's often not nearly as dramatic as some feature stories would have you believe. Although many journalists have portrayed extremes, profiling 5-year-olds with the body odor of a teenager and shopping for bras with their mothers before heading to kindergarten, such examples are truly exceptional. The facts of early puberty for most girls are much less intimidating. In fact, even the words "puberty" and "normal" are grossly misunderstood by many people because popular perceptions of what is meant by these terms don't reflect the scientific literature. The good news is that despite the media's somewhat sensationalistic slant on this rapid turn of events for modern girls coming of age, this book aims to quell fears that going through puberty early is necessarily "bad" (or that there's something "wrong").

That said, traditional wisdom about how to help a child through puberty falls short when it comes to caring for a girl facing this transition early in her life. Parents, teachers, and professionals who work with children need much more than advice on how to talk about physical changes and sex; they require a host of skills that will help them teach girls how to appreciate and love their changing bodies and nurture their evolving identities, and also to help girls manage the eventual health risks their early puberty might carry. (Often these conversations don't even mention the birds and the bees.)

Girls who enter puberty early fall into two categories: There are the rare girls with known disorders like Central Precocious Puberty, wherein a girl's pubertal process starts abnormally early for unknown reasons or due to a defect in the nervous system, and then there are the bulk of the girls, who simply develop on the early side of the normal curve. But defining this "normal curve" has been a moving target for us in the medical community. Continual shifts in our scientific thinking about what characterizes a healthy normal-but-early puberty have not only provoked some debate among the experts who study it, but also led to much confusion and misinformation among the public. Throughout this book, we will dispel myths that have unfortunately begun to circulate over the last decade, since "early puberty" became a popular topic for discussion.

Take a moment to consider some of the questions that are probably on your mind as you begin this book. Is soy really an estrogenic time bomb? Do hormones in meat and dairy hurt a girl's reproductive health? Can early puberty be stopped or reversed? *Should* it be? What's causing girls to start their pubertal process at younger ages today? How could things have changed so much in just one generation? These are questions we field routinely—from parents, teachers, school administrators, doctors, and health professionals—and we trust you'll be as surprised and reassured as they have been by our answers. For those who are seeking immediate solutions for guiding and nurturing rapidly developing girls, either because you work in some capacity with such girls or because you have a daughter of your own, we will provide highly practical strategies (e.g., lists of things to do or avoid and scripts for talking to girls) for supporting children going through this experience. Whether you care for a girl who is years away from puberty or one who is already in the throes of this important transition, this book will help you prepare for whatever lies ahead. We understand the unique set of challenges that arise when puberty begins for a girl who hasn't even begun to fathom what that means or what's ahead of her.

Before we present an overview of the upcoming chapters, let us tell you a little about ourselves. We've been working in the trenches of child and adolescent health in both clinical and research settings for years, nearly our entire professional lives, and between us, we have covered every angle of the early puberty phenomenon. In 2005, we— Louise Greenspan, a pediatric endocrinologist, and Julie Deardorff, a clinical psychologist—teamed up to study the complex nuances inherent in the new puberty, which eventually inspired us to write this manual for managing its potential effects, from blessings in disguise to serious hazards. People affected by early puberty, from panicked parents to educators and leaders in health care, have long urged us to combine our wisdom to create a scientifically grounded and practical book that addresses their concerns. And this is just what we've done. Even though we're still in the midst of our research and unveiling new insights every day, we've accumulated plenty of knowledge over the past decade to create an essential guide that can equip you with the information you need to traverse this terrain. Some of our most helpful information stems from the encounters we have had with individuals and families who live and breathe this new reality daily.

We should also add that aside from our professional jobs as doctors and scientists, we are mothers of girls, too. We go home every day to young daughters who are entering puberty themselves. We compare our notes and observations all the time from a deeply personal perspective, for we've pondered all of these emotional and sometimes thorny issues as parents as well as providers. And we practice the rules we preach in this book in the hope that our own loved ones will enjoy a most fulfilling, good long life.

A LITTLE BACKGROUND

Our journey started more than 20 years ago, before we were bona fide doctors, when a trailblazing woman made an important observation in the late 1980s and bravely spoke up about it. It is said that many great leaps in science have occurred when an alert person stumbled across a major discovery and recognized its importance. Marcia Herman-Giddens's chance observation was no exception. At the time a physician's associate working in the pediatrics department of the Duke University Medical Center, she began noticing that many young girls she saw in her clinic had started to grow pubic hair and breasts earlier than expected. Back then, the medical books asserted that, on average, puberty began for girls at age 11. But Herman-Giddens was seeing something else, so she started collecting data, and eventually led a study with the American Academy of Pediatrics that sampled a little more than 17,000 girls across the country who had undergone physical exams in their doctors' offices. The cross-sectional study had 225 clinicians at pediatric practices rate the level of sexual maturation in girls 3 through 12 years old. The assessment led her to discover that, among white girls, the average age of breast budding was not 11 years old, but just under 10 years old. Among black girls, it was a little under 9.

In 1997, when Herman-Giddens published these numbers in *Pediatrics,* she was unprepared for the firestorm that her research unleashed both within the medical community and among the public. Some dubbed the sudden fascination with the sexuality of young girls "the Lolita syndrome," after Russian novelist Vladimir Nabokov's famous book *Lolita,* published in the 1950s, about a controversial sexual relationship between a 30-something man and a 12-year-old girl. Health professionals and parents alike instantly became interested in Herman-Giddens's slide shows that featured the possible culprits: obesity, processed foods, plastics, and even child abuse and salacious media. The questions started to mount: Was the age of puberty really falling? Parents and teachers testified that it was, while many leading pediatric endocrinologists refused to accept the new numbers. A wide range of professional opinions swirled.

A few doctors were quick to try to discredit the Herman-Giddens paper, because there was much controversy and discussion among pediatricians about whether the results were valid. Her research didn't adhere to some of the rigorous aspects of the scientific method. She had collected data on girls at physicians' offices (what we in scientific circles call a convenience sample) rather than generating a more diverse sample from the general population. Meanwhile Louise, who was then in her pediatrics training at the University of California at San Francisco, started to see an increasing number of girls coming to the hospital clinics with early pubertal development, so to her the results "felt" right clinically. While Louise learned to evaluate and take care of these children, it was definitely a new world in her area of specialty.

The challenge was twofold: One was to determine if these girls actually had a hormonal problem, or if they were just starting puberty early and were otherwise healthy and "normal." The other was answering parents' questions about what may have caused their daughters' troubling transformations and determining how best to teach the girls ways to cope with the unexpected changes in their bodies. Parents would ask Louise if puberty had been triggered by hormones in the milk or meat they fed their kids, and what else they might have done wrong in their homes or parenting to have caused it. They'd describe mood swings and other emotional hallmarks of adolescence in their 7-year-olds, and they'd also talk about their struggle to find appropriate ways to broach the subject of puberty and sexuality with their 8-year-olds. Louise tried her best to reassure them, but without fully understanding the causes of this new pattern herself, she wasn't sure these assurances rang true.

In 2002, an opportunity to get to the bottom of all this finally presented itself in the form of the ongoing CYGNET study, one of the most sweeping scientific undertakings to date in the puberty realm and one that finally sheds light on how environment, lifestyle, and genes affect the age at which girls start puberty. CYGNET stands for Cohort of Young Girls' Nutrition, Environment, and Transitions (subtitled Environmental and Genetic Determinants of Maturation of Girls); it's funded by the National Cancer Institute and National Institute of Environmental Health Sciences and is based at the Kaiser Permanente Division of Research in Oakland, California, where we conduct our research under the leadership of Lawrence Kushi, ScD. The study follows 444 girls from across the San Francisco Bay Area who became participants when they were between 6 and 8 years old. Now, in 2014, the study is in its 9th year and the girls are between the ages of 14 and 16. Although the research is ongoing, we've amassed an enormous amount of insightful data thus far, which is featured in this book.

The CYGNET study is actually part of the Breast Cancer and the Environment Research Program (BCERP), a network of studies across the United States that are examining what factors affect the start of puberty in girls and how that may further affect the eventual risk of breast cancer. So in addition to our local CYGNET study, similar puberty studies are being carried out at the Cincinnati Children's Hospital Medical Center and at the Icahn School of Medicine at Mount Sinai in New York City, for a total of more than 1,200 girl participants nationwide. (It was from these three studies that our 2010 *Pediatrics* paper was published, which helped confirm Herman-Giddens's findings from more than a decade earlier.)

Meanwhile, Julie's work in adolescent clinical psychology naturally led her to the same phenomenon and search for answers. A clinical psychologist and faculty member in public health at the University of California at Berkeley, for many years Julie was the sole clinical psychologist at the University of California at San Francisco's community-based adolescent reproductive health clinic, the New Generation Health Center, where she fielded hundreds of referrals from doctors and nurses to assess teens who were struggling with body-image issues, self-mutilation, domestic and relationship violence, substance use, depression, and anxiety, as well as sexual and reproductive health issues. Early in her career, she was initially most interested in the behaviors and emotions that were triggered by early puberty, but in the wake of Marcia Herman-Giddens's provocative study, she was besieged with questions from parents, doctors, teachers, and academics about whether this was a real phenomenon and, if so, what was causing it. This flurry of questions inspired her to expand her research and delve further into the determinants of puberty. But she knew that without working across disciplines, it would be impossible to fully explore and understand them due to the medical intricacies of the potential causes and the need to better understand the role of hormones.

This led us to form the perfect match when we met in 2005; we knew that our individual areas of expertise complemented one another well.

WHAT YOU'LL FIND IN THIS BOOK

The two of us have now been collaborators for nearly 10 years. Over the last decade, we have forged many partnerships with researchers who specialize in such diverse fields as diet and obesity, chemical exposure and endocrine-disrupting chemicals, physical activity, and social justice and poverty issues—all of which lend clarity and insight to this befuddling topic. Among the projects we've been privileged to take part in are the CYGNET study and, of course, this book, in which we step outside academia to share with you what we've learned. It's been a thrilling journey, one that has taken many intriguing twists and turns through the years as new theories come into play and science tries to tease out details from very difficult questions—some of which cannot be answered through a standard scientific experiment. We are, after all, dealing with a multifaceted subject incorporating many forces. It took years for the collaborative group of epidemiologists, nutritionists, toxicologists, and clinical scientists (as we both are) on CYGNET and in BCERP to develop a common language for talking about puberty, growth, development, and even "environmental" concerns. To the toxin experts, environmental exposure initially meant chemicals in the diet, air, water, and household products; to us, this also encompassed the neighborhood and family environments, as well as the environmental factors that influence risk for overweight and obesity. Once we got on the same page about how to define the problem, though, there was no stopping us.

In the fall of 2013, a major new paper from CYGNET and our partners participating in the BCERP was published that further established that girls are starting puberty earlier. We had tracked breast development—a key marker for the start of puberty—among 1,239 ethnically diverse girls from 2004 to 2011. This was an important study because previous ones hadn't followed the same girls over time as they progressed through puberty while measuring the multitude of factors that we were assessing. We found the average ages for the onset of breast development were approximately 8 years 9 months for African American girls, 9 years 3 months for Hispanic girls, and 9 years 8 months for Caucasian and Asian American girls.

Now that we have documented evidence that girls are in fact developing breasts earlier, the conversation is focused on what is causing this change and what the health implications are. Generally speaking, puberty involves three momentous events for girls: breast development, pubic (and later armpit) hair growth, and eventually the beginning of a menstrual cycle. These events usually happen in that order over the course of about 2 to 4 years. But there's an interesting discrepancy. While studies have revealed that the average age of breast budding has dropped significantly since the 1970s, the average age of a girl's first period, or menarche, in recent years has fallen only slightly, from 12 years 9 months to 12 years 6 months. How to explain this inconsistency? Why would the early signs of puberty be starting earlier, but not necessarily menstruation? Put another way: Why would today's girls be experiencing an extended interval between the time their physical bodies begin to develop and when they reach full maturation and become capable of reproduction?

> **NEW PUBERTY FACT**
>
> Girls today tend to experience breast budding at a much earlier age than girls in the 1970s, but they don't necessarily get their first period that much sooner than their 1970 counterparts.

That's exactly what we're going to explore in this book, along with many other mystifying aspects of this phenomenon. And we won't be highlighting just what we've amassed in our own work. We draw on the ideas and "best practices" gleaned from the entire field, so you'll become privy to the knowledge of high-profile physicians and psychologists who specialize in this area and work daily with families, as well as of pioneering neuroscientists, epidemiologists, and behavioral researchers who spend their days buried in traditional lab experimentation and field-work to add clarity and perspective to this growing new reality.

In the first chapter, we'll describe the journey that science has taken to understand "the new puberty" as well as our own hunt for answers. Although much of the research has taken place over the past decade, we'll go back in time to post–World War II Europe to see how we can put the new puberty in perspective. By showcasing science from the past, we make relevant how to best manage the new puberty today and execute the strategies we recommend for doing that. In Part I, we'll address many of the questions that are foremost on the minds of parents, teachers, coaches, and other caregivers, such as why early puberty is occurring (and might be here to stay) and how to ascertain what could be triggering it. Then, in Part II, we'll cover everything you need to know about the appropriate actions to take, including whether to pursue medical intervention. We want to equip you with enough information to avert panic and give you step-by-step guidance to move forward with calm and confidence. You'll learn how to manage poten-tial risks coming from the environment, how to establish healthy life-style habits in young girls, and how to talk openly to girls about what's happening in their changing bodies. Throughout the book, you'll learn vital skills for building and maintaining emotional closeness, which is essential to the bond between a parent and an early developing daughter.

Among the topics we're going to cover in the pages ahead:

- Why girls are developing faster today than just a generation ago. What are the six surprising potential sources of early puberty?

- The three biological origins of early puberty in the body. Why is knowing where in the body early puberty originates a criti-cal key to shaping a girl's future health?

- What signs to look for to determine if a girl is going through early puberty and what steps to take if she is. Should a specialist be consulted for medical intervention? What are the risks of taking a wait-and-see approach?

- What effects early puberty can have on a girl now and in the future. Why are early bloomers at a much higher risk for behavioral problems like drinking and drug use, as well as medical health challenges such as obesity, depression, eating disorders, and, later in life, reproductive cancers involving the breast and uterus? How can you help mitigate these risks? Will early puberty propel her to start having sex sooner? How is early puberty affecting her developing brain?

- How to initiate and continue to engage in difficult conversations with daughters in early puberty. Why is it essential for parents to have conversations with their girls about puberty and certain aspects of sexuality, no matter how uncomfortable they can be, and why is it important to avoid the "wait until they ask" approach espoused by many books on the subject? How can parents build and maintain emotional closeness with prematurely developing girls? How can you set special limits for a girl going through early puberty and handle the inevitable blowups of a preteen?

- What preventive steps a parent whose child is years away from puberty can take. What are the top 10 principles a parent can follow to build emotional closeness and reduce the risk her prepubescent daughter will go through puberty early?

In proposing a new definition of puberty for the 21st century, we're going to demonstrate that early puberty cannot be blamed on a single trigger. Environmental toxins and foodborne chemicals are not the only potential culprits; strong social and socioeconomic forces and family stressors as commonplace as high levels of conflict can all come into play. The effects of obesity also can have an impact. Once equipped with the facts and a game plan, you'll discover that taking charge of a girl's pubertal experience is manageable (and doesn't entail an unrealistic change in lifestyle).

A quick note about boys: It's beyond the scope of this book to cover the pubertal process in boys today and whether or not they too are hitting puberty earlier than before. Boys typically experience puberty later than girls, entering this phase sometime between the ages of 9 and 14. Although some data suggest that they too are starting sooner today, the jury is still out, and future research will reveal the truth. Boys' biology is different, and they, therefore, respond differently to certain environmental factors; obesity, for instance, which may contribute to a girl's early puberty due to increased estrogen levels, might *delay* a boy's puberty due to the same increase in estrogen. The thinking used to be that late-blooming boys had a tougher time than early bloomers, but now there's evidence that early puberty can negatively affect boys in a number of ways, both behaviorally and emotionally. Although we won't address boys specifically in this book, much of the advice we provide—how to encourage healthy habits and build emotional closeness, for example—applies to them as well. So if you have a son or work with boys in some capacity, you'll still find useful advice in this book.

There's no doubt we have a lot to learn in the fields of science and medicine about how early puberty affects girls physically and psychologically, both now and in the long run. Many girls who start maturing by age 8 progress swiftly and have their first periods at about age 10, and some parents choose to medicate with drugs under a doctor's surveillance to slow it all down. Other girls progress through puberty more slowly (even if they start early), and most girls do fine under the proper guidance of parents who feel confident that their daughters will get through this early passage without major problems. Put simply, girls who start puberty early don't necessarily have a medical problem. You'd

NEW PUBERTY FACT

Just because a girl enters puberty early doesn't necessarily mean she has a medical problem.

be surprised by what patience, knowledge, and perspective can do to assuage worries and discomfort. The vast majority of girls who start puberty early do not require any medical treatment whatsoever. Once we take parents through what we call the process of normalizing, which is intended to reduce the anxiety caused by alarming statistics, rarely do we encounter families who continue to insist on drugs to delay puberty. Most parents adapt to the new normal and learn to cope with the pubertal shifts, helping their daughters adjust. Stated another way, this book is by no means an advertisement for medical intervention or a treatise on how our "toxic world," as it's often labeled in the media, is having an impact on our young generation. Instead, we strive to simply relay the facts and provide the context that a parent or caregiver needs to appreciate, understand, and effectively navigate the new puberty.

Like many girls who go through puberty early, Isabel—the 7½-year-old whose transition to puberty you read about earlier—had a happy outcome. Over time, her parents helped her cope with her changing body by engaging in continuous open dialogue that reinforced their emotional closeness, and they made a few lifestyle shifts at home to diminish some of the potential associated health risks and to prepare her for maturing early. This included paying closer attention to Isabel's diet as well as her exercise and sleep habits to help optimize her body's innate physiology and protect her from becoming overweight or obese. Although her parents assumed she'd get her period early too, it arrived when she was 11— only slightly sooner than the majority of her peers. Admittedly, Isabel was a challenging case for us doctors because at barely 7½ years old, she stood on the border that delineates those who are treated with medication and those who are not. Her parents initially wanted Isabel's puberty halted with drugs, but in the end decided to let her body continue on its own course. When she turned 10, her parents struggled to encourage her to wear age-appropriate clothing in the face of social pressures from a group of older friends, but they weathered that storm using some additional tips featured in these pages that are proven to work on kids of this age who think they should be shopping at Forever 21.

We all want our children to grow into healthy, joyful, thriving adults. This is especially true when it comes to raising girls today, for we live in a society that increasingly celebrates accomplished women and those who maximize their talents and strengths. But doing so requires completing a successful journey through one of the most confusing time periods in a young girl's life: puberty. And when it happens early, it can be grueling—but it can also be rewarding.

At this point, you may be asking: Is my girl going through early puberty? On the next few pages is a questionnaire that you can use to help you determine whether or not your girl has started puberty. This will give you a general sense of where she lies on that pubertal continuum and yield a base for perusing the rest of the book. We also invite you to go to thenewpuberty.com for additional support and access to more resources that are continually updated. There, you'll find a comprehensive list of studies—many of which are mentioned in this book—and downloadable materials that will help you tailor the information in this book to your unique circumstances.

Let's get started.

EARLY PUBERTY QUESTIONNAIRE

Is She Entering Puberty Early?

The following questions will help you to determine where a girl might be in her pubertal process and whether scheduling an appointment with a doctor for further investigation is necessary. In upcoming chapters, you'll gain a full understanding of the difference between "normal puberty" and "normal early puberty." You'll also learn about the rare potential causes of abnormal puberty. Whether or not you choose to speak with a health professional right away, this book will equip you with the information you need to work with doctors, ask the right questions, and confidently pave the ideal path for the girl in your care.

1. Is she more than age 8 with breasts and/or pubic hair?

If yes, then it's probably no problem; this is normal early puberty. Pay special attention to Part II, where we outline practical strategies for navigating the road ahead.

2. Is she more than age 10 and menstruating?

If yes, then it's probably no problem; this is normal puberty. Pay special attention to Part II, where we outline practical strategies for navigating the road ahead.

3. Is she 7 or younger with breast buds?

If yes, then there may be a hormonal issue; schedule an appointment with the pediatrician and pay special attention to Chapter 4 for in-depth information that will prepare you for the doctor's visit.

4. Is she 6½ or younger with pubic hair?

If yes, then there may be a hormonal issue; schedule an appointment with the pediatrician and pay special attention to Chapter 4 for in-depth information that will prepare you for the doctor's visit.

5. Is she 6½ or 7 with breasts or pubic hair?

If yes, then it might be a sign of normal early puberty or hormonal issues at play. Go on to Question 6.

6. Is she overweight?

If yes, these changes are less likely to be caused by hormonal issues, but you should see a pediatrician and pay special attention to our coverage of the role excess fat can play in early puberty (Chapters 1 and 3), as well as what to do about it (Chapters 5 and 6).

7. Does she have bad acne, unusual moodiness, or is she taller than expected and having an unusual growth spurt?

If yes, she might be experiencing puberty; schedule an appointment with the pediatrician and read this book for in-depth information about managing the road ahead and to help you prepare yourself with questions to bring with you to the doctor.

8. Is she less than age 10 and menstruating?

If yes, then it may be a hormonal issue; schedule an appointment with the pediatrician and pay special attention to Chapter 4 for in-depth information that will prepare you for the doctor's visit. The strategies that are outlined in Part II will help you to navigate the road ahead.

PART I

THE CAUSES OF EARLY PUBERTY

CHAPTER ONE

MOVE OVER, JUDY BLUME

How We Define Puberty Today

TAKE A MOMENT TO CAST your mind back to the days of your puberty. Can you remember the first signs? How about when your body started to change in ways that made you feel awkward? Did you wish puberty had occurred sooner, later, moved faster, or perhaps taken longer? Most of us hardly remember the nuances of the transition we made long ago unless it was a traumatic one. Women might be able to reminisce vaguely about buying their first bra and deodorant, talking about crushes with their friends, and wondering when they'd get their first period. Men often recall the year they outgrew all of their clothing and shoes as they gained several inches in height, followed by a significant deepening of the pitch of their voice. But most of us don't have a detailed enough memory of the process our pubescent bodies went through to feel confident about how to advise our children on it—or to know how worried we should be—if they experience puberty at an early age, before they're 10 years old.

As doctors who have dedicated much of our lives to the study of adolescence and in particular to the science of early puberty, we talk all the time with confused adults who seem to feel so far removed from the pubertal process that it's as if they never experienced it themselves. Whether we're talking with parents or principals, child advocates or other medical professionals, we're constantly reassuring them that in a lot of ways, puberty is still very much the same. It's a rite of passage that everyone goes through, one that is marked by dramatic physical, neurodevelopmental, and emotional changes that forever shift our physiology, psychology, and behavior. It's that inevitable stage in our lives when we transition from childhood to adulthood through a gradually progressing phase we traditionally call adolescence.

And for girls, puberty is unique. It not only foments a complex array of emotional issues but also heralds the development of visual cues of sexuality (e.g., breasts, wider hips) to a degree that boys just don't experience. Now that we're seeing more girls going through puberty at younger and younger ages, though, parents and teachers must address a constellation of challenges sooner than most are ready for. One can hardly call a 7- or 8-year-old a preteen, much less an adolescent, but when puberty comes knocking on a girl's door at this tender age, we as a society are compelled to redefine what it means to grow up. Unbeknownst to her, she is also forcing scientists to revise medical texts.

That's exactly what makes today's puberty unlike that of generations past. The subtle but undeniable features of puberty—usually breast buds and pubic hair—are appearing earlier in contemporary girls than they did in typical girls growing up just a generation ago. And the dynamics related to this change have been altered as well. While you might recall upgrading your wardrobe to reflect trends in the juniors department at roughly the same time that you noticed boys and your body began to look and feel different, today's young girls are experiencing an extended interval between the start of physical development and the emotional maturity to even harbor thoughts of dating.

For centuries, coming-of-age stories have been a popular subject for authors, playwrights, and entertainers. From Shakespeare to Louisa May Alcott, writers have shared the pains of growing up through stories of vivid characters that readers can relate to. Judy Blume may have made today's grown women blush when they first read her novels in the 1970s and '80s, but today, the changed facts of puberty for many young girls call for a whole new series designed especially for 8- and 9-year-olds. And many young girls now are probably discovering authors like Judy Blume *after* they've already started puberty.

Until the 20th century, puberty tended to coincide with a girl's teenage years, as her body and brain developed relatively in sync. But over the past 100 years, and particularly in the past 2 decades, the trajectory of the body's development began changing—making the process of beginning puberty at age 7 or 8 highly unsettling for a girl and for her caregivers (from parents to teachers to even medical professionals). Today, the same girl who's playing with dolls is also shopping for bras and asking questions about body odor and hair. And the adults in these young girls' lives are asking us if they should be thinking of these girls as tweens at these very tender ages and letting them buy into the entire tween culture. Or do they continue to treat their girls like the children they actually are? No wonder so many people are confused and uncomfortable about dealing with this topic.

JUST WHAT *IS* PUBERTY?

As with many words that are used in both medical and lay circles, "puberty" is a loaded term. And further confusing its definition are the subtle differences among what's considered normal, early, and abnormal.

Contrary to popular belief, puberty in a girl doesn't commence with menstruation. Scientifically speaking, puberty reflects the beginning of hormonal secretions from the pituitary—an exceedingly complex gland deep in the brain—leading to physiological changes that include the "turning on" of the sex organs to the point where the individual can procreate. But this obviously doesn't happen overnight, and the process varies enormously from girl to girl. Puberty is actually difficult to study; while a girl's age when she gets her first period is a clear benchmark, other steps in the development of young bodies— especially the changes that occur early on—are more gradual.

In other words, puberty is not like a single doorway to adulthood; instead, it's a long hallway. It's a process rather than a threshold. Every girl follows her own individual pathway. Some start with breast budding, while others sprout pubic hair first. In fact, the pubertal process happens twice in human development. In the womb, a girl's hormonal circuitry is first turned on and then turned off a few months after birth. We don't know the function of this "infant puberty," but we think it may prepare the endocrine (hormonal) system for reactivation in adolescence. Girls are born with their eggs in a sort of suspended animation in the ovaries until menarche.

From a scientific perspective, our understanding of puberty expanded over the past century, thanks to new technologies and pioneering doctors. During that same period, society changed dramatically as advances in medicine afforded us longer lives than any previous generation had. Once antibiotics and vaccines were introduced and our food supply multiplied thanks to the development of agricultural and manufacturing technologies, we grew taller and lived longer. Of course, greater access to foodstuffs and the rapid growth of the processed food industry also made for some unwanted outcomes, namely an escalating problem with overweight and obesity. Now the obesity epidemic has struck our children, too, and one of its manifestations appears to be the earlier onset of puberty, as we'll soon see.

Anyone who chronicles the subject of puberty usually starts the tale with the groundbreaking work in the 1940s of the late James M. Tanner, MD, an English pediatrician who is credited with creating modern standards for measuring a child's development. We still use his terminology in medicine today. Following Dr. Tanner's death at the age of 90 in 2010, Bruce Weber wrote about him for the *New York Times* in a beautiful essay that read like an ode: "Dr. Tanner was equal parts meticulous researcher and creative thinker whose interests lay where the fields of biology, psychology, and sociology intersect. He wrote widely, discussing, for instance, how the growth patterns of children can be powerful indicators of how their societies care for their young, and examining the connection between a child's physical and psychological development during adolescence." Weber went on to describe how, beginning in 1948, Tanner managed a study of childhood growth that the British government had commenced during World War II. Conducted among the residents of an orphanage in a small town north of London, it was supposed to record the effects of malnutrition on growth, but then progressed into a longitudinal study that involved photographing and measuring the same youths over several years.

Out of this pioneering study came a universal growth chart like those found in pediatricians' offices. But Tanner's chart, as Weber details, "expanded the range of growth patterns considered to be normal and led to the general understanding that neither early nor late maturation of a child is, on its own, an aberration." The study also established the now-famous Tanner stages—collectively, the Tanner scale—which define physical maturation as a sequence of bodily changes that occur during puberty. The stages are based on physical characteristics that one can see from a young girl's or boy's outer appearance: Girls are evaluated for breast development and the amount and length of pubic hair, whereas boys are similarly classified according to genital development and pubic hair growth. (Other signs, like voice change, the presence of facial hair, growth spurts, and even menstruation, are important physical milestones, but they're not the key measures when it comes to monitoring puberty.)

A girl in Tanner stage 1, for instance, is a preadolescent with no pubic hair whose breasts have not developed or changed since infancy. But a girl in Tanner stage 5, the last stage, has pubic hair that resembles that of an adult woman in quantity, type, and shape (the classic inverse triangle) and breasts that have fully developed. In this stage, there's a clear projection of the nipple, and the areola—the dark area surrounding the nipple—has receded a bit.

THE TANNER STAGES IN GIRLS

Tanner 1:	No changes since infancy (no pubic hair, no breast buds)
Tanner 2:	Breast budding, some pubic hair growth
Tanner 3:	Further enlargement of breast tissue, progression in the distribution and color of pubic hair
Tanner 4:	Increased breast size and elevation of the nipple area, adultlike pubic hair that doesn't reach the inner thighs
Tanner 5:	Mature female breasts, adultlike pubic hair and distribution with extension onto the thighs

Tanner also blazed trails in the study of childhood growth beyond just formulating pubertal growth charts. For example, he was among the first to investigate administering growth hormone to children with growth disorders and other developmental problems. His research findings have been embraced worldwide and have even influenced other disciplines, including sociology and economics. Tanner was revered for his theoretical musings. He asserted that the average height of a child during a particular time period in history was largely a reflection of their nutritional status during that era and that a person's adult height was determined not only by their genes but also by the adequacy of their nutrition early in life.

Puberty, like adult stature, involves both genetic and environmental forces. On the individual level, the exact age at which a girl goes through puberty is based on a number of factors unique to her. But on a societal scale, the mean age at which girls as a whole go through puberty is largely determined by environmental factors. Your DNA doesn't change much once you're born. But your environment does. And the two interact to influence how girls grow and develop.

As we'll stress throughout the book, race (or ethnicity) does not *determine* the timing of puberty, but in our culture it is *associated* with it. Early puberty's higher prevalence among certain populations, particularly African Americans and Latinos, likely has less to do with the underlying genetics associated with a particular ethnicity and more to do with social and environmental issues. Unfortunately, the risk factors for early puberty, such as obesity, disproportionately affect poor and minority populations in the United States. Social inequality in America remains a huge challenge today, and it rears its ugly head every time statisticians run numbers to understand demographics and related health risks in certain populations. Particular racial and ethnic groups have greater challenges from factors in the environment, such as the presence of pollutants, poor access to healthful foods, and exposure to hormone-disrupting chemicals, that may interact with genes to initiate puberty earlier than in children from other neighborhoods. (More on this in Chapters 3 and 5.)

NEW PUBERTY FACT

Puberty involves both genetic and environmental forces. Early puberty's higher prevalence among certain populations likely has less to do with the underlying genetics associated with a particular ethnicity and more to do with social and environmental issues.

The idea that the environment plays a large role in early puberty (and in health in general for that matter, regardless of age) is one that deserves more attention in research circles. Even though genes encoded by DNA are essentially static (barring the occurrence of mutation), the expression of those genes can be highly dynamic in response to environmental influences. This field of study, called epigenetics, is now one of the hottest areas of research. We believe epigenetic forces affect us from our days in utero until the day we die. There are likely many windows during one's lifetime when we are sensitive to environmental impacts, and puberty in particular represents a time of great vulnerability to concrete influences like synthetic chemicals and to less tangible ones, such as a lack of stability in the home and socioeconomic conditions. The multitude of neural and hormonal actions that control pubertal onset are susceptible to disruption and adaptation, especially by environmental changes.

Epigenetics is the study of sections of your DNA (called marks or markers) that essentially tell your genes when and how strongly to express themselves. These epigenetic marks control not only your health and longevity, but also how you pass your genes on to future generations. Our day-to-day lifestyle choices are now believed to have a profound effect on the activity of our genes. And this is true whether you're a 7-year-old on puberty's threshold or a 70-year-old at risk for a heart attack.

But what's empowering about this scientific insight is that we can change our health's destiny if we make the right lifestyle decisions. Now that we have evidence to suggest that the food choices we make, the amount of stress we experience, the exercise we get, the quality of our sleep, and even the relationships we keep affect which of our genes are activated and which remain suppressed, we can take some degree of control. And, therefore, we can help our young girls reduce their risks of developing too early or too quickly and possibly paying a health price as a result. Some experts suggest that we can change the expression of many genes that have a direct bearing on our health and longevity. What that really means is that our environment—in combination with our DNA—is the ultimate source of health or illness. This is true for defined diseases, such as obesity-related conditions, cardiovascular risk, and cancer, and for conditions such as early puberty that pose heightened health risks for these illnesses and other outcomes.

HOW EARLY IS "EARLY"?

As we mentioned briefly in the Introduction, the average age at which a girl first menstruates has fallen slightly in recent decades in Europe and America, as well as in developing countries in Africa and other places. But the age at which girls begin developing breasts and pubic hair has dropped more dramatically. Girls get their first period, on average, approximately 6 months earlier than girls did 40 years ago, but they get their breasts up to *2 years* earlier.

As noted in the Introduction, in the 1980s and '90s, Marcia Herman-Giddens noticed a surprisingly large number of girls with breast development or pubic hair as young as age 5 in her clinic at Duke University. Even though she was evaluating children who'd been sexually abused (a risk factor for early puberty, it turns out), as a mother herself, she became curious. "I was surprised that there was no data for the United States about the ages at which young girls were getting pubic hair and breast buds," Herman-Giddens, now an adjunct professor at the University of North Carolina, says today. She wanted to know: If she lined up a bunch of girls younger than 11, what would she find? How many would have signs of puberty and how far along in the process would they be?

In the journal *Pediatrics* in 1997, she published a game-changing study reporting that the average age of puberty in girls had dropped by

more than a year, compelling the field to redefine the biological bound-
aries of puberty and start asking questions. When Herman-Giddens
looked at the average age of puberty in a broad historical context by
reading the studies of other researchers, the stark change became even
more apparent: In 1860, girls got their first period around the age of 16.
By 1920, the age had dropped to 14; today, the median age for a girl's
first period is about 12½ years.

More than a decade after Herman-Giddens published her explosive
paper, we published our 2010 paper that confirmed the phenomenon of
earlier breast development among girls. Our findings actually showed
that the percentages of girls budding breasts by ages 7 and 8 were even
greater than Herman-Giddens's research had shown. Other studies have
also consistently indicated that puberty is occurring earlier, including
large population-based studies conducted in Western Europe beginning
in the 1990s. In particular, a 2009 study from Danish researchers put
the average onset of breast development at about a year earlier (9 years
10 months old) among girls studied in 2006 compared with those studied in 1991 (10 years 10 months old), and put the age of first menstruation
more than 3 months earlier (13 years 5 months for the 1991 group versus
13 years 2 months for the 2006 group). Similar results have been found
in studies of children immigrating to Sweden, France, Belgium, Switzerland, and the United States.

These studies nearly all agree on one thing: The discrepancies cannot be explained entirely by changes in nutrition, body weight, or body
fat percentage. Rather, they point to the powerful environmental
effects of changes that have taken place in
lifestyle factors, and perhaps psychological
conditions.

NEW PUBERTY FACT

A girl in 1860 got her first
period around 16. A girl in
1920 got it around 14. Today
she's likely to have a first
period closer to 12½ years.

As we continue to search for clues to early
puberty, we have to be realistic about the
complexity of it all—and rightfully so, Herman-
Giddens asserts. "People want a clear answer,
and there's no clear answer. A lot of factors

are interacting together, including some that we may not even be aware of yet. We need to move away from looking for single answers."

This is exactly what makes the whole notion of early puberty so difficult to comprehend. As human beings, we prefer explanations that show clear cause and effect, and when it comes to matters of health, we especially like to know that X causes Y, or that A triggers B, so we can attempt to control outcomes. But if there's one underlying message we doctors continue to glean from our own ongoing research and hear from other experts in the field, it's that the facts of the new puberty are far from rock solid.

THE THREE FORCES AT WORK IN EARLY PUBERTY

We'll be detailing all the potential triggers and causes of early puberty later on. But as a primer, let's briefly run through the three biggest forces at work.

Suspect #1: Excess Fat

The percentage of US children, including adolescents, who are obese has almost *tripled* over the last 30 years. A whopping one-fifth of children and adolescents are obese, and the timing of the obesity epidemic parallels the drop in the age of puberty. We've known since the 1960s

---

THE THREE MOST POWERFUL CULPRITS POTENTIALLY AFFECTING THE PUBERTAL PROCESS

- Excess fat (being overweight or obese)
- Exposure to chemicals that disrupt healthy human biology, especially the hormonal system
- Social and psychological stressors (e.g., early childhood trauma, poor familial relationships)

---

that sexual maturation is correlated more closely with body size (i.e., body fat) than with age. And this makes sense from an evolutionary standpoint, as we'll see shortly. Once a girl has enough body fat to meet the energy demands of reproduction, certain hormones responsible for sexual maturation start firing to prepare the body for this task.

Ethical issues make it impossible to conduct scientific experiments on the effects of overweight on the hormonal aspects of puberty in humans. It's also very difficult to tease apart the effects of other possible contributors to obesity, such as genetics, environment, and activity level, because these issues coalesce in any given individual and among various social groups. However, we do know from controlled animal experiments that under otherwise equivalent conditions, when the calorie load is greater, the chance of entering puberty earlier than normal is also greater.

Extra body fat has consistently been found to be a driving factor in early breast development. It's well documented that obese and overweight girls develop significantly earlier than girls of normal body weight, regardless of ethnicity. One study of 3,000 girls born in the 1980s showed that for every point increase in body mass index, the age of menarche dropped by about a month. Studies also indicate that a girl's weight even by age 3 can predict her prepubertal weight and her chances of going through puberty before her peers.

One reason why excess fat can be so problematic for girls is related to a specific hormone called leptin, which plays a leading role in appetite suppression and how and where the body stores fat. Leptin reduces feelings of hunger by acting on specific centers in the brain. When we've satisfied our body's need for fuel, leptin gets released so we can stop eating; more specifically, when fat cells fill up and start to expand, they secrete leptin, which acts as your brake at the table. And since leptin is produced by fat, higher levels of it are usually found in obese people, though their bodies don't respond normally to it (hence their difficulty with controlling caloric intake). It turns out that leptin and puberty share a special relationship, for research has found that the leptin level rises before puberty. So, having more fat cells means more leptin secretion, allowing puberty to start sooner. Interestingly, studies in mice show that when they are born without the ability to produce leptin, they become obese, but they don't go through puberty. The same is true for people who are born with a genetic defect that disrupts their leptin production.

But obesity alone doesn't fully explain early puberty. If it did, then we wouldn't see girls with healthy body weight develop earlier than in decades past. So there must be other factors.

"I'm convinced that obesity is an important part of the story," asserts Paul Kaplowitz, MD, chief of the division of endocrinology and diabetes at Children's National Medical Center in Washington, DC. "But I'm no longer convinced it's the whole story." Kaplowitz, who was among the first to report on early puberty and is the author of the 2004 book *Early Puberty in Girls,* says he would have blamed just obesity a few years ago, but now he admits that there's much more to it. And in the decade since his book came out, studies have not only magnified the complexity of it all but also shown that the general increase in the body mass indexes of girls over the past 15 years has not been great enough to account for the younger onset of breast development over that same time period.

Suspect #2: Exposure to Chemicals That Disrupt Healthy Biology

Kaplowitz highlights another essential fact to consider: exposure to possible environmental culprits starting as early as in the womb. Indeed, by the time a girl begins to develop at age 8 or 9, she's been exposed to so much, from the moment of conception onward, that it's virtually impossible to know what, exactly, could have triggered the early puberty. As we'll discuss later on, fetuses and babies don't have fully developed defense systems capable of neutralizing chemicals that can be harmful, so they are much more vulnerable.

Today there are an untold number of synthetic chemicals in our environment, many of them present in the things we touch, breathe, and consume. Traces of 232 synthetic chemicals have been found in the umbilical cord blood of infants at birth, and close to 800 chemicals are known or suspected to be capable of interfering with our hormonal system in some capacity. (In our ongoing BCERP study of 1,200 girls nationwide, we've found detectable levels of every chemical that we've tested for—even those that were banned years ago, since the body can store certain chemicals for a surprisingly long time.) But only a small fraction of these substances have been tested for their endocrine-disrupting effects in laboratory animals. In other words, the vast majority of chemicals in current commercial use have not been fully analyzed for their effects on human health (we'll go more deeply into this in Chapter 5). This lack of data means there's significant uncertainty about the true extent of risks from chemicals that could potentially disrupt the endocrine system and cause health challenges as diverse and severe as diabetes and cancer.

Among the chemical pollutants that scientists are currently studying to see whether they affect pubertal timing are flame retardants; substances used in making plastics, including phthalates, parabens, and phenols such as bisphenol A (BPA, a common ingredient in plastics and aluminum cans, which the FDA banned in sippy cups and baby bottles in 2012); pesticides; detergents; tobacco compounds; and heavy metals such as lead and cadmium. Often called endocrine-disrupting chemicals, or EDCs, these can interfere with the body's natural hormones and are therefore of particular interest to scientists. Some of these chemicals may also contribute to obesity, perhaps by stimulating areas in the brain responsible for appetite, or disrupting other hormone levels.

Because estrogen lies at the heart of a female's reproductive biology, we also think that environmental chemicals can lock on to estrogen receptors in the body, producing an estrogen-mimicking effect. This may help explain why girls experience much earlier breast development but not necessarily much earlier menstruation. Breast tissue is more sensitive to estrogen than menstruation is. And the fact that girls can develop true breast tissue at much younger ages over a short period of time also points to an environmental impact.

Studying the effects of chemicals on the body is as challenging as studying the effects of obesity. There are many variables, not to mention many chemicals, whose potency must be examined alone and in combination with others. The few epidemiological studies that have been done offer mixed results, and adding to the confusion is the fact that studies contradict each other. While it's likely that hormone-disrupting chemicals are part of the story, fat tissue is itself a hormone-secreting organ. So another part of this incomplete tale is a potential feedback loop: a perfect storm in which the same chemicals that impact estrogen metabolism may cause girls to accumulate more fat tissue, which in turn releases more estrogen. Environmental chemicals and increased fat tissue could very well be changing girls' hormonal milieu and the ways their bodies are exposed to hormones. Put simply, obesity plus the chemicals potentially lead to problems.

NEW PUBERTY FACT

Obesity and exposure to environmental chemicals create a vicious cycle whereby the chemicals that influence hormones can lead to more fat tissue, which in turn releases more hormones to interact with those chemicals.

Another complicating variable is that there could be an as-yet-unidentified "window" of exposure that makes a difference. Perhaps, for example, exposure to a particular substance early in life or in utero has a significant effect but less of one when puberty is approaching. Again, more research is needed to eliminate many of the uncertainties. We also need more consistent study methods; the usefulness of some research has been limited because some chemical exposures must be tested through blood while others are more effectively tested in urine. So if a study looks only at exposures through blood when the urine should also be tested, those results won't be totally accurate.

It's all the more interesting to note that most chemicals in use today were developed after World War II, a time line that's consistent with the earlier onset of puberty. However, Herman-Giddens is quick to point out that during this same time period, so much else has changed in our society as well it's hard to weigh culpability. For one, our food environment has been transformed dramatically, with processed and high-calorie junk foods and drinks dominating our diets— all readily available at low cost and most marketed to kids. In addition, many communities lack the infrastructure to encourage physical activity. Most neighborhoods are perceived to be less safe for children to play in compared to a generation ago. Schools no longer offer sufficient phys ed courses, or even recess time. Computers, televisions, tablets, smartphones, and the like further discourage physical activity (and could even be exposing kids to light waves that can adversely affect brain chemistry). Although the debate over the impact of chemical exposure on puberty will continue until scientists learn more, there's a lot we can do to mitigate these potential influencers regardless of whether they turn out to be harmful.

Suspect #3: Social and Psychological Stressors

A third area of study into early puberty is determining the influence exerted by a girl's physical, social, and emotional environment. Although medical researchers were once very skeptical of this theory, a large body of research now supports the notion that excessive stress early in life can indeed affect the timing of puberty. In response to danger and instability, the body may trigger hormonal responses to cue puberty.

We've reported from our own studies, for example, that children who have a high sensitivity to their circumstances (as measured by biological reactions to stress) are more likely to undergo puberty earlier if they also have poor familial relationships. But stressful relationships in families aren't the only documented sources of instability that can influence puberty. As Chapter 3 will show, stress can stem from low emotional investment on the part of parents or an absentee father (girls who from

an early age grow up in homes without their
biological fathers are twice as likely to experience menarche early as are girls who grow
up with both parents), living with a depressed
mother, and experiencing significant early-
childhood trauma (such as sexual abuse).
Some studies even show that the presence of
a stepfather in the house might correlate

> **NEW PUBERTY FACT**
>
> **Just as early puberty
> increases the risk for social
> challenges, problems in the
> social environment increase
> the risk for early puberty.**

with early puberty, but these findings have been mixed. (And for the
record, based on the existing research, absentee mothers don't seem to
increase the risk of early puberty among girls.)

In addition to the vicious cycles we've already mentioned that
might influence puberty, there's one in the social realm, too: Social
problems don't just increase the risk for early puberty, early puberty
increases the risk for challenges in the social arena as well. We know
that, on average, girls who develop ahead of their peers have more anxiety, a higher incidence of depression, poorer body image, and more
eating disorders. They are more likely to experiment with drugs and
alcohol sooner, as well as lose their virginity sooner. They are at risk
for having more sexual partners and more sexually transmitted diseases as a result of starting to have sex earlier.

However, we want to stress that there's a big difference between
early puberty and early sexuality. While some studies show that early
maturers will engage in sexual acts earlier than later bloomers, it's not
as early as you might fear. Moreover, a 9-year-old girl who has entered
puberty is not necessarily having sexual thoughts. This is where many
adults get the facts of puberty wrong. We shouldn't confuse a young
girl's early physical development with full sexual maturation. Even
though she has started to grow breasts and has pubic hair, sex is still
likely the furthest thing from her mind, unless there are other factors in her environment that are encouraging these age-discordant
thoughts (e.g., exposure to inappropriate media, older peers, sexual
abuse). Yes, she will start to have sexual desires at some point down

NEW PUBERTY FACT

Nobody knows exactly what starts puberty or what awakens this complex neurohormonal machinery. The process can take 2 to 4 years or more from the onset of breast development to a girl's first period, and it can take a few more years for a girl's menstrual cycle to become regular.

the road, but it doesn't mean that she will act on them (and there's a difference between having a crush and having sexual thoughts). Sexual desire is also a process that evolves over time. It's totally normal, natural, and healthy. Just as puberty isn't one event, neither is the development of sexuality. Put another way, although puberty does entail sexual maturation, this doesn't happen all at once the moment a girl first starts to get pubic hair and breasts. It's a long process (remember, too, that menarche—the first sign of reproductive capacity—occurs far later in the pubertal process). You won't have to be prepared for the sex talk until long after you've addressed those first signs of puberty (and we'll help you with that in Chapter 8).

PUBERTY REMAINS SOMEWHAT OF A MYSTERY

Of course, if we knew more about human development in general, questions about early puberty would be easier to answer. Think about it: Puberty happens when a body reaches that critical point where certain genetic, physiological, and environmental stimuli intersect—and all of it happens according to a biological calendar set over the long course of human evolution. The hormones involved in this transition have been well studied, but exactly how they are awakened, how they interact with one another, and how they are influenced by the environment is still largely unknown. Moreover, we don't know exactly what percentages of various aspects of the pubertal process are genetically driven and how much each pubertal marker is governed by the environment throughout this long pathway. For different aspects of puberty (e.g., breast development, menstruation), various forces are likely at play. Consistent data suggests the age when a girl first men-struates, for instance, is determined roughly 50 percent by her genes (when her biological mother first got her period). There is a documented heritable effect in terms of menarche. But this is likely to be weaker for breast development today, which appears more strongly influenced by environmental factors. Studies of breast development for two generations of women (mothers and their daughters) would help us understand how much of timing of breast onset is inherited.

In much the same way that physicists are trying to understand how the "big bang" created the universe, scientists like us are still trying to discern what conditions must be met to instigate the body's equivalent of the big bang, puberty. We can clearly describe puberty's events and characteristics, but we can't explain its true origin. And because of this, a lot of myths about puberty persist.

Take, for instance, the notion of "raging" hormones. As we'll see in the next chapter, hormones alone are rarely to blame for a youngster's behavior. Although we tend to think of people at certain developmental stages or times of the month as being "hormonal," this is misleading and even backward. For instance, women who experience premenstrual syndrome (PMS) are often said to be hormonal, but hormone levels are actually low during this time period. Similarly, in the postpartum period of motherhood, when depression can occur, sex hormone levels are low, not rising. Contrary to popular wisdom, it's when certain sex hormones are *highest* that most women report psychological well-being and feelings of attractiveness. This is when women are ovulating or, if pregnant, during the second, "glowing" trimester.

So things are not always as they seem. Just as with women and PMS, pubertal kids aren't destined for certain behaviors because of elevated or "raging" hormone levels. Remember this nugget of wisdom as you read this book. Later on, we'll be busting a few more myths and ultimately empowering you to help your young girl take advantage of this very unique time in her life.

THE EVOLUTIONARY PERSPECTIVE

Before diving into the potential consequences of early puberty, let's take a look at the evolutionary view to deepen your understanding of early puberty and further assuage your fears.

Historically, the ability to reproduce at a younger age indicated that a female had optimal nutrition (and therefore adequate body fat) to support the demands of reproduction. The anthropological and evolutionary perspectives have proposed some intriguing new theories that scientists are just beginning to explore. Among them: Is early puberty simply a product of human evolution? That is, are we just reproducing effectively and efficiently in response to certain environmental and biological circumstances?

To answer this question, we turned to Jay Belsky, PhD, an expert in child development and family studies at the University of California at Davis. He's taken a keen interest in the study of how things like day care and the relationship between parents and a child during infancy and early childhood can affect that child's path and health later in life. He's also well known for his evolutionary theories about why a human body would mature more quickly or sooner than expected. According to Belsky, Mother Nature is all about "live fast and die young." Nature doesn't really care whether you live to the age of 100. It just wants you to reproduce. So if entering puberty early causes greater health risks later in life, including the chance of dying from breast cancer at a younger age, so what? It's all about trade-offs. Nature isn't there to protect you when you're too old to have biological children. Only when an individual's survival is truly at stake—in extreme famine or war, for instance—will the body protect itself and turn off its procreational powers. Conversely, if certain stressors are present, such as the environmental factors that might contribute to early puberty, then the body might decide to mature quickly so it can accomplish the ultimate goal of reproduction sooner. "It's reasonable to [believe that] environmental toxins can change physiology and alert a body that the world is dangerous and it needs to develop and reproduce earlier," he asserts. But Belsky sounds a very positive note: We as adults and parents can act as the primary buffers between children and what they experience and are exposed to, particularly early in life and during the prepubertal period. Parents and the family provide a child with what Belsky calls the ultimate psychological nutrient.

This perspective is indeed provocative, because puberty is triggered by an interaction between nature and nurture, and as human actions modify our physical world, we force the body to make adjustments. Most people don't understand evolution, Belsky asserts. They think our outcomes are largely predetermined by genetics, which remain relatively static. But this couldn't be further from the truth. We are among the most adaptable species on the planet. We adapt to external pressures that arise in our environment as it changes (or we change it). Viewing our ever-adapting biology in this way permits a nonjudgmental assessment of early puberty. Perhaps a girl going through early puberty is simply an adaptation to our modern environment.

Our job as evolving beings is to ensure that the new puberty brings about optimal, healthy outcomes for girls over their lifetimes. The new puberty may have its pluses from an evolutionary perspective, but as the next chapter will show, it also has minuses for health and behavioral outcomes in adolescence and later in life. Remember, puberty is not just a physical transition but also a social one. It's supposed to presage a switch to adult social roles. But what happens when a little girl whose favorite retailer is American Girl suddenly finds herself among peers who shop at Urban Outfitters?

CHAPTER TWO

7 GOING ON 17

The Potential Repercussions of Early Puberty

TO GET A QUICK SENSE of the vast array of issues that relate to puberty today, consider the following questions we have fielded from parents.

My 9-year-old daughter just started to wear a bra, and I noticed her underwear has some off-white stains. Every day she worries that she's going to get her period in the middle of class. How can I prepare and reassure her? Her 4th-grade teacher is male.

My 10-year-old daughter is really self-conscious about her weight and developing breasts. She used to talk about feeling fat, and I reassured her that she wasn't. Now she won't talk to me about it. How do I broach this or help her without making a bigger deal out of it or having her shut me out? Because she's developing earlier than her friends, I also worry about the sexual attention she may be unknowingly drawing, too.

My husband and 11-year-old daughter are far less close since she started developing. I think he feels uncomfortable hugging

her and being affectionate the way he used to be. Is it normal
for fathers to withdraw during this time?

Before my daughter entered middle school, I noticed
that her relationships with her friends became much more
complex. She often comes home teary and doesn't want to talk
about it. I'm not sure how to help her because she just gets
angry with me when I try to broach it.

My daughter has said several times that she "just wants to die"
or "wishes it were over," but I don't know how seriously to take
this. It usually happens when she's frustrated or mad and
honestly, I think she's just being dramatic and wants attention.
Is this just because of pubertal hormones? Do I ignore it?

CLEARLY, A LOT IS GOING on in a girl's life when she starts to develop. The above scenarios reflect just a few of the issues we encounter daily in our clinical work with families. Puberty, as you learned in the previous chapter, isn't a doorway. It's a long hallway that can be easy to navigate at times and much harder at others. And it goes way beyond just the physical changes classically associated with the experience, such as budding breasts and the onset of acne. There are social and psychological components to this important transition, and they are all the more complex when a girl is young. Once a girl is biologically able to reproduce, nearly every system in her body has gone through years of transformations that have changed her brain, heart, lungs, and musculoskeletal system. And while experiencing these changes can be unsettling for any individual girl, it's also usually completely ordinary.

Puberty does not occur in a vacuum; it's experienced within a diverse and continually changing social environment. Most girls are very good at navigating the psychosocial dimensions of puberty as they come to grips with their developing bodies and learn to manage feedback from their environment, including friends, parents, teachers, the wider culture, and the media. But to understand why some individuals are more challenged by the risks of puberty than others demands that we look at the bigger picture, the one that goes far beyond just biological—namely, hormonal—changes.

If you've paid attention to some of the more alarming media reports about adolescent behavior over the past couple of years, then you're likely concerned about how such trends relate to the new puberty. Disturbing news reports about teens developing eating disorders, sexting, using social media and the Internet to explore their sexuality, and experimenting with drugs and alcohol make it seem like these issues are increasingly prevalent and happening at ever-younger ages. However, the opposite is true: Teens are actually *less* likely to engage in unhealthy behaviors than they were a few decades ago. Antismoking campaigns, for instance, have led to a decline in youth smoking. So where—and more important, *how*—does the new puberty play into these trends?

Although entering puberty early in today's society can seem like stepping into a minefield, it needn't be an ill-fated journey. One of the most important messages we want to convey is that *context* matters for how an individual fares, and it's likely that it matters a lot. Many of the emotional and physical health risk factors that early puberty poses can be mitigated by the simple power of a girl's physical, emotional, and peer environments, plus adequate family support.

Just because an early bloomer is, for example, statistically more prone to depression and anxiety disorders doesn't mean she'll inevitably experience those conditions or have suicidal thoughts. For one, several factors beyond just early development can play into these behaviors, which makes identifying cause and effect all the more difficult. Both environmental and genetic forces are at play here. And secondly, there's a lot we can do as adults to help steer a girl in the right direction and avoid some of these pitfalls—regardless of nature's forces. As the University of California at Davis child development expert Jay Belsky said, we can provide the "psychological nutrients" that young girls need to thrive in spite of the presence of circumstances linked to certain risks.

Being at a higher risk for a health condition or behavior does not equal destiny. This important fact bears repeating. Julia Graber, PhD, perhaps said it best when we interviewed her. Graber, currently a professor of psychology at the University of Florida, has dedicated her life to examining how the timing of puberty can have lasting effects on a young individual's mental health, social environment, and health outcomes. She asserts: "We need to be on the lookout for these augmented risks for early-maturing girls, but realize that it's not inevitable. There are lots of points for intervention." There isn't a direct link between early puberty and the behavioral issues these girls are at greater risk for, Graber stresses. Although girls are at a higher risk for depression when they go through puberty early, you can't blame hormones or their social environment alone. A does not always lead to B.

The medical literature divides the negative potential repercussions of early puberty, many of which are long term, into two major categories: behavioral issues and health conditions. Obviously, these categories are related, since behavior influences health. If a girl abuses alcohol, for example, she's more likely to suffer the physical health consequences during adolescence (such as the increased risk of depression) or in adulthood (such as the increased risk of liver disease and cancer). So keep that in mind as we explore both categories of risks.

BEHAVIORAL HEALTH RISKS ASSOCIATED WITH EARLY PUBERTY

Behaviors and problems that tend to emerge during adolescence, regardless of pubertal timing, include body-image issues and eating disorders, substance abuse, poor academic performance, deviant activities such as delinquency and aggression, and "internalizing symptoms" such as depression, anxiety, abdominal pains, sleep disturbances, headaches, and upset stomachs. Generally speaking, internalizing symptoms are the effects of behavioral or psychological problems that are experienced inwardly as opposed to outwardly (i.e., acted out). Worry, fear, feelings of self-loathing, self-injury, and social withdrawal are additional examples of internalizing problems. And unfortunately, girls who start puberty early are more prone to develop both negative behaviors that are focused inward, toward themselves, and those directed outward, toward others.

It's no secret that adolescents are more vulnerable to developing psychological and behavioral problems than children are. This may well have been true since humans first began roaming the earth. And having one problem can certainly result in having more. Take, for example, social anxiety, which is well known to sometimes lead to related problems such as underachievement in school, smaller social networks and fewer close friends, poor social skills, and even depression. It's characterized by persistent fear of social or performance situations in which there's a chance of being embarrassed. As with depression, social anxiety disorder is more common in adolescent girls than in boys (in fact, depression is more prevalent among adult women than men, too, as are panic disorders and social phobias).

We don't know exactly why internalizing symptoms increase more in girls than in boys at puberty. Differences in sex hormones could be a factor. We know that estrogen, for example, interacts with serotonin, a neurotransmitter involved in controlling moods, sleep, and appetite, and could contribute to social phobia in girls. But at the same time, girls face more stressors during puberty than boys do, simply because of their gender, independent of hormones. These include being overly self-conscious or dissatisfied with their bodies in part because of the prevalence of unrealistic media images, being restricted or discriminated against in some way due to their sex, and receiving unwanted sexual attention. This last factor can be especially true for girls whose early physical development naturally attracts older boys. Or their emerging sexuality may elicit negative responses, including from other girls, as they are judged for weight gain and their rapidly changing bodies.

BEHAVIORAL HEALTH RISKS ASSOCIATED WITH EARLY PUBERTY

- Body-image issues
- Eating disorders
- Substance abuse
- Poor academic performance
- Deviant activities such as delinquency and aggression
- Internalizing symptoms (depression, anxiety, worry, fear, self-loathing, abdominal pains, sleep disturbances, headaches, upset stomachs, self-injury, social withdrawal)

So it's really no surprise that numerous studies have shown girls with early puberty experience higher rates of depression and anxiety. They also exhibit increased rates of smoking and delinquent behavior, as well as earlier sexual experiences (though, again, very young bloomers won't necessarily be contemplating sex). Of course, girls who befriend trouble-makers or live in disadvantaged neighborhoods are also at further risk for deviant behavior during adolescence. They are more likely to experiment with alcohol and marijuana early if it's available and to socialize with older kids.

While there remains some debate over whether these emotional and behavioral problems last into adulthood, two large studies, one from the United States and one from Switzerland, that recently evaluated young adults in their late teens and early twenties reported higher rates of substance abuse and depression among those who went through puberty early. Another study of US undergraduate students found higher rates of eating disorders and anxiety in early-maturing women (and men, too). In addition, early-maturing girls reportedly have lower academic achievement in the long run. Such studies suggest biological and social transformations that happen during puberty put very young adolescents at higher risk for poor outcomes, presumably because they are too developmentally immature to deal with these changes. Their brains, in a sense, aren't up to speed with their physical bodies. Also, it's still unclear how early use and abuse of substances affect a developing younger girl's brain. Future research may find that they have much greater long-term impacts, especially on the developing brain, when they occur earlier than they would if an individual started trying alcohol or marijuana later, as a teenager or young adult.

We'll examine just what's going on in the young person's brain in Chapter 7. Many people fail to realize that while the physical attributes of puberty—pubic hair and breasts, growth spurts, and eventually periods—are indeed a big deal, the biggest changes are actually taking place deep within the recesses of the brain. But this is where context really counts. It's well documented that family relationships profoundly influence how girls thrive regardless of the timing and speed of their physical development. And for this reason, researchers like us are staunch advocates of starting in the home when it comes to addressing early puberty and finding ways to mitigate its risks. Our own studies, in addition to others, have highlighted the importance of building good, strong, high-quality family relationships that include structure, clear expectations, warmth, and attention to what's called emotional regulation, or the ability to control or modify one's emotional responses.

It should come as no surprise that regardless of a girl's maturation time line, children who enter adolescence with poorer-quality family relationships or preexisting emotional problems are likely to continue to have more challenges in terms of their mental health and their familial and social relationships. And as Julia Graber's research has shown, early maturers, particularly girls, often experience poorer-quality relationships than other youth during adolescence and even young adulthood. We can't ignore the additional impact of the psychological and social stress and hormonal changes that a child may undergo in the throes of puberty, for these can also adversely affect their relationships.

We also cannot forget this critical fact: The influence of the parent–child relationship on child development (both physical and psychological) *does not begin at puberty.* No doubt puberty may impact the course of a child's psychological development and therefore family relationships, but family relationships can also have an indelible impact on the timing of puberty itself, including when it commences. In 1991, Drs. Belsky, Temple University's Laurence Steinberg, and University of Nebraska anthropologist Patricia Draper were among the first to posit that stressful family environments lead to earlier puberty and earlier sexual experiences among girls. By "stressful family environments," we mean homes in which there's a lot of turmoil and argument and not a lot of affection or warmth.

> **NEW PUBERTY FACT**
>
> The impact of the parent-child relationship on development begins long before puberty starts.

Belsky's more recent research has shown that girls who were "insecure infants" (i.e., they had less confidence in the availability and support of their parents) hit puberty earlier and got their periods sooner than girls who had been "secure" infants raised in warm, loving, safe households. This remained true even after he accounted for the mothers' ages at menarche, thus correcting for that hereditary factor. In fact, several studies (including our own) have consistently demonstrated that an absentee father during childhood and/or a low quality of family interactions actually *predict* earlier maturation in girls.

Before moving on to the physical health risks, we should add that lots of doctors and educators, ourselves included, are working hard to dispel the myth that once children hit adolescence, their relationships with their parents inevitably go down the tubes. To the contrary, they don't "tank inevitably," as Graber points out. She asserts: "Conflicts probably do increase because young adolescents want to have more autonomy and they want to be treated like teens instead of children. They also want more self-control. But that doesn't mean that family relationships have taken a downward spiral."

And indeed, just as we can mitigate the behavioral and psychological risks that accompany puberty by nurturing our family relationships, we can also prevent our relationships from taking an adversarial turn.

PHYSICAL HEALTH RISKS ASSOCIATED WITH EARLY PUBERTY

Of all the health risks an early bloomer courts, the one that gets the most attention and creates the most concern is the increased risk of reproductive cancer, especially breast cancer. The link between early menarche and breast cancer in adulthood, continues to be widely studied. Epidemiologic studies have revealed that girls who get their periods early have up to a 30 percent increased risk of breast cancer as adults, although estimates vary widely. One pooled analysis reported that each year the age of menarche was delayed reduced the risk of pre-menopausal breast cancer by 9 percent and the risk of postmenopausal breast cancer by 4 percent.

Of all the pubertal markers, menarche proves to be one of the best-established risk factors for breast cancer in part because even years later, a woman can typically recall the age at which it occurred. A 1989 report from the Breast Cancer Detection Demonstration Project first suggested this association when it studied 284,000 women, some of whom had started their periods before age 12 and others who had started after age 14. It found that women whose menstrual cycles began before the age of 12 were at a higher risk for breast cancer than those who started later. Now informally known as the Gail model after its lead researcher, Mitchell Gail, MD, the Breast Cancer Risk Assessment Tool predicts who is most at risk for breast cancer based on certain risk factors such as age, number of blood relatives with breast cancer, age at first giving birth (or never having had a full-term pregnancy), and age at menarche.

> **NEW PUBERTY FACT**
>
> A girl who gets her period early could face an increased risk of breast cancer later in life.

Additional studies now reveal that a girl's age at peak growth (when she goes through her biggest growth spurt to reach adult height) is also an indicator of her risk for breast cancer later in life. The sooner she reaches her adult height, the higher her risk. And clearly, both of these—peak growth and menarche—are among the milestones of puberty. We also know that ovarian cancer risk seems to be higher when a girl gets her period sooner, and this risk appears to be directly linked to the increased number of ovulatory cycles: Some studies have shown that each full year of ovulation increases ovarian cancer risk by 6 percent.

Just what does puberty have to do with breast cancer risk? You'd think we'd know the answer to this question by now, but it's still an active area of research, and it's possible that a constellation of factors combine to determine any given girl's risk. One of the predominant theories points to lifetime exposure to estrogen. Robert Hiatt, MD, is a University of California at San Francisco professor and the chair of its department of epidemiology and biostatistics. Hiatt studies what roles the environment and early-life exposures of various kinds play in the risk of developing breast cancer later in life. "We've known for a long time that girls who go through menarche early are at higher risk for breast cancer. Conventional wisdom says more cyclic estrogen and more menstrual cycles are a strong risk factor for breast cancer," Dr. Hiatt asserts. "So the fewer cycles [in a lifetime], the better—that is what has been believed generally."

Another factor that scientists (including Hiatt) continue to talk about is exposure to environmental "insults" during the rapid biological changes a girl experiences when she develops early. With puberty, breast tissue grows exponentially as the mammary gland undergoes extensive changes to eventually become an adult female breast comprised of mature breast tissue. This creates a "window of susceptibility" during which exposure to harmful substances might be able to permanently mutate a girl's genes, altering her susceptibility to abnormal cellular growth and cancer in adult life.

What's more, growth factors that impact a girl's height and bone mineral density could also play a role in her lifetime cancer risk. We know, for example, that obese and tall children generate higher levels of IGF-1 (insulin-like growth factor 1) in response to growth hormone than do short and normal-weight children. IGF-1 is a hormone similar in structure to insulin that plays an important role in childhood growth. It may be behind the link between menarche and breast cancer. Investigations into which is the better predictor—age of menarche or age of peak growth—for future cancer risk show that early rapid growth puts a woman at greater risk, perhaps more so than when she gets her first period. One study found that the risk of breast cancer increased by 11 percent for every 5-centimeter increase in adult height. Similarly, if a woman reached her maximum height at or before age 12, her risk of breast cancer was increased. Several studies have also documented a relationship between greater bone mineral density and later development of breast cancer. Bear in mind that the majority of bone mineral content is deposited during the pubescent years, peaking shortly after an individual experiences the final growth spurt to reach adult height.

To be clear, just because a girl experiences puberty earlier or over a longer period of time doesn't mean she will outgrow her peers and become a 6-footer. To the contrary, early puberty can *prevent* a girl from reaching her maximum height potential. Though many children who enter puberty early might for a time be taller than their peers because they have their growth spurts sooner, they actually can wind up shorter because the opportunity for growth is shorter; their bones are not given adequate time to grow to their genetically determined length. Indeed, hormonal pressures can trump genetics.

It should also be noted that adult height is associated with cancer risk in general, regardless of when puberty takes place. In 2013, researchers at the Albert Einstein College of Medicine in New York published an analysis of 20,928 postmenopausal women that showed the taller a woman is, the greater her risk for a number of cancers, including breast, colon, and skin cancer. Although we don't know why cancer risk is associated with tall stature, it's been suggested that hormones and growth factors that spur both height and cancer cell development are involved. Another theory is that height increases the surface area of the body's organs, resulting in a greater number of overall cells and thus a higher risk of malignancy. The taller and bigger one gets, the more cells the body has, which literally creates more room for error, if you will. This helps explain why we've documented an association between an increased risk for several types of cancer among females and height.

Obesity is another clear risk factor for cancer and other diseases. Obesity likely contributes to early maturation for reasons we'll be exploring, while maturing early also increases a girl's risk of becoming obese and having a higher body mass index (BMI) as an adult. It's also a risk factor for weight-related illnesses in adulthood such as insulin resistance and metabolic syndrome, a group of risk factors that increase the chance of developing heart disease, diabetes, and stroke. It's well documented that girls who develop pubic hair early and also menstruate early are at greater risk for developing cardiovascular disease and diabetes than are girls who go through puberty later on. The hard part, though, is teasing out the details to know which is more influential in the long run: the early puberty due to higher weight, or the excess childhood weight that brings on weight and metabolic conditions in adulthood. Further research will help us understand this better.

An analysis from the Bogalusa heart study found that children with higher BMIs had earlier pubertal onset, and earlier puberty was linked with having a higher BMI as an adult. And in adults, extra weight alone raises the risk of cancer regardless of when puberty took place. Many studies have indicated that overweight and obesity are associated with a small increase in the risk of postmenopausal breast cancer, but according to some studies, a *reduced* risk of premenopausal breast cancer. So once again we're left with a confusing array of factors to reconcile about all these pathways, both direct and indirect. Some studies are now showing that when researchers factor out an individual's weight in childhood, early puberty doesn't appear to be a strong independent risk factor for adult obesity.

We should add, however, that there's still a lot of debate about this, and making matters even more confusing is a long-term study of more than 61,000 Norwegian women that found that the earlier a girl got her period, the earlier she died; in this particular study, each year of decrease in age at menarche was associated with an average increase of 2.4 percent in death rate. Similar conclusions were drawn from a study that involved 55,128 Japanese women who were ages 40 to 79 in 1988–1990 and were monitored through December 2006. When the researchers adjusted for age, menopausal status, and BMI as well as lifestyle factors such as smoking, alcohol use, exercise, and sleeping hours, they found evidence that early menarche is associated with an increased risk of all-cause mortality (that is, death regardless of cause). More specifically, they found that women who got their periods before the age of 12 were more likely to die sooner than the women who got their periods after the age of 13. But these researchers admitted that they haven't identified how age at menarche impacts a woman's longevity. Further study of these associations, including the results of our own CYGNET study investigating how environmental exposures and biological and socioeconomic factors influence the transition through puberty and potential breast cancer risk, should prove illuminating.

The relationships noted between very early weight gain and puberty and subsequent obesity, metabolic syndrome, and increased mortality indicate that the profound effects of rapid

---

ADULT PHYSICAL HEALTH RISKS ASSOCIATED WITH EARLY PUBERTY

- Reproductive cancers, especially of the breast and ovaries
- Obesity
- Insulin resistance and diabetes
- Cardiovascular disease
- Short adult height

---

weight gain during childhood could be resulting in adverse hormonal or metabolic "programming" that persists throughout life—making weight loss and a healthier metabolic profile all the more difficult to achieve.

DON'T JUMP TO CONCLUSIONS

We should distinguish causation from correlation. Knowing the difference between the two will help assuage your fears about these behavioral and health risks.

"Correlation does not imply causation" is a popular phrase used in science to emphasize that a correlation between two variables does not necessarily mean that one directly causes the other. In a widely cited example, numerous studies once showed that menopausal women who were taking combined hormone replacement therapy (HRT) had a lower incidence of coronary heart disease. This led doctors to suggest that HRT was protective against heart disease. But randomized controlled trials—the gold standard in science—conducted to verify that this was the case revealed something different: HRT caused a small but statistically significant *increase* in the risk of heart disease. This prompted scientists to take another look at the earlier data, which showed that the women in those initial epidemiological studies who were taking HRT were more likely to be from higher socioeconomic groups. This meant they were more likely to practice healthier diet and exercise habits than the average woman did. So, the use of HRT and the decreased incidence of coronary heart disease were associated due to a common cause—the superficial relationship was attributable purely to the benefits of having a higher socioeconomic status rather than because they were cause and effect.

If we were to ask you if sugary foods cause obesity in kids, or if watching too much TV causes children to perform poorly in school, you wouldn't be able to say definitively yes or no once you thought about it. Why not? Because you'd recognize that there are many potential influences on a kid's weight or academic prowess. The child could counteract her obesity risk despite eating a lot of sugar by getting plenty of exercise and eating an otherwise healthy diet. And who's to say that bad report card isn't the result of a hostile household environment or a learning problem, regardless of the amount of TV watching? Here's another analogy to think about: We used to assume that ulcers were caused by stress and spicy foods, because we noticed there was a strong correlation between the independent variables—stress and spicy foods—and the dependent variable of ulcers. But we know now that most ulcers are caused by a bacterium, *Helicobacter pylori.* Although natural stomach acids and spicy foods can irritate the already damaged digestive tracts of people who have ulcers, they don't directly cause ulcers.

The subject of early puberty, like the stories of HRT and stomach ulcers, is laden with a lot of misinformation. Incorrect conclusions made in light of one or two studies can rapidly become conventional wisdom. What happens is that the media often simplify scientific findings from a single study, which the public then interprets as being definitive. This unfortunately leads to the proliferation of broad, unsubstantiated claims that reflect false cause-and-effect relationships. (Scientists, on the other hand, do the opposite—they are extremely cautious about overinterpreting their study results as sure things until the findings are replicated many times.) So we need to be careful about how we talk about and address these risks. Because not all early maturers have behavioral and health problems (and, conversely, because not all of those who *do* have behavioral and health problems are early maturers), other variables must be involved. And while people tend to cast blame on early puberty when discussing the chance of having a negative outcome of some kind, they forget about how much power certain lifestyle practices can have in significantly reducing all of these risks. They also tend to forget that puberty is normal. That's right: *Puberty is normal even when it arrives early.*

PUBERTY IS NORMAL!

Now that we've covered the main behavioral and health risks associated with early puberty, we want to emphasize the normalcy of puberty itself. This can help you better manage all those risks in the context of a "new normal." Indeed, girls who go through puberty early have to cope with what may seem like a laundry list of additional challenges so they can enjoy healthy, long lives. But no matter what age a girl is when she enters puberty, much of her journey will share very similar characteristics with those of all pubescent girls. And this is especially true when it comes to how they behave as they mature.

As mothers in the 21st century, we're acutely aware of how much has changed from a parental standpoint since we were kids. It used to be that parents encouraged kids to perform for adults (cue the image of the piano recital) and otherwise not have much to do with adult conversation. But we make sure that we let our daughters know that what they have to say is important and could actually influence the way we think about something. We stay open to the possibility that they could change, or add to, the way we see the world. This goes a long way in our daughters feeling seen and heard, and building our relationship and their self-confidence. In Part II, we'll be going into greater depth for establishing these important bonds and leading them through a journey that might have some behavioral challenges.

It's somewhat contradictory that we expect our toddlers to misbehave, yet we want our pubescent children to act like angels. Seeking autonomy and independence is a natural and healthy part of the developmental process. It defines adolescence and facilitates a lot of positive change. For example, parents hope that their adolescents are able to do their homework on their own, get dressed in the morning without assistance, and eventually make their own lunches and get to school by themselves if possible. So, while as parents we expect and even welcome these helpful changes, we must remember that kids will also want to make some of their own decisions in other realms of life. Sometimes those realms can be intimidating for parents, however, and fear and conflict can arise.

As kids mature, they often see things differently than their parents do, and they begin to negotiate with them. On the positive side of this process is independent and creative thought in school and in schoolwork. Adolescents are able to problem solve and learn from trial and error on their own. As this newfound independence is emerging, though, a parent's job is to support the child and guide him or her to make good, safe decisions, not dangerous or risky ones. Unfortunately, kids often need to learn by experience, and we can't watch them all the time. As adolescents get older, they spend less and less time with us and more time in school and with friends.

We love how Bruce Ellis, a University of Arizona evolutionary developmental psychologist, articulates the normalcy of puberty: "Everyone talks about early puberty as a crisis, but no one really talks about the function or purpose of puberty. We need the functional perspective to explain what these changes mean and how they play out. Puberty is fundamentally a transition from a prereproductive to a reproductive portion of the life span. . . . The person is entering the breeding pool and developing the social and physical abilities to attract mates, and all of the changes that take place to make this happen can be understood within that framework." As examples, he cites the typical pubescent's huge growth spurt, the dramatic increase in the number of calories consumed (which supports the physical growth needed to compete with other adolescents), and the changes in sexual motivation as well as shifts in sensation seeking and aggression.

All of these transformations, however fast or slow, are completely normal. And as for why puberty now seems to have speeded up, it's

because we're living in a world that supports
these changes with, for example, extraordi-
narily improved medical conditions, good
hygiene, increased access to calories, and a
more sedentary lifestyle of reduced physical
activity. These factors combine to generate a
powerful force favoring early puberty.
"We've always had the potential to go
through puberty this early, but it's never
happened in history," Ellis says. "This set of
circumstances is highly novel in terms of our
evolutionary environment."

NEW PUBERTY FACT

Entering puberty early isn't
necessarily bad; today's
trends could simply reflect
a powerful set of environmental forces that the body
is responding to and that
favors early development.
We know very little about
potential advantages it may
confer and these are
understudied.

Which likely means that early puberty
may not be bad or harmful. It's simply a product of where we are on the
evolutionary continuum.

One of the most fascinating conversations in scientific circles is the
one about the mismatch between our "Stone Age genes" and "space
age" circumstances. As many books, and especially diet books, have
pointed out, today we're living with genes that were programmed during prehistoric times when food was scarce and, therefore, having
access to ample calories was the body's opportunity to build fat stores
for survival. This reality has unique repercussions for children going
through puberty, which is a time when physiology and metabolism are
impacted by remarkable forces. The so-called thrifty gene hypothesis
helps explain some of the biological pressures stimulating early maturation. We still have a hunter–gatherer genome; it's thrifty in the sense
that it's programmed to make us fat during times of abundance. Genet-
icist James Neel, MD, PhD, first described the hypothesis in 1962 to
help explain why diabetes has such a strong genetic basis and results in
such negative effects. According to the theory, the genes that predispose someone to diabetes—the "thrifty genes"—were advantageous
long ago. They helped one fatten up quickly when food was available,

since long stretches of food scarcity were inevitable throughout much of human evolution. But once modern society changed our access to food, the thrifty genes, though no longer needed, were still active. Today, they are essentially preparing us for a hypothetical famine that doesn't arrive. Many scientists believe that our thrifty genes are partially responsible for the obesity epidemic, which is closely tied to the development of diabetes. Researchers are also studying how the environment of a growing fetus in utero can be having a direct impact on how that baby's genes will express themselves later and impact the risk for conditions like obesity.

We are designed not only to fatten up whenever possible, studies show, but also to reproduce as early as we can. Back in the Stone Age, a woman would have had her first baby at a younger age and breastfed for longer than are typical today, thereby reducing her body's exposure to certain hormones that would have increased her lifetime risk of cancer. Today, however, women tend to delay childbirth and breastfeed for a shorter period of time. They also don't have as many children as their cavewoman counterparts, who were either pregnant or nursing during most of their reproductive years. This, combined with the possibility of getting one's period at a younger age than a cavewoman, sets the stage for elevated health risks.

One final matter we'd like to point out in this chapter—to emphasize the normalcy of puberty—is that it's frequently misunderstood as a time when a child is melodramatic and behaves uncontrollably thanks to hormones running amok. Elizabeth "Birdie" Shirtcliff, PhD, is the author of major scientific papers that have demonstrated the environmental and psychosocial impacts this phase of life has on adolescents, especially with respect to stress physiology. Based at Iowa State University, where she's an associate professor in the department of human development and

NEW PUBERTY FACT

Hormones don't create emotions, but hormones can intensify existing emotions.

family studies, she finds herself constantly setting the record straight about puberty's hormonal impacts. She puts it bluntly: "Once puberty kicks in, there's a tendency to think that kids will be out of control." She explains that hormones don't *cause* emotions—they intensify the emotions that are already there. "If a girl is calm and rational," she says, "then she won't suddenly become wild and irrational. But if a girl is already struggling, or she's emotional, or [she's] put in advanced social situations, then [certain hormones] can exaggerate those emotions."

Shirtcliff's remarks are highly relevant to anyone worried about difficult behavior from early-maturing girls, for the inevitable hormonal changes are normal, and not doom laden. And, she says, an adult can help a girl navigate puberty despite the commanding presence of these hormones. "You can't control the hormones," she says, "but you can, to an extent, control the context." As parents and adults who work with children, we can create the proper supportive structure that will help prepare a maturing girl for the rigors of adolescence and all the social situations and peer-related demands it will bring. After all, as Shirtcliff points out, "You can't lock them away. When they are calm, don't disregard their opinions. Give them more grown-up roles so they can practice controlling their behavior. Then they'll be more likely to control themselves in situations that are emotionally charged."

That's just a taste of what's to come when we cover the how-tos of nurturing girls as they navigate puberty.

CHAPTER THREE

NATURE VERSUS NURTURE

An In-Depth Look at Puberty Prompters

IF YOU WERE TO ASK people on the street what causes early puberty, you'd hear plenty of theories, from hormones in our meat and dairy products to an overload of plastics, pesticides, and soy. Here are a few anxious questions we hear on a regular basis.

> *My 4th-grader came home today with spotting in her underwear. Is this because I only recently changed to eco-friendly shampoos and I've messed up her hormones?*

> *I'm a single mom who has heard that girls will go through puberty earlier if there's no biological father in the home. I have a 5-year-old daughter, and I'm worried. Is this true?*

> *I'm a 3rd-grade teacher in a school that has a diverse student body, with kids from various backgrounds and family income levels. Why do some of my girls develop faster than others?*

> *My mom thinks my niece's early puberty is because she was fed soy-based formula as an infant. Is it?*

My sister-in-law insists that her kids never eat anything
from a plastic container. Is she crazy?

BECAUSE OUR GENETICS CAN'T POSSIBLY CHANGE as rapidly as puberty recently has, scientists are trying to determine what it is in the environment that might be the main culprit. But the potential environmental factors don't include just belching chemical plants, processed foods, and plastic water bottles.

As clinical researchers, when we use the word "environment," we're not talking solely about things you can consume or are exposed to via air and water. "Environment" represents a number of less tangible elements, such as the location of the family home—is it in the country, the suburbs, or an urban area? Who is living in the house? Is a girl's biological father living there? Are the parents happy and engaged or stressed and emotionally distant? Is the neighborhood safe? Are there opportunities to play nearby? How much disposable income is available? Indeed, one's "environment" encompasses a lot.

Amidst all the facts we've learned from medicine and scientific research, we've probably heard every urban legend out there, and we marvel at some of the measures desperate parents will take to try to stall or thwart their young girls' development. Whether it's purging all plastics from the house and buying 100 percent organic everything, forcing their girls to consume herbs touted to eliminate estrogen, or insisting that their daughters exercise like athletes and train for 5-K runs, parents who take extreme measures can drive themselves (and their children) crazy by attempting to control a very natural process. While some parents don't do much at all, those who do take action often resort to faulty measures, especially once puberty has already commenced, and eliminate the wrong culprits from their households and their children's diets.

They also may be very confused about what should be considered normal and whether to take action. A 7-year-old sprouting pubic hair may be more common or even the "new normal," but whether or not it's "okay" is another question. An 8-year-old with the bust of an 11-year-old and a moody 9-year-old with acne may also be considered standard in media portrayals, but many adults still think that's not okay. So how do we rectify this disconnect between what's "normal" and what's "okay"?

To answer that, we must first turn to the potential environmental causes of early puberty and see where we can intervene to limit unhealthy exposures. In some cases, however, in the absence of any medical emergency, this may entail accepting a young body's natural (albeit early) transition. If we as parents and caretakers learn how to decipher between the more tangible, modifiable environmental factors that we can control—such as diet and exposure to substances known to disrupt a developing body's natural biochemistry—and the less easily modifiable factors, like family income or the proximity of a girl's school to the nearest freeway, then we can gain the upper hand in coping with a girl's maturation no matter how or when her body decides to bloom. We also can work on our relationships at home to provide the best, most nurturing environment possible before puberty starts and during this transition.

And so in this chapter, we're going to explore what environmental elements could be instrumental in early puberty. You've already gotten a primer on the potential triggers of early puberty (see "The Three Forces at Work in Early Puberty" on page 13), but now let's comb through the details in greater depth in preparation for Part II, where we will offer solutions for confidently managing and taking control of early puberty. Here, we're going to separate the hype and hyperbole from the truth, starting with the common misconception about one sign that causes many parents to panic: pubic hair.

IS IT REALLY PUBERTY?

Because pubic hair reflects the presence of androgens (male hormones) and the first true sign of puberty in girls is estrogen secretion, it is inaccurate to associate pubic hair with puberty in a girl. Rather, it means that her adrenal system is waking up and producing hormones that trigger the appearance of pubic hair—which is often (but not always) due to obesity and insulin resistance.

Some breast development may not be caused by true puberty either—the hormones responsible for this change are not coming from the pituitary. As we'll describe in the next chapter, real puberty cannot commence without gonadotropin-releasing hormone (GnRH), which is released by the brain. GnRH acts like a switch that turns on the pituitary gland, which then sends a message to the ovaries to produce estrogen, which causes breasts to grow. But the estrogen that is causing breast growth in some young girls may be coming from elsewhere, such as from the girls' fat tissue or from environmental sources. So if that estrogen production didn't start with GnRH release, it's not "real" puberty. And if breast development isn't caused by GnRH being released from the brain, then it doesn't automatically lead to early puberty. (A doctor can usually identify the biological origins of early puberty; see Chapter 4.)

Frank Biro, lead author of our 2010 *Pediatrics* paper that confirmed earlier breast budding in young girls (see Chapter 1) and one of our colleagues monitoring girls in the Breast Cancer and the Environment Research Program, began to suspect that estrogen had sources in the body other than the pituitary after the release of a groundbreaking study by a colleague, Dr. Anders Juul. In Juul's study, published in 2009, some of the girls with early breast development had surprisingly low levels of estradiol, the predominant form of estrogen in a female's body from puberty through menopause. Biro had noticed a pattern like this in our data as well as in other data of his own, indicating to him that estrogens not produced by the ovaries could be causing the early breast growth. In other words, the pubertal changes might not be originating in the girls' brains but rather in other sources inside or outside the body. He is now performing tests on our data to see if he can determine their origins.

The idea that estrogen-like chemicals and/or fat cells producing estrogen in a child's body can be enough to cause breast development is troubling. On the one hand, it might reassure the physician and parents that a girl doesn't have a pituitary tumor or another medical condition. However, if a girl is 9 but looks older, she may be medically healthy, but in a social context it doesn't make any difference what type of estrogens started her breast growth. She may not be interested in boys yet but she could find herself in complex social situations where older peers are attracted to her and she feels pressured to engage in early experimentation with alcohol or sexual activity. Also, she may no longer perceive herself as the 9-year-old she is and instead start to wrestle with a poor body image or, on the flip side, begin acting older because she gets positive attention for it.

Regardless of how or why these physical changes happen, the question remains: What environmental factors could be exerting power over a developing human body? So let's turn to the possible perpetrators holding the remote control to our girls' puberty. And we'll start with the most obvious and fiercest one of all: obesity.

OBESITY AND INACTIVITY

The link between obesity and puberty starts at a very young age. Paul Kaplowitz, the Children's National Medical Center physician introduced in Chapter 1, has written extensively on this topic over the past decade. An article he published in *Pediatrics* in 2001 was among the first to support the idea that an increase in obesity might be driving the trend for the earlier onset of puberty. Since then numerous other studies and scientific discussions have confirmed this link. A girl's body mass index in early life (whether at 5 years, 3 years, or even 9 months of age) is indeed associated with earlier pubertal timing. This fact has led pediatric endocrinologists to move away from their previous idea that once a girl's body reaches a certain body mass, puberty assuredly starts (this was known as the critical-weight theory). Now we refer to the critical-*fat* theory, for we now believe that *fat tissue,* not simple body mass or poundage, initiates a feedback loop that spurs maturation. And the reason for this is that fat releases the hormone leptin, which not only may contribute to early puberty, but also causes higher estrogen levels that encourage the buildup of more fat tissue—and, therefore, more leptin and estrogen. It's a self-propagating cycle that continues until the body is biologically mature.

The fact that obesity is a cause of early breast development was established in 2007 when Joyce Lee, MD, and her colleagues published a seminal study in *Pediatrics*. Lee, a pediatric endocrinologist at the University of Michigan, teased apart the chicken-or-egg problem to show that weight gain can lead to early puberty (for example, early breast development) and early puberty then can lead to more weight gain.

Let's back up a moment to underscore how fat tissue can play so powerful a role in regulating biological development. Most people assume that fat is just stored calories or "excess" that serves no purpose other than to pad us for a rainy day when food is scarce. But contrary to popular belief, fat cells are not inactive. Our total body fat mass can be thought of as our largest endocrine (hormonal) "organ," much bigger than our pituitary, adrenals, thyroid, and sex glands combined. Fat generates a multitude of substances, including enzymes, hormones, and chemical messengers, that can have a commanding role in our physiology and biochemical processes. Many of these molecules, like estrogen and leptin, can promote more fat storage. In fact, fat continually signals the body to create more fat cells to store more energy. A fact that is less well known is that the fat-loving ("lipophilic") synthetic chemicals we consume in our diets (e.g., additives, preservatives, stabilizing agents, residues from pesticides, etc.) and that enter our bodies from the environment in other ways often get stored in fat as well. These chemicals can further aggravate the body's biology by promoting even *more* fat storage and disrupting normal hormonal activity. There are other factors that can also contribute to the chaotic signaling, such as too little sleep and too little exercise—topics we'll get to later.

At the opposite end of the spectrum, we know that certain external forces, such as excessive exercise, can exert effects that *delay* puberty. Ice-skaters and gymnasts, for example, are famous for having extremely immature-looking bodies that defy their chronological ages (with teenage Olympic gymnasts often looking like 7- or 8-year-olds), and menarche in these girls is often delayed by years. Why? For the same reason that overweight girls experience puberty sooner: fat mass. Girls who exercise to extremes (and may suffer from eating disorders as well) tend to have lower fat masses and thus lower levels of hormones related to puberty. While we wouldn't recommend starting girls on restrictive diets or excessive exercise regimens, establishing healthy levels of exercise early in life may be one of the interventions that could help prevent early puberty or slow down the puberty already in progress.

The reason obesity can be so calamitous to a developing human being isn't just because excess fat can interfere with many bodily

---

OVERWEIGHT AND PREGNANT: A RECIPE FOR EARLY PUBERTY?

Is an overweight mother-to-be putting her unborn daughter at risk for early puberty? Possibly. In one of our recently published studies, we analyzed data from 2,497 mother–daughter pairs from the 1979 National Longitudinal Survey of Youth. We determined that women who were overweight when they became pregnant and those who gained excessive weight during pregnancy had higher odds of having girls who got their periods earlier. Why? Overweight mothers could potentially be passing along metabolic disadvantages to their daughters that put them at higher risk for obesity and diabetes. Moreover, women who develop diabetes when they are pregnant (a condition called gestational diabetes) expose their babies to higher insulin and glucose levels in utero, which has been linked to a higher risk of developing early pubic hair. The study of passing along such "environmental" effects despite one's fixed DNA is now a burgeoning field called epigenetics.

---

functions that in turn spark disorders and disease but also because, as we have already mentioned, certain environmental chemicals tend to be lipophilic, meaning that they accumulate in the endocrine glands and in fatty tissues such as the breasts. What's more, when the liver is overloaded with toxins to process, it can be less effective at clearing them from the body, especially excess estrogen. This may partly explain why anecdotal evidence suggests that a diet free of processed foods and refined sugars and high in fiber can delay puberty. It's not the sugar that triggers puberty per se, just as it may not be the fiber itself that potentially protects against early puberty; a healthy diet supports a well-functioning body, and a well-functioning, healthy body is less likely to suffer from metabolic disorders like diabetes and obesity.

EXPOSURE TO POLLUTION, CHEMICALS, AND HORMONES

Even though there is not yet definitive evidence in humans that specific environmental chemicals are a big factor in early puberty, there is plenty of convincing proof from animal studies and recent human studies to raise a red flag. But the guilty culprits might not be the ones you assume them to be. Every day, we find ourselves correcting misconceptions about what constitutes a true "chemical exposure" (to what people loosely call a toxin) that might trigger hormonal issues and impact the pubertal process in young girls. We also find that the media love to feature extremist views, like fearmongers claiming that we live in a "toxic soup" that is making us sick and, at the other extreme, those insisting that environmental concerns are blown out of proportion and we should trust the government to regulate what we eat and drink. These misguided voices only further polarize and misinform the public. To counter them, let's take a tour of the main suspects, starting with one that makes for a lot of confusion: soy.

Soy

Soy has gotten a bad rap because it contains plant estrogens that for a time were demonized for supposedly mimicking female hormones. But soy that comes from natural sources—so-called soy isoflavones such as tofu, edamame, and soy milk (as opposed to manufactured soy products like soy protein isolate, found in energy bars and processed foods that replace meat protein with soy)—are perfectly healthy. Although plant estrogens do bind to estrogen receptors in the body, they have very weak effects and are not true "hormone mimickers" in the same way as, say, synthetic chemicals that can profoundly change the body's natural hormonal machinery. In fact, natural soy may actually *protect* a girl from developing prematurely, and in some instances may delay puberty. The theory is that the early exposure to natural soy may lead to the body being less sensitive to estrogen receptors and thus make one less sensitive to estrogen later in life—hence less breast cancer. This may also work with breast development. Recent evidence from our own CYGNET work led by nutritional expert Lawrence Kushi at Kaiser Permanente's division of research suggests that this is likely the case. He says, "[Studies show that] women who ate more soy during adolescence had a lower breast cancer risk. Given that, we expect there to be some delay in puberty age onset in girls. And we have data to show that soy can confer some delay." He also dispels the myth that eating soy after you get breast cancer can increase your chance of recurrence. "Not true," he states. "[Those women] actually have a *lower* risk of occurrence."

However, it's well known that girls who consume more natural soy products also tend to gravitate toward more healthful diets generally (more fiber, less meat) and have lower body weights. These related influential nuances are challenging to tease apart—for instance, as noted above, a higher-fiber diet is associated with delayed puberty.

Hormones in Dairy and Meat

Another misunderstanding that we constantly encounter among even the most well-informed and best-educated adults is that hormones found in milk and meat, as a result of how cows and cattle are raised to yield more product, are biologically villainous. While that's not necessarily fiction, it's not entirely accurate, either. Some substances in milk may have very weak estrogenic effects in humans but probably are not responsible for interrupting normal hormonal signaling and activating early puberty. And to be clear: Some cows are injected with a hormone called recombinant bovine growth hormone (rBGH) that is related to the human form of growth hormone; however, since growth hormone is not a major player in triggering puberty, we have no reason to believe rBGH is a factor either. We also don't have evidence that naturally occurring hormones in beef and dairy have negative effects.

Both naturally occurring and added hormones that end up in these products are quickly degraded in the stomach.

True Endocrine Disruptors: Xenoestrogens

The real offenders are chemicals in the environment that, once ingested, *act like* hormones. Hence their name: hormone mimickers, technically known as xenoestrogens. These are not hormones per se, but they are so similar to estrogen in structure that they bind to estrogen receptor sites throughout the body, causing reactions similar to those of estrogen. Endocrine-disrupting chemicals include antibiotics (found in meats and dairy products), bisphenol A (BPA), tobacco, phthalates, flame-retardants, pesticides, and polychlorinated biphenyl compounds (PCBs). Even lavender and tea tree oil can have potent effects as estrogen mimickers, so their use by young children should be avoided.

> **NEW PUBERTY FACT**
>
> Antibiotics cause animals to grow larger and mature earlier, so they may act like endocrine-disrupting chemicals in humans.

As scientists, we can't conduct traditional experiments to determine whether or not and how these chemicals affect young bodies—it wouldn't be ethical to test certain exposures on a group of children and see what happens. So instead, we often resort to analyzing data gathered from accidents, such as one in 1973 in Michigan, when cattle were unintentionally fed grain contaminated with the flame-retardant PBB, an estrogen mimicker. As a result, the PBB wound up in the meat and milk products from these animals. The girls born to pregnant women who had consumed those products started menstruating, on average, a year earlier than their peers. A similar incident occurred in a population of Puerto Rican children during the mid-1980s. There, mothers and their children unknowingly consumed meat that contained high levels of estrogen-mimicking phthalates (plasticizers), and an epidemic of early pubertal development was documented in both the girls and boys.

Xenoestrogens Found in the Home Environment

Xenoestrogens are on the rise in our environment, and they are not easy to avoid. However, it's unclear at what levels these chemicals become toxic (produce unhealthy outcomes), particularly in young, developing girls. Animal studies can get us only so far in understanding what might be a safe versus an unsafe dose. Many pesticides (such as DDT), industrial chemicals, cosmetics, toiletries (such as scented body lotions), and plastics contain xenoestrogens. All of these chemicals also find their way into our water supply, and many of them don't readily break down into harmless forms and are "bioaccumulative," or stored in the fat of animals in increasing amounts as you move up the food chain (and ultimately are stored in our own fat tissue). They also tend to accumulate in the soil and in the underwater sediment where small organisms live and feed. And many of these chemicals are discharged into the environment legally, so they are difficult to control or remove. They are also hard to ban because they're used in so many products.

Even though some of these estrogen-mimicking chemicals have a short half-life (the time it takes for a chemical to lose half of its potency), many persist at high overall levels because they're continually flowing into the environment. And they are ubiquitous—found in everything from plastic toys to foods, cleaning agents, and nonstick coatings on pans to medical supplies. Young girls who love to play dress-up with sparkly makeup and perfumes are exposed to xenoestrogens every time they use popular cosmetic products, many of which contain estrogen-like compounds. Even conscientious parents may have a tough time finding beauty products that are chemical free. But as we'll see in Chapter 5, that doesn't mean all is doom and gloom. We can choose which items we buy, and companies are increasingly moving to create safer products.

The cumulative effect of multiple exposures to many estrogen mimickers has been a concern for years among researchers. For example, take the ubiquitous compound BPA. More than 93 percent of Americans have traces of this chemical in their bodies. BPA was first made in 1891 and used as a synthetic estrogen drug for women and animals in the first half of the 20th century until it was banned for medical use due to cancer-causing effects. (It was used in women to treat numerous conditions related to menstruation, menopause, and nausea during pregnancy and for the prevention of miscarriages; meat producers injected animals with the chemical to promote growth.) In the late 1950s, commercial manufacturers started putting BPA in plastics after chemists at Bayer and General Electric discovered that when BPA was linked together in long chains (polymerized), it formed a hard plastic called polycarbonate that's strong enough to replace steel and clear enough to replace glass. It soon found its way into electronics, safety equipment, automobiles, and food containers. Since then, BPA has been used in many common products, from cash-register receipts to dental sealants. More than a million pounds of the substance is released into the environment each year. The BPA found in plastic food containers has been shown to generate hormonal imbalances in both women and men. Such imbalances in females not only can play a role in the orchestra of biological events leading to early puberty but also may contribute to infertility and breast cancer later in life. Still, BPA is just one of many chemicals we encounter in daily life. Although it's increasingly being phased out of commercial products and the food supply thanks to aggressive consumer lobbying, there are thousands of other xenoestrogens continually inundating our environment that can be equally as harmful.

In Chapter 5, where we cover all the steps you can take to minimize harmful exposures to probable "puberty prompters," we'll see how three key factors come into play: the timing of the exposure, the dose of the exposure, and the route of exposure. We suspect that there is a big difference between a 5-year-old girl and a 50-year-old man consuming estrogen mimickers, much in the same way that lead paint chips can do serious damage to a baby's developing brain but leave a middle-aged individual unharmed. The windows of greatest susceptibility to endocrine-disrupting chemicals may be during fetal development and again during puberty. Of course, the dose received also is a key factor, because the level of exposure affects the extent to which a person is impacted. And the route of exposure is important, too. Since toxins can enter the body in a variety of ways—through the skin, lungs, and via a number of sources like food, air, and water—we can reduce some exposures by choosing safer cleaning supplies and skin-care and beauty products, as well as through diet. (The skin is the largest organ in the body, so young girls can get a sizable dose of external chemicals through this route.)

If we can intercede, we can substantially reduce—but probably not eliminate—these damaging exposures. Even by installing air and water filters in our homes and minimizing our use of all products known to contain suspicious chemicals, it's hard to control pollutants that we inevitably encounter in daily life. But we can, with relative ease, make a few shifts in what we purchase to limit the ways potentially harmful chemicals gain entry into the body.

THE SOCIAL LIFE: STRESSORS AT HOME

Although extremely stressful events like famine or war often delay puberty, ongoing chronic stress and conflict can push the body's puberty trigger early. A group of related theories ties this to evolution, as described earlier: In tough times, a species' survival is best served if its offspring mature (and hence reproduce) as soon as possible. So the body of a girl living under stressful circumstances might mature as quickly as possible with the idea of giving her the best chance to reproduce and propagate the species.

In another study, published in 2011, Bruce Ellis, the evolutionary developmental psychologist introduced in Chapter 2, and his colleagues (including one of us, Julie) showed that 1st-graders who were more sensitive to stress (based on how their hearts and cortisol levels responded to environmental challenges) entered puberty earliest when raised in difficult homes (i.e., homes where there were more negative interactions and less warmth). But stress-sensitive kids raised in positive, supportive homes were the latest to develop. Evolutionary psychology again suggests that a stressful and unpredictable childhood characterized by low parental investment pushes a body toward early reproduction; if life is hard or unpredictable, it's best to mature young.

While on the surface such a theory seems plausible, and even with many of today's families enduring extreme pressures of various kinds, it's very hard to prove and, therefore, quite controversial. A related theory explains how children's biological stress reactions may change in response to adversity. Remember that "stress" can encompass a multitude of circumstances, from physical or sexual abuse to poverty. According to the research, early exposure to stress in the family environment may influence how the body behaves biochemically in response to stress, which may subsequently accelerate hormonal responses related to puberty.

Supporting this is the fact that many studies have shown that girls who grow up in families that are less stable and experience higher levels of conflict have an increased likelihood of entering puberty and getting their periods earlier. Conversely, girls who grow up in warm, stable, loving homes may enter puberty later. Similar effects have been documented in animal studies led by Michael Meaney, PhD, and his team of scientists at McGill University in Montreal. The female pups of mother rats that lick and groom their offspring (analogous to expressing warmth in human families) enter puberty late. Meaney and colleagues have also found that the quality and quantity of the maternal care given by rats changes their female offspring's neuroendocrine responses to stress. These researchers and others are extending this work to humans to examine the effects of early-life stressors on pubertal development.

We know that stress has major health repercussions, from raising levels of the stress hormone cortisol to fanning the flames of inflammation that can have a negative impact on health over the long run. The stress response, which typically starts with the release of cortisol to trigger the self-preserving fight-or-flight impulse, may be helpful in the short term, but over the course of a lifetime, it can raise the risks of developing certain health conditions, such as cardiovascular disease and cancer.

Two researchers, Bruce Ellis and Jacqueline Tither, launched a study published in 2008 that examined 160 sibling pairs in New Zealand. They discovered a prevalence of early puberty in girls whose parents divorced when those girls were prepubertal (around age 5½ on average) and whose fathers were considered to be seriously dysfunctional (meaning they abused drugs or alcohol, were violent, attempted suicide, or spent time in prison). Curiously, this effect was not seen in their older sisters, who had already started puberty and were approximately 12 years old at the time of the divorce; in other words, the older girls' pubertal experience wasn't affected by the divorce (we'll discuss why later). Clearly the age of the girl and the timing of her parents' divorce—and the intensity of the paternal dysfunction that preceded it—played key roles in prompting menstruation almost a year earlier, on average, in the younger siblings.

NEW PUBERTY FACT

A child's responses to stress may affect pubertal timing.

Tom Boyce, MD, and Bruce Ellis have also suggested that there may be an "orchid" and "dandelion" phenomenon at work here. In other words, certain kids are resilient regardless of their circumstances; kids who show low stress reactivity appear to weather family conflict like dandelions weather storms—the stress doesn't have as detrimental an impact on them, and puberty is unaffected. Alternatively, orchid children, who react more strongly to stress physiologically, tend to blossom in optimal conditions (i.e., warm, loving families). But these kids wilt when the conditions get rough, and they are more likely to enter puberty early. Therefore, knowing how reactive your child is to everyday stress may be an essential tool in helping her weather the physical and emotional impacts of stress. As a parent, you can provide your child with a warm, nurturing, and safe environment, particularly in the early years of life that are so important. No matter how chaotic the outside world is, parents can exert this power while their children are still young. Little is known about the effects of the classroom environment, where kids eventually spend most of their time when they aren't at home. However, extending the same logic indicates that safe and nurturing classrooms (and even neighborhoods and communities) also have a protective effect.

A big question in research now: Are kids orchids or dandelions from birth? Is this a trait you're born with, like the color of your eyes, or is it a function of the early environment, with the stressors encountered early in life, perhaps even in utero, shaping a child's biological responses to stress? Current signs point to both.

But as we mentioned earlier, such theories are challenging to prove. Researchers showed that children adopted from orphanages in developing countries, who have experienced significant stress during early childhood, are also at greater risk for early puberty once they're living with Western families. One explanation for this is that their bodies opened the hormonal floodgates once the chronic stressors of life as orphans were *removed*. This explains the results of the study mentioned before that revealed different timing for puberty in older and younger daughters of divorced parents. While both sisters experienced high levels of chronic stress, the younger girls' bodies reacted to the relief the divorce provided by deciding it was an advantageous time to reproduce. The older sisters' bodies, however, didn't experience that relief before their pubertal years, so their hormonal floodgates opened significantly later.

Interestingly, there's evidence linking a mother's depression with early development in her daughters. Studies going back to 2000 have looked at whether a mother's stress or mood disorder could cause earlier puberty. (In fact, depression in any family member may trigger early puberty in a young girl if there's a high level of family dysfunction as a result.) Although a direct cause-and-effect relationship is difficult to prove, researchers have linked a strong early bond between mother and baby to *later* pubertal onset, suggesting how parents can give their girls the best start possible.

Research has shown for decades that girls who grow up from an early age in homes without their biological fathers are twice as likely to experience menarche early (before age 12) than those who grow up with both parents under the same roof. Some researchers also report that the presence of a stepfather in the house correlates with early puberty, but the findings are inconclusive. How can a biological father living in the home protect a young girl from early puberty? The answer is not clear, but some researchers believe having Dad in the home exposes the girl to his familiar pheromones. (Pheromones are chemicals we all release into the air that are thought to stimulate hormonal reactions in others.) Animal studies show that when the urine of strange males is placed in the cage with prepubertal females, the females' fertility is stimulated earlier. A father's familiar

NEW PUBERTY FACT

A girl who grows up without her biological father in the home is twice as likely to get her first period before age 12.

scent, then, might have the opposite effect. Although this idea is intriguing, it's currently impossible to verify it in humans. More research needs to be conducted on the senses before such a definitive conclusion is reached.

Other researchers have examined whether a father's absence—or a mom's single parenthood—is correlated with lower income, poorer diet, and obesity and whether these issues then forecast earlier puberty. Studies currently under way are seeking to determine which aspects of the family environment explain the effects an absentee father has on his daughter's pubertal course.

We are often asked by couples with adopted children and same-sex couples with biological or adopted kids what they can expect for their daughters, but research in such families is too scanty to permit conclusions. Also, parents who are divorced often ask about the effects of Dad's part-time presence in joint-custody or equal-care situations. The research here is also thin, but we can surmise that even in these circumstances, having a very involved parent in a child's life can be protective.

MEDIA

It's common knowledge that kids in our society are exposed to more "sexualized" information and images today than in the past. Social media, the Internet, and cable TV have all contributed to this effect. These technologies give everyone access to all types of content like never before, but they also give rise to two unfortunate results: accidental exposure to inappropriate material and a trickle-down effect produced by the sheer amount of sexualized content in our culture that ends up being partially geared toward—and marketed to—pre-teens and kids. Think about the sexy clothing made for toddlers and "bralettes" for 5-year-olds. Or the images and behaviors seen on television shows for tweens that younger girls may watch, too (and let's not forget Miley Cyrus's live performance on broadcast television at the

MTV Video Music Awards in 2013). But can early exposure to sexual content trigger the body's pubertal processes?

Truth be told, we don't have enough evidence for a definitive answer. Some experts—like Marcia Herman-Giddens, the woman who first brought the phenomenon of early puberty into view for society and the medical community—believe that the media's culture of hypersexualization could be one of many factors triggering early maturational processes in children. She thinks violent, sexualized, and consumer-driven images "spill over into everything that they buy, eat, wear, and do," and the media's depiction of children as sexual beings is "a phenomenon that goes hand in hand with the actual earlier physical development of children, especially girls." But such a connection has yet to be studied. Herman-Giddens further cautions that even if seeing sexual content affects a girl's sex hormone levels, it doesn't mean this could act as a trigger for early puberty. "Nonetheless, it is an area that needs to be researched," she asserts.

One intriguing facet of this conversation that rarely gets mentioned but is worth noting: Could exposure to the *hardware* that supports these media—such as computer screens, tablets, and television sets—be having an adverse effect that has nothing to do with the content streaming through them? Possibly. It turns out that limiting the time an early-blooming adolescent spends in front of a computer screen achieves more than curtailing their access to inappropriate Web sites, racy YouTube videos, and general overconsumption of media. New studies show that the pineal gland—a small, mysterious endocrine organ in the brain that produces several hormones—is highly sensitive to certain wavelengths emitted from digital screens. This partly explains why teens who use computers, tablets, and smartphones late at night can have a difficult time going to sleep, as these devices stimulate the pineal gland and disrupt its production of melatonin, the sleep-inducing hormone. This lack of sleep can lead to other problems like poor academic functioning, memory issues, car accidents, and substance use (such as abuse of caffeine or prescription medications to stay alert or marijuana or alcohol to facilitate sleep). There is also some speculation now that some types of artificial lighting affect puberty (more on this later). For these reasons, in Chapter 6 we recommend setting "screen time" limits in addition to monitoring what they are watching and where computers are kept in the home.

POVERTY

We've already touched on the fact that the girl who grows up in an impoverished family or neighborhood in the United States or other developed country is at an increased risk for early puberty. But there's an interesting paradox here: Extreme poverty of the sort characterized by malnutrition and severe psychological strain due to acute stressors like famine, epidemic disease, and war has been shown to *delay* puberty, whereas poverty of the variety typically found in developed nations may trigger early puberty.

As we've described, when there are not enough resources to fuel a human body, Mother Nature won't support reproduction (or its maturation). But when there are plenty of resources in the form of calories and just enough stress to prompt survival responses, early puberty is stimulated. And it's in industrialized nations where we find people who are both overfed and undernourished—where obesity rates are high and frequently correlated with a lack of adequate resources to support healthier habits.

ETHNICITY

We saved this factor for last since it's a highly convoluted topic involving everything from socioeconomic forces to potential genetic ones. African American and Hispanic girls tend to start puberty (as measured by breast development) 6 months to a year sooner than their

Caucasian counterparts, and it's not necessarily due to their DNA. The dramatic disparity between the experience of puberty among blacks and Hispanics and their white or Asian peers may be partially genetic and largely related to social determinants. (For the record, there are genetic differences that seem to predispose African Americans to insulin resistance and hypertension, for example, and in general, this population has higher BMIs even in the healthy range. But it's hard to separate out other purely genetic risks that are not worsened by social disparities.)

Put simply, there's more going on from an environmental standpoint among African American and Hispanic girls that could be pushing those pubertal buttons. A lack of financial resources and poor access to healthful foods in low-income neighborhoods lead to a higher propensity to be overweight or obese. Due to historical and current social injustices, there's a higher likelihood of having an absentee

IS THERE A WEALTH EFFECT?

Some research—currently in its infancy—is examining whether and how wealth may play a role in affecting girls' puberty. We know that wealth may be associated with some of the other factors that appear to trigger earlier maturation, such as unlimited access to electronics, less sleep (particularly in overachieving and overbooked kids), and stress related to the drive to succeed. However, on the flip side, wealthy families have the resources to eat more healthful foods that don't contain endocrine-disrupting chemicals (EDCs), limit financial strain, buy environmentally friendly beauty and cleaning products, and have more access to safe places to play and recreate. As such, lack of resources or poverty seem more tightly linked to the stressors proven to influence early puberty than wealth does. This may partially explain why ethnic minority girls in the United States are experiencing puberty at earlier ages than their non-Hispanic white counterparts.

father in African American households, and families of color endure more stressors from the environment, including greater exposure to environmental hazards in certain geographic areas, racial discrimination, job insecurity and financial strain, neighborhood crime, single motherhood, fewer opportunities to play outside, etc. In other words, girls of color are experiencing not one or two risk factors associated with early puberty, but a maelstrom of conditions all at once. Just as rising rates of obesity are distributed disproportionately throughout the United States, with higher rates in lower socioeconomic communities, so too is there a correlation between rates of early puberty and ethnicities with higher rates of poverty.

IT'S NORMAL—BUT IS IT OKAY?

As you can probably conclude by now, it's hard to put a finger on a single trigger for early puberty; instead, exposure to a variety of influencers is likely the driving force behind this phenomenon. The other critical message to take away is that many of these potential factors are interrelated. A stressful home life, for example, can exacerbate obesity, just as much as obesity may compound the effects that environmental toxins have on the body. And the chance that a young girl is exposed to toxins is often linked to her family's economic resources and her parents' education. These intricate relationships make the study of early puberty all the more challenging—and endlessly fascinating.

It's important to remember that heightened risk factors are *not* causal—in other words, just being exposed to a potential peril does not doom a girl to early puberty. There are key protective elements that appear to offset these dangers, and we will describe them in detail in the upcoming chapters. For those dealing with girls who have already started puberty, you cannot stop the process, but you can certainly influence what happens farther down the road. It may sound obvious, but if a girl is living in a supportive family environment where she is eating family meals, getting regular sleep, and being encouraged to participate in sports and be active to stave off obesity, a parent can wield a good deal of control—including with very young girls who haven't even begun to show signs of puberty. Early breast growth is not a sure sign of trouble ahead. It doesn't automatically signal that she will leap from the first signs of early puberty to having body-image issues or depression, starting to smoke or drink, and seeking romantic involvement with older youths.

To some extent, pointing a finger at all the potential triggers for early puberty is a moot endeavor for parents. What's most important is that you learn how to manage this phenomenon so your girl can take advantage of its hidden blessings while avoiding its common pitfalls— to make it normal *and* okay.

Our girls knew about puberty long before they heard about it in school. They were even comfortable saying words like vagina, breasts, pubic hair, and penis aloud. And thanks to our early teachings, they view puberty as something normal and special, rather than something odd and embarrassing. We hope that perspectives like this can help change the culture in schools and make it okay to talk about these matters in real ways.

So, it's important to note that after running down the list of possible risk factors, we are often asked by confused parents why *their* daughter entered puberty early. We hear time and time again about early-maturing girls whose mothers were late bloomers, who were raised in stable and intact families, who eat well, exercise, aren't overweight, and get plenty of sleep. Well, that's the nature of science and medicine. We can identify risk at the population level and then study how it might apply to individuals, but each individual is unique. There are no formulas for how and when girls enter puberty.

TOP THREE WAYS TO PREVENT OR SLOW DOWN EARLY PUBERTY

- Help a girl establish healthy habits that will keep her fit, well rested, and at an ideal weight.

- Limit exposure to synthetic chemicals that may disrupt healthy human biology.

- Work toward maintaining a loving, supportive family environment.

PART II

STRATEGIES TO HELP GROWING GIRLS THRIVE

CHAPTER FOUR

IS TREATMENT NECESSARY?

How to Know When to Medically Intervene

MEET MAYA, A 7-YEAR-OLD AFRICAN AMERICAN girl whose mother brings her to the pediatrician with concerns over pubic hair development and worsening body odor that started when she was 6. Although Maya is a very active girl who enjoys dance classes twice a week in addition to PE, she's always been on the heavy side, and her pediatrician has voiced concern over her increasing body mass index. Maya is tall compared to her peers, but she's not experiencing a growth spurt. A bone age x-ray, which reveals how physically mature she is based on the development of her bones, confirms that her biological age is the same as her chronological age, but a blood test shows an elevated level of a hormone coming from her adrenal glands that's related to puberty. Other tests performed to rule out serious hormonal anomalies are normal. Maya's pediatrician counsels the family on dietary changes to address her weight gain and does not refer her to a specialist for puberty. Maya develops breasts at age 8½, and gets her period a few months before turning 11.

Should Maya have seen another doctor? Is she a classic case of early puberty? Could her parents have delayed her body's development? And if so, would this have been a good idea?

Before addressing such questions, we should define puberty from a biological standpoint so you can understand how doctors think when they see a girl like Maya. As we outlined in the Introduction, puberty is a long process that entails a well-defined sequence of events starting with certain physiological changes that kick in before visible changes are present and ending with a girl being able to have a child. And that process has been starting at younger and younger ages for girls today. Although in the past, earlier puberty often occurred with improved health and better nutrition, today's early puberty likely reflects different forces working on the human body. The obesity epidemic and an overabundance of calories no doubt play a role.

For someone like Maya, her weight likely awakened her adrenal system, leading to her pubic hair and body odor, but not necessarily real puberty. And her increased height at this stage followed her weight naturally, though she'll likely be outpaced by peers who start puberty later on. Why does this happen? We'll take you on a guided tour of a young girl's body to help you figure out exactly where your girl is on the puberty spectrum from a medical standpoint and learn how to properly manage her development, whether that includes medical intervention or not. From working with thousands of parents and children, we know that one of the most unsettling and stressful aspects of dealing with early puberty is simply getting past the initial phase of gathering information and becoming confident that you know what to do next.

PUBERTY'S SILENT BEGINNINGS

People commonly think that a girl's puberty starts with the onset of her period, or menarche. But that's one of the final events in a long process that begins years earlier. The medical term for the onset of puberty is actually "gonadarche" ("gonad" refers to the reproductive glands and "arche" is from the Greek word for "beginning" or "onset"), which occurs when the pituitary awakens the gonads—the ovaries in girls and the testes in boys. The pituitary gland is a pea-size structure situated behind the eyes that secretes hormones as directed by the hypothalamus. Although the pituitary usually steals all the credit for being the master hormonal gland, in reality it's the servant of the hypothalamus, which is among the most ancient structures in the human body (we inherited the hypothalamus from lower vertebrates, and research has traced this portion of the brain back to wormlike marine ancestors that existed tens of millions of years before mammals emerged). Roughly the size of an almond, the hypothalamus sits in the middle of the brain and is responsible for releasing chemicals that regulate bodily functions. Think of it as a sort of traffic control center for your entire body, presiding over a wide range of physiological functions throughout our lives, including body temperature, thirst, hunger, moodiness, water balance, circadian rhythms, puberty, arousal and sexual function, and even contractions during childbirth. We owe much of our experience of pleasure, aggression, stress, embarrassment, and aversion to our hypothalamus and the hormones it triggers. It's fully functional at birth, and one of its most important jobs is to link the nervous system to the hormonal system, also known as the endocrine system.

The endocrine system controls development, growth, reproduction, and behavior through an intricate, balanced orchestration of hormones. On a basic level, hormones are your body's messengers. Typically produced in one part of the body, such as the thyroid, adrenal, or pituitary gland, they pass into the bloodstream and then travel to distant organs and tissues to modify their structures and functions. They act like conductors of an orchestra, telling your body what to do and when so it can run effectively. Hormones are as much a part of your respiratory, cardiovascular, nervous, muscular, skeletal, and digestive systems as they are a part of your reproductive system.

As previously mentioned, puberty begins with gonadarche, when the hypothalamic–pituitary–gonadal axis is activated. That's when two hormones are pumped out by the pituitary: luteinizing hormone (LH) and follicle-stimulating hormone (FSH). LH and FSH cause the ovaries to produce estrogen and progesterone, which are necessary for female sexual characteristics such as the breasts to develop; LH and FSH also signal the testicles to produce testosterone, which is responsible for developing male sexual characteristics like larger testes.

Historically, gonadarche typically began between the ages of 8 and 13 years in females and 9 and 14 in males. Breast development, or the-larche ("thel" comes from the Greek word for nipple), is the clinical sign doctors look for to diagnose the onset of puberty. Your pediatrician will distinguish between true breast development (that is, the growth of glandular breast tissue) and fat accumulation, which is often mistaken for breast development, by examining the breast, since the two feel different. Fat is soft, whereas breast tissue is firmer. This isn't something we recommend that parents do, even mothers. It's best left to well-trained doctors who can tell you which of the five Tanner stages of breast development your girl is in (see Chapter 1); stage 1 is prepubertal, whereas stage 5 is an adult.

As we highlighted in Chapter 3, the appearance of pubic hair isn't always a sign of puberty. It *does* happen with true puberty, but it also can result from a different process that starts in the two adrenal glands rather than in the pituitary. Each adrenal gland sits atop one of the two kidneys, which are located about halfway down the torso, near the bottom of the rib cage. The adrenal glands are small, but they are potent. And when they awaken, in a process called adrenarche or sometimes pubarche, they start to secrete hormones, some of which cause pubic hair development. In other words, the growth of pubic hair can precede breast development, the latter of which is usually triggered by the pituitary.

The adrenals are key glands in both developing children and fully

MILESTONES OF PUBERTY

- Gonadarche (go-nad-ar'kee): Luteinizing hormone (LH) and follicle-stimulating hormone (FSH) cause the ovaries to produce estrogen.

- Thelarche (thee-lar'kee): The onset of female breast development

- Adrenarche (ad-re-nar'kee): The onset of armpit and pubic hair, acne, and body odor

- Pubarche (pew-bar'kee): The appearance of pubic hair, occurring as part of adrenarche

- Menarche (meh-nar'kee): The onset of menstruation

grown adults. In addition to producing hormones, they help to determine your energy level; control inflammation; induce the fight-or-flight stress response; and balance the levels of fluids, minerals, and blood sugar. Different sections of the adrenals produce different hormones. The part involved with pubic hair development is the outer layer, called the adrenal cortex, and among the many hormones it secretes are cortisol, testosterone, epinephrine, and DHEA (dehydroepiandrosterone, which is used to make estrogen and testosterone). It is DHEA that is responsible for the development of pubic hair. Adrenarche starts when DHEA (and sometimes testosterone) begins to rise, and the glands' production peaks in an individual's early twenties. Adrenarche prompts the development of armpit and pubic hair, changes in sweat glands and body odor, and, often, acne.

As mentioned, adrenarche often occurs earlier than gonadarche. Although in the past thelarche and adrenarche usually happened after the age of 8 in girls, nowadays they typically start between the ages of 7 and 10 in females, and a year or 2 later in males. As noted in the Introduction, our 2010 study found that at age 7, more than 10 percent of Caucasian girls in America had started growing breasts, along with almost 25 percent of African American girls and 15 percent of Hispanic girls. And at age 8, those percentages had spiked to a whopping 18, 43, and 31, respectively.

Another major event in puberty is a growth spurt that changes a child's size and body composition. In the past, this has typically occurred at about age 12 in girls and age 14 in boys, but a girl who enters puberty early will probably have that initial growth spurt by age 10 and be much taller than her peers for a while.

Weight and height share a unique relationship in puberty, with growth typically following weight gain. This explains why obesity can cause a girl to have an early growth spurt, but wind up not being as tall as her normal-weight peers because the excess weight shortens the duration of the growth spurt. Again, a bone age x-ray can help a doctor figure out where a girl is on the puberty spectrum. A simple x-ray of the wrist and hand, it allows bones to be evaluated for their maturity (i.e., how much they have developed), with early maturation indicating that the girl has been producing estrogen for longer. It also can show how much growth potential a child has before reaching his or her full height.

The growth plates of the bones can be seen in the x-ray. An x-ray of a 5-year-old girl's wrist typically shows a lot of black, which is cartilage, a flexible connective tissue that is replaced by bone as she develops. The growth plates of a 15-year-old girl, on the other hand, appear white because they are done growing. Children with early-maturing bones stop growing sooner. For example, a 10-year-old with the bones of a 13-year-old may be the tallest girl in her 5th-grade class, but she will stop growing and could be outpaced by her peers who mature later on and continue to grow. (By the way, we don't recommend that normally developing girls have bone age x-rays because there is no reason to expose them to the radiation. The procedure is safe, of course, but it's necessary only when a doctor is trying to diagnose early puberty—not so parents can find out how tall their child will be!)

Every girl's pathway through puberty is different. For some, pubic hair comes first; for others, it's breasts. But the pathway a girl takes can result in her having certain health risks. As you know from the previous chapter, the girl whose breasts develop sooner is more vulnerable later in

NEW PUBERTY FACT

Early breast development may be associated with a higher risk for estrogen-related diseases like breast cancer later in life. Early pubic hair growth is associated with a higher risk for metabolic disorders like diabetes and heart disease.

life to estrogen-related diseases like breast cancer. And the girl who gets pubic hair first is more at risk for metabolic disorders such as obesity, diabetes, and heart disease. If pubic hair appears at an early age, she also has an increased risk for polycystic ovarian syndrome, an imbalance of female sex hormones, when she is older. Symptoms, which usually begin a few years after she has her first period, include acne, stubborn weight gain, irregular periods, and increased hair growth on the face, chest, around the nipples, or on the lower abdomen. Pubic hair growth in overweight or obese girls may be caused by insulin resistance, which is having a high level of the hormone that escorts the energy from the carbohydrates in food into the cells for use.

DO YOU NEED TO SEE A DOCTOR?

Although we recommend that any parent who's concerned about early puberty first schedule an appointment with the child's primary pediatrician, we've included a flowchart on page 82 that can help you understand what your next step should be and where your girl likely is in her pubertal process.

DO YOU WORRY SHE'S GOING THROUGH PUBERTY EARLY?

Yes

Then you need to see the pediatrician—asking the question merits the appointment

The Possibilities Based on Age

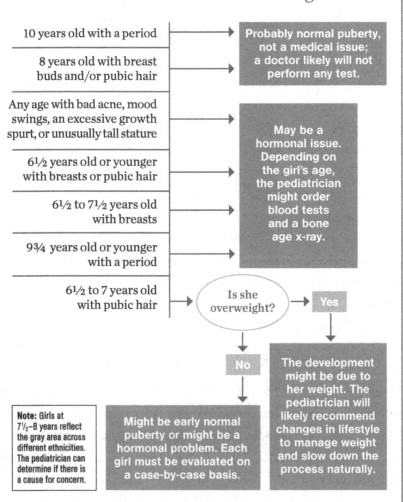

10 years old with a period

8 years old with breast buds and/or pubic hair

→ Probably normal puberty, not a medical issue; a doctor likely will not perform any test.

Any age with bad acne, mood swings, an excessive growth spurt, or unusually tall stature

6½ years old or younger with breasts or pubic hair

6½ to 7½ years old with breasts

9¾ years old or younger with a period

→ May be a hormonal issue. Depending on the girl's age, the pediatrician might order blood tests and a bone age x-ray.

6½ to 7 years old with pubic hair

→ Is she overweight? → Yes

→ The development might be due to her weight. The pediatrician will likely recommend changes in lifestyle to manage weight and slow down the process naturally.

No ↓

Might be early normal puberty or might be a hormonal problem. Each girl must be evaluated on a case-by-case basis.

Note: Girls at 7½–8 years reflect the gray area across different ethnicities. The pediatrician can determine if there is a cause for concern.

HOW TO PREPARE

A trip to the pediatrician can be very difficult emotional terrain for a girl to traverse. A parent—typically the mother—shouldn't make a big deal about going to the doctor, rather just tell the girl that she is going to have a routine checkup and that the doctor will examine how she is developing. It's fine for a parent to ask a daughter, "Have you noticed any changes in your body lately?" This can help you gauge where a kid is in terms of what she knows and has been experiencing. But she may lack the right vocabulary and be embarrassed or uncomfortable about using new terms she will encounter now, like "breasts," "pubic hair," "BO," "discharge," or "vagina." When Louise sees a girl for the first time, she uses age-appropriate dialogue, and often finds herself saying things like "Mikayla, do you know why you're here? I'm a special kind of doctor who looks at growth and development in children. Your body is changing in a way that usually happens to girls when they are a little older."

It's perfectly fine, too, to address matters privately with the doctor first, especially if there are behavioral issues or the child is having emotional problems because of the experience. Every family is different. Some also involve Dad if everyone—especially the girl—is comfortable with it.

WHAT THE DOCTOR WILL DO

Each girl must be looked at as an individual, because the decision to medicate depends on a host of factors such as her age, rate of development, current height, and emotional maturity. There are risks and long-term side effects for both giving medications and forgoing treatment. When a pediatrician suspects early puberty, the first step will likely be having the bone age x-ray we've described. If a young girl's bone age is older than her chronological age, the next step is usually a blood test, or possibly referral to a specialist like Louise, a pediatric endocrinologist who will take charge of the testing and diagnosing. To gather information, this specialist will ask questions such as:

- Was the child born premature or small for her gestational age?
- Did Mom have diabetes when she was pregnant?
- When did you notice breast development?
- How long has she had pubic hair?
- Is acne or body odor present? Any changes in mood?
- Is there any family history of early pubertal development?

The doctor will also examine the child, and perhaps order additional blood tests for hormone levels.

One test commonly used to detect puberty by measuring hormone levels is what's called a stimulation test. This involves giving the child a dose of a medicine that mimics gonadotropin-releasing hormone (GnRH)—the initiator of true puberty—and then checking blood samples drawn at timed intervals to see how the body responds. (Note: This test will *not* induce puberty.) GnRH, which is produced by the hypothalamus, stimulates the pituitary gland to produce sex hormones. The way the body responds to this hormonal test can help the pediatric endocrinologist decide whether there is indeed early puberty, and if so, whether the cause is the brain (the pituitary), the body (the ovaries or elsewhere), or something outside the body (the environment).

PUBERTY FROM THE PITUITARY. If early puberty is being triggered by the pituitary, the doctor will probably order a brain MRI to check for any abnormality such as a tumor. Ninety-five percent of the time, however, the MRI is normal, and there is no true cause found. Then the doctor and the family need to discuss what the options are, depending on the age of the child, how long she's been in puberty, and her health risks. Clearly, there's a difference between a 6-year-old starting puberty and an 8-year-old. If medication to slow down or halt the changes until the child reaches an appropriate age for puberty is decided upon as the best course, it can be given by injection every 1 or 3 months for as long as needed. Another option is an implant placed under the skin of the arm that is changed annually. This treatment is called GnRH analogue therapy, and the most popular drugs in use are leuprolide (Lupron Depot) and histrelin (Supprelin LA). These drugs are also used to treat advanced prostate cancer in men and endometriosis or fibroid tumors in women, and they are safe for children in whom the pros of intervening outweigh the cons. On average, about 6 months after stopping the medication, the process of puberty resumes.

If a girl was in very early puberty when diagnosed, her doctor might stop the medication when she reaches age 10 to allow nature to take its course. If she was diagnosed later in the pubertal process, however, her doctor might wait until she's 11 to avoid compromising her final height. Most girls are not medicated beyond age 11 so they can be in sync with their peers and their bones can develop normally. Some of the side effects include vaginal bleeding during the first month of treatment and mood changes in response to the hormonal shift. If the drug is used for too long, it can prevent the bones from growing as strong as they might. But a vigilant doctor can prevent this, too, by closely monitoring the child.

Although intervention of this kind is in a girl's best interests when it's necessary, this is the case for a very small number of them (to date, it's unclear how many girls are medicated; studies haven't been done to determine that). Medication is the exception, not the rule.

PUBERTY FROM THE OVARIES OR BODY. Puberty starting from somewhere in the body other than the pituitary calls for tests to rule out ovarian tumors and cysts that may warrant surgery. Very rarely, the cause can be a genetic defect or mutation such as McCune-Albright syndrome, a genetic disorder affecting the bones, skin pigment, and hormones that trigger premature puberty. In most cases, however, the early puberty is deemed normal and, *when appropriate* due to concerns about, for example, a girl's final height, medication is prescribed to manage the signs. Again, just because a girl is going through puberty early doesn't mean she should be treated.

PUBERTY FROM THE ENVIRONMENT. As you might expect, this is the hardest type of early puberty to diagnose and manage. Sometimes the environmental culprit is relatively easy to identify and eliminate, such as when environmental factors cause a cluster of cases in the same geographic area. In 1979, for instance, the medical journal the *Lancet* described an outbreak of breast enlargement in several hundred Italian children at one school, probably caused by estrogen in the foods the children ate after the hormone had been added to the feed of cattle and poultry to increase their muscle mass. Similar epidemics in Puerto Rico and Haiti were tracked by the US Centers for Disease Control and Prevention in the 1980s.

More recently, in 2006 doctors at the University of Massachusetts reported that first a preschool-age girl and then her kindergarten-age brother had begun growing pubic hair and having genital enlargement. It turned out that their father was using a concentrated testosterone skin cream he bought on the Internet for cosmetic and sexual performance purposes, and the children had absorbed the testosterone through normal skin contact with their father. The boy also developed some aggressive behaviors. Sex hormones are easily absorbed through the skin and don't degrade as readily as many other hormones do. This wasn't an isolated case; many more have been reported since then.

In 2007, the *New England Journal of Medicine* reported yet another disturbing case, in which seemingly innocuous products containing lavender and tea tree oil acted like estrogen when the two were combined. Researchers at the University of Colorado documented several cases of young boys with marked breast enlargement after using shampoo, hair gel, and a skin balm containing these ingredients, which are widely used and present no problem for adults. Unlike in the siblings' case, however, these instances resulted not from the passive transfer of hormones from a parent to a child, but rather from the boys' own use of these products. But like the siblings, when the boys stopped using the products, their breasts decreased in size. The National Institute of Environmental Health Sciences in North Carolina tested the oils on human breast cells grown in test tubes and confirmed that lavender and tea tree oil together are xenoestrogenic, meaning that the combination has the same effect on the cells that estrogen does. As you learned in Chapter 3, a substance that has the power to mimic a hormone is called an endocrine disruptor.

Doctors and scientists have been concerned about the prevalence of endocrine-disrupting chemicals (EDCs) in the environment for some time now and rightfully worried that children might be at higher risk for early puberty as a result. These chemicals, some of which are natural, like lavender and tea tree oil, are pervasive today, finding their way into scores of cosmetics, beauty products (e.g., lotions, bath oils, and perfumes), plastics, certain drugs, and even the food supply and water. That said, there's a lot we can do to prevent excessive exposure to these chemicals, and while total elimination of EDCs is virtually impossible, it helps to know that by controlling the things we can, parents can indeed have a substantial impact on a girl's developmental health. In a perfect world, a child would never encounter chemicals that can change her physiology. But the bigger problem, as we'll soon see, is that because some of these chemicals can be stored in fat cells, the more overweight a girl is, the more likely it is that she may be affected by environmental chemicals. Still, we can practice certain habits that will tip the scales in favor of good health.

TO TREAT OR NOT TO TREAT?

Let's consider two similar cases with different outcomes. Eva was 5 years 4 months old when she started complaining of a painful lump on her chest as well as growing pains in her legs. Her mother took her to the pediatrician, who noted that the girl had grown significantly in the 9 months since her last well-child visit and on examination found Eva to have Tanner stage 2 breasts. A bone age x-ray revealed her bones to be very mature. The pediatrician sent Eva to the pediatric endocrinologist, who agreed with the physical exam and calculated that if no treatment was started, Eva would be 4 feet 7 inches tall as an adult—much shorter than her genetic potential. Blood tests confirmed that the puberty was coming from her pituitary. An MRI was normal.

Kayla, meanwhile, was 6 years 5 months when she started to have acne and body odor. Shortly after that, her mother noted that she had breast budding and had grown to be one of the taller girls in the class. A physical exam and review of her growth chart at the pediatrician's office confirmed this, and the pediatrician found that her bone age was mildly advanced, at age 7 to 8 years. Kayla was referred to the pediatric endocrinologist. The mother told the specialist that Kayla was having mood swings—she was acting like a cross between a 2-year-old and a 13-year-old, as she described it. The specialist estimated that even without treatment, Kayla would be a normal height for her family, about 5 feet 1 inch.

NEW PUBERTY FACT

Early puberty affects two sets of girls: those who have no biological abnormalities and are naturally entering puberty on the early side and those who have an abnormality that is causing their pituitary to make puberty hormones early in what is called Central Precocious Puberty.

So, how were these two girls treated? Eva, the younger of the two, was diagnosed as having Central Precocious Puberty, though no true cause of the early puberty was determined. Due to her young age and the fact that she faced a much greater risk for short stature as an adult, Eva was treated with puberty-halting drugs while Kayla was not. Both girls had good outcomes. Eva took the medicine until she was 9½ years old, when she decided she was sick and tired of the shots, and when her best friend got her first bra. Eva got her first period a year later, at age 10½. Kayla continued to be the first in her class to go through puberty and got her period shortly after her 10th birthday.

There are no hard-and-fast rules for treating early puberty. Every girl must be evaluated by a pediatrician (and pediatric endocrinologist as needed) and treated on an individual basis. Remember, girls who enter puberty early are categorized broadly as either those with diagnosable disorders like Central Precocious Puberty, and those who simply develop on the early side of the normal curve. Central Precocious Puberty is the condition that affects girls whose puberty is triggered by a pituitary abnormality. The origin of this malfunction most often cannot be identified, but it could be caused by a type of brain tumor that's usually benign, a brain abnormality that was present at birth, brain or spinal cord injury or irradiation, or a rare genetic disorder. In most of these cases, a doctor will prescribe medication to slow down or halt the pubertal process until the girl is older. But the vast majority of girls today who go through "premature puberty" are *not* in this category. They are among a growing number of girls who are blurring the line between what's been considered "normal" and atypical. And now there is no discrete age that separates the two.

The best course of action will be decided upon by the doctor and parents of an early-blooming girl. Among the many factors to be weighed in addition to age, height, and weight are:

- Where the girl is along the pubertal continuum.
- How fast she is progressing.
- How she is adapting socially.

Many doctors take a wait-and-see approach and monitor the girl closely. Paul Kaplowitz, a Children's National Medical Center pediatric endocrinologist and one of the chief experts in this field, does this in his practice; after examining a girl whose parents are concerned about early puberty, he usually asks them to come back in 4 to 6 months so he can evaluate how fast the girl is progressing. "I do not feel that there is an absolute age cutoff for when puberty is too early," he says. "I generally do not start testing unless the girl is Tanner [stage] 3 or 4. I've gotten away from one age defining 'normal' and 'abnormal.'" He adds, "In most cases, girls are tall when first evaluated, and even if they stop growing 2 years earlier than average, [height potential] is often not the issue. So I spend a lot of time with parents talking about whether it's okay for a 9- or 10-year-old to have a period. In many cases, with adequate preparation from the parents, these girls do fine, though girls who start their periods before age 9 often have a hard time coping." (Kaplowitz also questions the studies that point to there being social consequences to early puberty, such as an increased risk for substance abuse or delinquent behavior. He wonders, "How do we know that these kids who enter puberty early wouldn't have developed these problems regardless?" It's a good point, one that highlights how difficult it is to isolate all the variables.)

Of course, the wait-and-see approach requires patience. Parents who feel some anxiety or even hysteria about their little girl developing should rest assured in the interim that early puberty can be totally normal. Moreover, as we'll show you in the next chapter, they can make certain lifestyle changes that will naturally avert some of the risks involved for a girl who starts puberty early.

Parents are the ultimate guardians of their child's well-being. It's never easy to discuss early puberty with your child (especially when you thought that dreaded sex talk was still many years away), but it's essential to teach kids what they can expect and to reassure them that they are *normal*.

Remember: *The vast majority of girls going through puberty early do not need to be medicated and do not have an identifiable medical problem* causing Central Precocious Puberty. We only need to support them and teach them that they can cope with their body's natural process—and to manage our own anxiety when we're talking with them and with medical practitioners when our girl is present. A lot of kids will need psychological support, however, which can start with the adults in a girl's life—parents, guardians, extended family, teachers, coaches, and mentors. And if her emotional or behavioral problems are bigger than this support structure can handle, parents can reach out to a school counselor or psychologist (more guidance on this will come later).

For those who *do* need medical intervention, the treatment is safe, and we know a lot about how to manage it in the best interests of the child. The first thing we do as doctors is to help families look at the situation as an opportunity rather than something to fear. There's absolutely no reason to panic. The experience can be full of benefits, too.

NEW PUBERTY FACT

Most girls who enter puberty early do not have a medical problem and do not need drugs.

SHOULD YOU GET A SECOND OPINION?

What happens if you feel like your pediatrician is ill equipped to diagnose early puberty? Or what if he or she doesn't want to send you to a specialist when you feel it would be appropriate? Frankly, as with any condition, some doctors have more experience dealing with early puberty than others do, and your general pediatrician might not be up to snuff in this department. If you feel that your daughter is not getting the kind of care she needs, then seek help elsewhere.

It may also be useful to get a second opinion from another pediatrician before seeing a specialist. Many pediatricians work in groups today, so you can likely get another pair of professional eyes from within the same medical office. Doing this can even help reduce your anxiety. Asking questions is a sign that you're on the right path to a solution, even if that solution turns out to be simply accepting that your girl is maturing earlier than you did.

CHAPTER FIVE

HOW TO MANAGE ENVIRONMENTAL RISKS

Practicing the Precautionary Principle

THROUGHOUT HISTORY, EVENTS AND ACCIDENTS have clued us in to how environmental factors can impact health over the short and long term. Since World War II and the bombings of Hiroshima and Nagasaki that unleashed toxic levels of radiation, for example, we've known that such exposures can lead survivors to develop cancers later in life. Women in Hiroshima and Nagasaki who were under 20 when the atomic bomb was dropped had higher rates of breast cancer as older adults than women who were older at that time. After the tragic nuclear accident at Chernobyl in the Ukraine in 1986, large numbers of people were exposed indirectly through food contaminated with radiation and through inhalation of radioactive material in the air. Again, scientists have documented higher rates of breast and thyroid cancer among Ukrainian women today who were exposed in their youth, as well as birth defects among children whose pregnant mothers were exposed.

And most everyone remembers the story of DDT, the pesticide

sprayed in neighborhoods across America in the 1950s and '60s that caused a fivefold increase in breast cancer before age 50 among women exposed during childhood and early adolescence. Although it's banned now in the United States, DDT is still used throughout the rest of the world, especially in Africa and Asia, and is the subject of international debate because its effectiveness in killing the mosquitoes that carry the deadly malaria parasite must be weighed against the dangers it poses. Panels of scientists continue to recommend that it be used only as a last resort due to its adverse health effects, which go beyond just increasing cancer risk. Exposure to DDT is also associated with reduced fertility, genital birth defects, diabetes, and damage to developing brains.

The potential hazards of exposure to endocrine-disrupting chemicals (EDCs) can be seen vividly in animal populations. In Florida during the early 1980s, large spills of the pesticide dicofol caused male alligators' bodies to become "feminized"; the pesticide acted like estrogen in their reproductive tracts and essentially turned them into semi-females. As recently as 1994, scientists found that chemicals from plastics manufacturing plants that acted like estrogen had contaminated sewers in England, causing male fish to develop into females. Although we don't know for sure what levels of daily exposure to xenoestrogens might interfere with children's reproductive development as it does with animals, the previous chapter's descriptions of children exposed to high levels of EDCs who experienced physical changes like breast and pubic hair growth are cautionary. Clearly, the health of our environment can factor mightily into the health of our bodies—especially the bodies of children.

As noted in Chapter 2, childhood is a special "window of susceptibility" when youngsters' physical immaturity, high rate of growth through rapid cell division, and small body masses cause them to react to smaller amounts of harmful substances than adults do. Brenda Eskenazi, PhD, is a professor of epidemiology at the University of California, Berkeley School of Public Health, where she also conducts research on environmental health and the impact of certain chemical exposures on cognitive function, child development, and reproductive health. She underscores the fact that children's bodies haven't developed enough to produce enzymes that can neutralize or make these chemicals less toxic. Eskenazi, along with experts like Mary Wolff, PhD, at Mount Sinai Hospital in New York, is conducting some of the leading-edge research in this area of children's health. Ask them about the effects of chemicals on little bodies and they will tell you that proportionate amounts of certain chemicals have much more harmful effects in developing children than they do in adults.

Exposure to nuclear fallout or DDT is an extreme environmental event. But the devastating ramifications seen with those toxins bring to light other questions: How much should we worry about everyday potential environmental hazards, such as chemicals like BPA used to make shockproof plastics, and foods from livestock treated with antibiotics? We live in a world where the use of chemicals is widespread, yet most have not been adequately tested for potential health effects. Some of these common chemicals could be toxic. But keep in mind that research on the *potential* for certain chemicals to act like hormones and disrupt a child's developing hormonal system is still new, and many studies' results conflict. Just because we have evidence showing that a chemical can act like estrogen in the body doesn't necessarily mean it's triggering early puberty.

Needless to say, we can't live in a bubble or drive ourselves crazy trying to control everything by changing our lifestyle overnight. Balancing our legitimate concerns about chemicals with our dependence on them in our daily lives is what we're going to tackle in this chapter. We'll start with some bad news but then move on to the empowering information that will help you do something other than just worry.

THE BODY BURDEN

Just how toxic our planet has become is hotly debated. It seems like every day we read a new report about a potential association between a health condition and a chemical or contaminant in our environment. Over the past 30 years, more than 100,000 chemicals have been approved for commercial use in the United States. Among these are more than 82,000 industrial chemicals, 9,000 food additives, 3,000 cosmetic ingredients, 1,000 pesticide active ingredients, and 3,000 pharmaceutical drugs. Only a very small percentage of them are regulated for safety by the Environmental Protection Agency (EPA) or the Food and Drug Administration (FDA). In fact, due to funding constraints and industry litigation, in the years since the 1976 Toxic Substances Control Act (TSCA) was passed, the EPA has been able to require safety testing on only about 200 of the 84,000 chemicals listed on the TSCA chemical inventory.

But in some ways, our children are growing up in a much cleaner environment than we did, thanks to tighter regulations and cleaner technologies. We can be confident that water coming out of nearly any tap in the United States will not give you a stomach-churning illness; choking smog, like the kind you see in China today, has been much reduced by implementing stricter emissions standards on manufacturing and cars (and unleaded fuel); and rivers don't catch fire due to high levels of chemical pollution like they did in the '60s. At the same time, however, newly created chemicals that seem safe in the short term could have health effects that don't show up right away. So while the risk of being exposed to a chemical that's immediately toxic is arguably lower than it was in the last century, we still need to be concerned about the possible dangers of substances we've had small exposures to over a long time period.

Although scientists have been measuring industrial pollutants in our environment for decades, only recently have we begun the process of monitoring the so-called body burden, the levels of toxins in tissues of the human body. This biomonitoring, for which blood, urine, umbilical cord blood, and breast milk are analyzed, is being conducted by several high-profile institutions and research organizations on an ongoing basis, including the Centers for Disease Control and Prevention (CDC) and the National Institute of Environmental Health Sciences, established by the National Institutes of Health (NIH) in 1961.

Many other research organizations are also conducting ongoing studies, and then there's the collaborative Human Toxome Project of the nonprofit organizations the Environmental Working Group and Commonwealth, begun in 2000 to analyze human tissues for industrial chemicals found in foods, air, water, and consumer products. The project's research involves participants of all ages (from newborns to the elderly) from across the country. All of these biomonitoring projects say that the bodies of virtually every US resident, regardless of location or age, contain measurable levels of synthetic chemicals, many of which are fat-soluble and therefore stored in fatty tissue. However, in most cases we don't know if they are harmful at these—or any—levels. And that's why more scientific research into their health effects is sorely needed.

NEW PUBERTY FACT

People living in industrialized nations have an average of 700 synthetic chemicals in their bodies from food, water, and air. Most of these chemicals have not been adequately tested for health effects.

THE LIMITS OF MODERN TESTING
AND REGULATION

Testing for toxins in the body isn't as easy as you might think. First, we have to know what to look for, and second, we need to measure certain toxins using methods currently available. But more important than merely detecting chemicals is uncovering how exposure to them affects the human body.

Keep in mind that studies report averages according to sex, age, and ethnicity; obviously, they cannot predict the body burdens of individuals. Everyone's body reacts differently to external stimuli, including the effects of combinations of various stimuli. Because of this, regulatory standards for limiting exposures to pollutants in food and water may not protect certain vulnerable populations, such as children or those with chronic illnesses or genetic issues. The unknown effects of combined exposures are one of Eskenazi's many concerns. An article published in the *Nation* explained the problem well: "Throughout the course of a day, people may eat several different types of produce, each of which may bear traces of one or more pesticides. They encounter other types of chemicals as well—from antibacterials in soaps, to plasticizers in foodware, to flame retardants in the furniture. 'By day's end, you've got a combination of chemicals and an unknown level of risk,'" it quoted Eskenazi as saying. The epidemiologist admits that she could spend several lifetimes trying to unravel the knot of potential influences on a girl's development. Scientists are just beginning to study genetic factors, too. In addition to a person's DNA conferring vulnerability to one toxin or another, future research may also find that a particular gene interacts with a particular chemical to increase one's risk for a specific health problem.

One of our biggest concerns as scientists regarding toxins in the environment is that we humans are at the top of the food chain and, therefore, exposed to larger amounts of toxic substances as the result of a process called bioaccumulation. Meat, dairy, and fish consumption is one significant way we are exposed. For example, certain kinds of fish can concentrate chemicals in their tissues exponentially, to a level greater than the concentration found in the surrounding water. On land, some livestock eat grains sprayed with pesticides and then store those toxic substances in their fat, along with potential chemicals like hormones, antibiotics, and other additives that are given to them. Consuming these products can expose you to chemicals used along the entire agricultural chain.

When researchers examine blood and/or urine for chemical contaminants, the ones that most alarm scientists and environmentalists alike because of their potential endocrine-disrupting properties include bisphenol A, a xenoestrogen that's used in many consumer products, and polychlorinated biphenyls (PCBs), a class of chemicals used in hundreds of industrial and commercial products and banned decades ago, though people continue to test positive for it today. Another class of chemicals that turns up in human samples is phthalates, which are used to soften plastic and are a primary component of polyvinyl chloride. Phthalates, which we first mentioned in Chapter 1, are prevalent in products such as adhesives, personal care products, shower curtains, garden hoses, and vinyl siding and flooring (it's the source of that "new car smell").

Exposure to these and other toxic substances is greater in low-income communities than elsewhere, revealing the demographics of environmental health inequities. One of the reasons ethnic minority groups and the poor have poorer health outcomes—including a higher likelihood that girls will enter puberty early—than other groups may be because they are more frequently exposed to multiple environmental hazards. People of lower socioeconomic status typically live closer to sources of pollution such as highways, hazardous waste sites, industrial facilities, and pesticide-sprayed fields and lack access to health-promoting resources like healthful food, green spaces, preventive health care, and recreational programs. It's a Molotov cocktail that can disproportionately affect disadvantaged populations when interventions and buffers aren't in place, and we as a society must address this inequity.

According to Rachel Morello-Frosch, PhD, a professor of environmental science, policy, and management at University of California at Berkeley, we need to map out which communities are the most vulnerable and start by intervening there with effective strategies that can improve existing conditions and prevent future harm. This can reduce not just the number of environmental stressors in those communities but also their dosage.

The Dosage Makes All the Difference

It's the dosage that makes something a poison. In other words, just because a girl is exposed to a chemical or she eats an apple that has been sprayed with synthetic pesticides doesn't necessarily mean that she'll be harmed or that it will affect her pubertal process. But how do we know how much exposure translates into a problem in any given individual, particularly a child? Most people assume that to affect health you must be exposed to a large amount of a toxin. This is not always the case. Chronic long-term exposure to even the smallest amount of a chemical, as can be the case in low-income communities can be harmful to a person's health and/or change one's "normal" developmental path—particularly if he or she happens to be sensitive to it.

The other two elements, as you know by now, include the timing of the exposure and route of entry. Exposure to EDCs can have a dramatically different effect depending on a girl's age (i.e., what stage of development she is in), how long she is exposed, and how these compounds were introduced. Evidence suggests that many chemicals are most damaging to a developing child in utero. And a young girl exposed to EDCs in a certain product she uses daily might be affected more than she would have been if she used the product only once. In addition, the effect of a chemical can differ when it's ingested through the digestive tract, lungs, skin, and mucous membranes of the mouth and nostrils.

Moreover, as previously mentioned, chemicals can impact a body in unanticipated and even unknown ways, especially in combination with other chemicals. Unfortunately, we cannot predict who will be sensitive to which substances, at which dosages, and in what concentrations.

The technical word for this is "synergy." In the world of chemistry, synergies are what make two seemingly innocuous chemicals harmful. Let's say you have a chemical that's considered to be a 1 on a hypothetical danger scale of 1 to 10 (with 10 being the most dangerous), while another chemical is a 3. But when combined, the resulting chemical is a hazardous 9. This synergy brings the number of potential chemical toxins to a nearly infinite number. As Randall Fitzgerald notes in his *Hundred Year Lie,* "What distresses and perplexes me is the realization that even if government had the resources to thoroughly conduct widespread safety testing—which it doesn't—our technology is too primitive to detect all of the synthetic chemicals in combination or to complete the task within our own lifetimes or even within the life spans of any of our grandchildren."

NEW PUBERTY FACT

Studies have found an average of 232 chemicals in the umbilical cord blood of newborns.

In the last month of a woman's pregnancy, her baby's umbilical cord pulses each day with the equivalent of at least 300 quarts of blood. This cord is the developing baby's lifeline, delivering life-giving nutrients that support growth. We used to think that cord blood was protected from most chemicals and pollutants in the environment thanks to the placenta. But science has now shown that the umbilical cord isn't safeguarded and that the placenta isn't the formidable shield we thought it to be. A steady stream of industrial chemicals and pollutants can indeed cross the placenta, just like residues from cigarettes and alcohol. Our federally funded biomonitoring studies organized by the NIH and CDC demonstrated this when they found chemicals in cord blood and breast milk, and other cutting-edge studies also have proven that wombs are no safe haven. Our body burden actually begins to accumulate *prior to* birth, before the completion of the blood–brain barrier, which eventually will prevent most substances from being absorbed by the brain. And this body burden can last a lifetime.

A BIG DOSE OF REALITY

Before you pack up the car and think about living off the land in a remote shack in the woods, let's get one thing straight: You can't avoid exposure to toxic substances by moving to a far-off location. You can't even seek safety in the Arctic Circle; the by-products and chemicals from industrial centers have landed in this pristine area of the world via air currents. Dust particles grab onto chemicals and travel north to colder climates, which explains why animals and humans who live in the most desolate patches of the globe—thousands of miles from sources of pollution—are showing signs of significant contamination. Beluga whales accumulate such high levels of PCBs in their fatty tissues that in some cases their carcasses might even qualify as hazardous waste. Inuit women who live in the seemingly unspoiled northern regions of the world have been shown to have PCBs in their breast milk, and research suggests that these exposures are affecting the health of their children.

Although we assume our elected representatives will protect us and not let harmful chemicals be used or sold in this country, that assumption is false. Regulations have yet to catch up with what scientists have been discovering about the harmful effects of toxic chemical exposure. The 1976 TSCA gives the EPA what the agency calls "broad authority to identify and control substances that may pose a threat to human health or the environment." But large loopholes nonetheless exist. For example, the act grandfathered in some 62,000 chemicals already in use, which precludes them from having to be tested. Since then, Congress has frozen or cut the EPA's budget for the past decade. One reason for this is because some members of Congress place a higher priority on protecting industry and business interests than on public health. Budgetary constraints and capitulation to special interest lobbies also blunt the effectiveness of other federal agencies that regulate chemicals, including the FDA, which enforces the regulations on the levels of chemicals, pesticides, and other additives permitted in foods and drugs; the USDA, which regulates agricultural use of pesticides (along with the EPA), hormones, and antibiotics; and the Department of Labor, which enforces the Occupational Safety and Health Act of 1970 to address, in part, exposure to toxic substances in the workplace.

What all this means is that it's impossible to know exactly how many synthetic chemicals exist in the world today and which ones are truly harmful. Moreover, myriad political interests influence the standards and enforcement of laws and regulations.

"THERE'S NO SMOKING GUN"

Now for some better news. When we spoke with University of California at Berkeley's Kim Harley, PhD, who studies the effects of EDCs and prenatal exposure to pesticides and other environmental contaminants, she set the record straight: "People think the associations are clear and obvious—that EDCs are proven to disrupt puberty. But the literature is conflicting and confusing and not complete." She further explained that what scientists observe in animals after exposures, such as reproductive disorders or the feminization of males, doesn't necessarily mean it also happens in humans. "At this point, we don't have much evidence that EDCs are causing earlier puberty in girls. There's no smoking gun. We will keep conducting studies and keep looking at this issue—but for now, the evidence isn't strong." Moreover, Harley pointed out that doing this kind of research in humans is difficult and said that some of the studies that have been conducted are flawed. She even went so far as to say that, although there are lots of animal studies showing the endocrine-disrupting effects of BPA, there is little evidence that BPA can cause early puberty in humans. And she posed a good question: "If we buy a BPA-free bottle, what chemical has replaced that BPA? It doesn't work to be regulating on a chemical-by-chemical basis. When one chemical goes, what it is replaced with is a related chemical that may have similar effects."

Ken Cook, the president and cofounder of the Environmental Working Group (EWG), shares similar views: "There are so many questions about what is really going on. There's so much we don't know—so much of the evidence is suggestive but not definitive." Cook contends that the government is not regulating chemicals that could be problematic and that the EPA not only labors under budgetary constraints but sometimes also caves in to pressure from the chemical industry. The hardest chemicals to regulate are those that require more evidence definitively linking them to a human health condition. He stresses, too, that it takes so long to get regulations in place that we as consumers have to take matters into our own hands. In his words, "Legal is not always safe."

Legal is not always safe. We think that speaks volumes about the potential hazards we all face in our environment, children and adults alike, and how we should approach protecting ourselves. Cook's group is committed to gathering data and making it available via tools the public can use to limit our exposures to certain foods, household goods, and cleaning and personal care products. (Note that they aren't the only ones undertaking this task: The EPA, European Union, and World Health Organization have all ramped up their efforts to gather data on "contaminants of emerging concern" like BPA, pharmaceuticals, and personal care products.)

We use the EWG's user-friendly Web site (ewg.org) ourselves to search for the safest foods and products and recommend that our patients and fellow parents do the same. And we are huge fans of Cook's advice: "Try and shop your way around products or behaviors that are sources of exposure to toxins." He recommends starting with one particular product type rather than trying to overhaul everything all at once. "Think through what you are eating, think through what you are cleaning with, think through the consumer products you are bringing home." And for young girls who are entering their preteen years, thinking about the beauty products you'll encourage them to use and teaching them to be attentive to the types of products they are using and their ingredients, to read labels, and so on may be a good place to start. (See the list on page 111 for a cheat sheet of things to avoid.) Those who are willing to dig a little deeper into the issues should check out the EPA's databases on pharmaceuticals and personal care products at epa.gov/ppcp/. From there, you can enter NIH and international databases, including trade industry Web sites in Asia and Europe. And a quick and easy phone app is available to help you shop. We also have a resource list at thenewpuberty.com.

Obviously, it's not just children who can benefit from a cleaner environment. All of us will reap the rewards of living in a cleaner, healthier world, and tools like these empower us to choose safer products and practices while we push for policy change. Because even though these strategies help, policy change is still needed. We cannot simply shop our way out of unwanted chemical exposures.

PRACTICE THE PRECAUTIONARY PRINCIPLE

All of these unanswered questions about chemicals and whether or not they have a biological impact mean that we would do well to practice the precautionary principle: When in doubt, use a safer alternative. We don't have a definitive answer to the question of whether a chemical or combination of chemicals causes or accelerates early puberty, especially when it comes to less clear-cut environmental perils (e.g., phthalates, chemicals found in many common household products, and antibiotics in meat and milk). So we need to use common sense and avoid or limit products that may be problematic. Remember, it can take years for studies to gather enough evidence for the government to justify writing new or stricter regulations and even taking dangerous goods off the market. So the best we can do today is use sound judgment based on the science we have. Put simply: Don't wait until something is officially labeled "dangerous" to eliminate it from your life; if the evidence available from reliable sources (such as those listed in "How to Be a Smart Consumer" on the opposite page) suggests that certain products or chemicals could well be hazardous, then work to avoid them.

Note, too, that following these tips will be good for not only you and your family but also the environment and community in the broader sense. For instance, eating organic foods is arguably healthier for you than eating conventionally grown food and also a way to increase demand for it in the marketplace, reduce the use of pesticides, and protect farmworkers, who are exposed to much

NEW PUBERTY FACT

When in doubt, take it out. If a product *may* be harmful, try to avoid it.

HOW TO BE A SMART CONSUMER

Shopping with a view to avoid a long list of ingredients can be tedious and impractical, and labels and ingredient lists can be difficult to read, let alone understand. Keep it simple by buying goods that are as close to their natural state as possible—ones that haven't been processed, treated, grown, manufactured, or infused with chemicals in any way. In addition to the tips coming up in the next section, we recommend bookmarking these top online resources for navigating labels, claims, and brands.

- Environmental Working Group: ewg.org
- Toxic Matters from University of California at San Francisco's Program on Reproductive Health and the Environment: prhe.ucsf.edu/prhe/toxicmatters.html
- Healthy Child Healthy World: healthychild.org
- National Institutes of Health (NIH) Household Products Database: householdproducts.nlm.nih.gov
- Children's Environmental Health Center at Mount Sinai Hospital in New York: atmountsinai.org, search for "Children's Environmental Health Center"
- Zero Breast Cancer Organization: zerobreastcancer.org /get-informed/resources

And remember to go to our online destination at thenewpuberty.com for a regularly updated list of resources.

higher levels of these chemicals than anyone else. In this way, we can encourage changes in the practices of industry and agriculture. Also remember that everyone who has kids or who works with kids has a voice. You can advocate for change in your local community by speaking up. Some legislative changes at the local level and beyond have come about solely as a result of public outcry.

Use the EWG's Web site and other reliable resources to learn more about which products you should be replacing with safer alternatives. In addition, don't forget to refer to the resources listed in "How to Be a Smart Consumer" on page 107, many of which provide practical tips and advice. Our partners and colleagues at Zero Breast Cancer, for instance, offer excellent fact sheets on puberty and chemicals.

What follows are our top recommendations for safer living.

Food and Drink

INGREDIENTS

- Minimize use of canned, processed, and prepared foods. Cans are often lined with a BPA-laden coating, and processed foods are more likely to contain artificial ingredients like chemical additives, preservatives, colorings, and chemical-based flavors. And it's hard to know exactly what's in prepared foods you find at market buffets and in ready-made products.

- Cook more from scratch so you know what's going into your food, but don't use nonstick pans or cookware. Teflon-coated wares contain perfluorooctanoic acid, or PFOA, which the EPA has labeled a likely carcinogen.

- Eat less meat and processed foods and more natural, plant-based foods—to avoid bioaccumulation of chemicals.

- Go organic whenever possible and wash your fruits and vegetables thoroughly—even those you peel—especially the top 20 "dirty" ones. (See "Top 20 'Dirty' Fruits and Vegetables," opposite.) This helps limit the consumption of pesticides and herbicides that can mimic hormones.

- Eat more whole fruits and vegetables. This will not only improve the nutrition of the entire family but also boost your girl's intake of fiber, which has been shown to offer some protection from early menarche. This may be due to fiber's ability to bind to estrogen and escort it out of the body so there is less of it in circulation. Even if you can't afford to buy all of your fresh produce organic, don't limit your intake of fresh fruits and vegetables. Just make sure you wash it well with water, or try an organic commercial fruit and vegetable wash. (Find ideas for making your own wash at thenewpuberty.com.)

TOP 20 "DIRTY" FRUITS AND VEGETABLES

Buy these organic whenever possible to limit your exposure to chemical pesticides.

Apples	Cherry tomatoes
Strawberries	Hot peppers
Grapes	Blueberries (domestic)
Celery	Lettuce
Peaches	Snap peas (imported)
Spinach	Kale and collard greens
Sweet bell peppers	Cherries
Nectarines (imported)	Nectarines (domestic)
Cucumbers	Pears
Potatoes	Plums

The Clean 15 tested as having the lowest levels of pesticides, so if you can't buy organic, these are among your safest choices: sweet corn, onions, pineapple, avocados, cabbage, frozen sweet peas, papayas, mangoes, asparagus, eggplant, kiwifruit, grapefruit, cantaloupe, sweet potatoes, and mushrooms.

*Source: ewg.org/foodnews/list.php

- When you do eat beef and poultry, choose low-fat, antibiotic-free, 100 percent organic meats. In fish, choose wild, which often have lower levels of toxins than farmed fish (for a list of sustainably caught fish that contain the lowest amounts of toxins, visit the Monterey Bay Aquarium's Seafood Watch at seafoodwatch.org).

- Buy organic milk (more on this in the next chapter).

- Limit sugar, which is among the most problematic ingredients fueling the obesity epidemic among children. Replace sugary snacks and beverages with healthier alternatives, such as water flavored with lemon or lime slices instead of soda, which is a blend of chemicals and sugar.

- Get to know your local farmers. Opt for locally sourced foods that are farmed organically or with minimal pesticides. Check out the nearest farmers' market and start shopping there.

- Encourage community gardens in your neighborhood. If you have the opportunity to join one, do so, or start your own. Studies show that kids eat more fruits and vegetables if they know where they're grown.

STORAGE

- Don't microwave foods in plastic, which can release nasty chemicals that are absorbed by the food. Microwave in glass containers.

- Avoid storing food in plastic containers and plastic wrap made from PVC (which has the recycling code "3").

- Ditch plastic water bottles (or at least avoid plastics marked with a "PC," for polycarbonate, or the recycling label "7"). Buy reusable bottles made of food-grade stainless steel or glass.

Bath and Beauty Products

INGREDIENTS

- When it comes to toiletries, deodorants, soaps, and beauty products, look for the genuine USDA organic seal and choose products that are safer alternatives (go to ewg.org for lists and resources). Avoid the following ingredients, many of which are potential EDCs:

  Triclosan and triclocarban (antibacterial hand soaps and some toothpastes)

  Tea tree oil

  Lavender

  Formaldehyde and formalin (nail products)

  Toluene and dibutyl phthalate/DBP (nail polishes)

  "Fragrance" and "parfum"

  Parabens (propyl-, isopropyl-, butyl-, and isobutyl-)

  PEG/ceteareth/polyethylene glycol

  Diethyl phthalate

  Sodium lauryl sulfate/SLS, sodium laureth sulfate/ SLES, and ammonium lauryl sulfate/ALS

  Aluminum chlorohydrate (deodorants)

- Find phthalate-free personal care products by using the EWG's Skin Deep Cosmetics Database: ewg.org/skindeep.

SUN PROTECTION

- Use hats and sunshirts on your kids rather than sunscreen every time you're in the sun. Many sunscreens on the market today (including ones labeled "safe" by the FDA) contain suspect chemicals and EDCs. It pays to invest in this type of protection, so buy the safest sunscreen you can even if it costs a lot more. The Environmental Working Group stays on top of the research and the products that are available. Go to ewg.org for updated lists and warnings. On her own fair-skinned children, Louise uses EWG-approved sunscreen on the face, a hat and sunglasses, and a rash guard or swim shirt. Many manufacturers offer specially designed shirts that appeal to kids and preteens and are not expensive, especially when you factor in what you save on sunscreen. And dermatologists prefer these, because they block out all of the sun's harmful rays, unlike sunscreen. Another bonus: No more reapplying lotion on a squirmy kid! As children get older, they may not like the shirts as much, but reminding them that they don't have to reapply sunscreen if they are covered up might make them more amenable to wearing them. At some point, however, a girl will likely prefer to wear a traditional bathing suit, and that's when you should help her use safe sunscreen responsibly.

Household Goods

CLEANING

- Reduce toxic dust and residues on surfaces by regularly using a vacuum cleaner with a HEPA filter. Toxic dust and residues that you cannot see or smell come from furniture, electronics, and textiles.

- Whenever you buy household cleaners, detergents, disinfectants, bleaches, stain removers, and so on, select ones that are free of synthetic chemicals (basically, anything that looks suspicious in the list of ingredients). Do not depend on labels that say "safe," "nontoxic," "green," or "natural," because these terms have no legal meaning. Read labels carefully and pay special attention to warnings. Don't buy any products labeled "poison," "danger," or "fatal" if swallowed or inhaled. Avoid anything with the following ingredients: borax, boric acid, diethylene glycol monomethyl ether, 2-butoxyethanol (EGBE), and methoxydiglycol (DEGME). For more details and product information, go to ewg.org.

- Change air-conditioning and heating filters every 3 to 6 months and have your home's HVAC ducts cleaned yearly. Naturally ventilate your house frequently by opening the windows. Avoid air deodorizers and plug-in room fresheners. Indoor air is notoriously more toxic than outdoor air due to all the particulate matter that comes from furniture, electronics, and household goods.

- Wet mop floors and wipe down windowsills weekly to capture dust particles that might contain toxins.

BUYING

- Ideally, you should sleep on a mattress made of natural material, like organic cotton, or wool. Natural latex is another good option. Conventional mattresses are made from polyurethane foam that disintegrates over time, releasing tiny particles that may be harmful.

- Until you can buy new all natural or organic mattresses, buy 100 percent all-natural covers that fit snugly to prevent off-gassing chemicals from passing through the sheets. And use hypoallergenic pillows filled with natural fibers such as cotton, wool, or feathers.

- The next time you're in the market for a new couch or bed, choose goods made without toxic adhesives and glues (such as

Synthetic carpets are magnets for dust and toxic chemicals and can off-gas chemicals for years that can affect the health of sensitive people. Opt for natural hardwood floors or carpets made with all-natural fibers that haven't been treated with flame-retardant or stain-resistant chemicals.

those containing formaldehyde), hard plastics, synthetic wood or particleboard, and treated wood, all of which may off-gas harmful chemicals.

- When purchasing clothes, fabrics, upholstered furniture, or mattresses, choose items that are free of synthetic flame-retardant, stain-resistant, and water-resistant coatings. Avoid reupholstering foam furniture, since foam can disintegrate.

- Hire an expert to replace old carpet; the padding may contain polybrominated diphenyl ethers (PBDEs). If you do it yourself, protect yourself using gloves and an air-filtering mask. Also avoid buying new synthetic wall-to-wall carpet, which off-gases.

- Speak with your local garden store or nursery personnel for recommendations on pesticide- and herbicide-free products you can use in your garden to control pests. And don't use leaded pottery (hardware stores have inexpensive, easy-to-use kits to see if your favorite flower bowl has lead in it).

IN GENERAL

- Wash your hands! This is one of the oldest strategies in the book, and it works.

The goal is to do the best you can based on what you can afford, what you're willing to change, what groups like the EWG report, and so on. No one can avoid all risks, and many of us are limited by financial constraints. And that's okay. Don't feel overwhelmed or depressed by thoughts of toxins getting the upper hand. We have to keep things in perspective, too. If your daughter is playing soccer and it's 100°F, let her use the plastic water bottle that might contain BPA if it's the only one available. Balance what you need with what you'd like to achieve— a safe and comfortable lifestyle that's healthful and fulfilling.

Finally, remember that as adults, we are the role models. We can't say one thing and do another. How you live your life has the most influence on your child. Clean up your environment for your kids but also for the benefits that you, too, will reap.

CHAPTER SIX

LIFESTYLE MATTERS

Establishing Healthy Habits

EARLY PUBERTY, AS YOU KNOW by now, does not typically occur from a single toxic influence, lifestyle issue, or dietary flaw. Rather, many different environmental exposures—chemical, psychosocial, and nutritional—are likely interacting to accelerate maturation in some girls, bringing along with it the associated risks for health and well-being. This is why strategies to avoid or combat these environmental stressors must entail a multifaceted approach.

Now that you've considered how to alter your surroundings to reduce your girl's exposure to chemicals and substances that could cause problems in her developing body, it's time to work on matters related mostly to lifestyle. This includes focusing on dietary choices, how much activity and sleep she gets, as well as what she is exposed to in the media. Emotions must also be attended to because a healthy emotional environment is arguably the most essential ingredient in raising healthy, resilient girls, regardless of whether they mature early, on time, or late.

EAT RIGHT

It's really true that you are what you eat, and the adage "food is medicine" dates back to ancient Greece and the era of Hippocrates, the father of modern medicine. The challenge in addressing matters of diet today is to teach good habits without talking about "dieting" in the weight-loss sense. As adults, if we're overweight, we of course turn to an effective dieting strategy to reach a weight goal. But this shouldn't be the case for kids, especially girls, who unfortunately face more challenges with body image as they develop and, therefore, must be carefully protected from developing an unhealthy relationship with food.

How your girl learns to relate to food in these years will likely form her lifelong habits. Healthy eating habits should begin with breast-feeding or bottle-feeding. (For the record: Breast is best, but not always possible. The jury is still out about cow's-milk versus soy-based formulas. Speak with your doctor if you are debating between the two types of formula.) Once a child is eating the same foods as the rest of the family, those healthy habits will be reinforced as a matter of course. Do your best to have everyone—including Mom and Dad—eating the same way. As mothers ourselves, we've taught our kids how to look at lists of ingredients and be aware of what they are eating or buying. We also talk to them about how organic food—or food that is grown without pesticides—is particularly good for the farmworkers whose exposure is high if pesticides are used and the workers are in the field all day. Also it's important to avoid saying that you're "on a diet" when you mean you're trying to eat healthier, because language like this can set your child up for a poor relationship with food and even contribute to eating disorders like anorexia nervosa and binge eating. Food should never be used as punishment or even as a reward, as some parents do— when, for instance, they potty train with candy. Instead, food should be revered as a positive by making eating about nourishment, enjoyment, and energy—the way to grow strong and smart. So it matters what's in the house, what's available to children in the kitchen, what they're being fed at school and in after-school programs, and what kinds of habits other household members are keeping.

When people ask us for the "best diet" to follow, it is hard to know how to answer, but in general we recommend a Mediterranean-type protocol. A lot has been written about the benefits of this way of eating, which is famous for being rich in olive oil, nuts, beans, fish, whole grains, and fruits and vegetables. It emphasizes eating a variety of plant foods while reining in consumption of red and processed meats and high-fat dairy products. It also encourages making foods tasty using herbs and spices instead of salt and unhealthy fats. In March 2013, the *New England Journal of Medicine* published a seminal study showing that people ages 55 to 80 who ate a Mediterranean diet had as much as a 30 percent reduced risk for heart disease and stroke than those on a typical low-fat diet. They also had a lower risk of death from cancer, as well as a reduced incidence of Parkinson's and Alzheimer's diseases. It's highly probable that children with health challenges would also benefit from eating this way. The Mediterranean diet excludes processed foods and focuses on healthy (and delicious) fats from nuts, seeds, and fish, plus carbohydrates from grains and whole

TOP FOODS OF THE MEDITERRANEAN DIET

- whole fruits and vegetables
- whole grains
- nuts
- beans
- legumes
- seeds
- olive oil
- fish and seafood
- poultry, eggs, cheese, and yogurt in moderation
- meats and sweets less often

fruits and vegetables. It provides the body with the nutrients it needs to run optimally. These include essential fatty acids to fuel the brain and tamp down inflammation and natural fiber to support digestive health and manage blood sugar.

To be clear, the Mediterranean "diet" isn't necessarily a weight-loss plan. It's a way of eating that certainly can lead to weight loss, but it is at heart a food lifestyle with documented health benefits. In fact, the Dietary Guidelines for Americans now recommends it as an eating plan that can help promote health and prevent disease. The beauty of the Mediterranean approach to eating is that your entire family can enjoy it and it leaves plenty of wiggle room for occasional splurges. If you follow its tenets most of the time while allowing treats occasionally, your girl will avoid eating the large amounts of junk so many kids consume today—namely, processed, refined foods filled with the Big Three: sugar, fat, and salt. And because you'll be eating as close to Mother Nature as possible, you'll avoid not only potential EDCs, but other "obesogens"—a term for substances that promote obesity, coined by biologist and University of California, Irvine, professor and researcher Bruce Blumberg, PhD. Obesogens, which include pesticides, herbicides, fungicides, and antibiotics that can mimic and confuse sex hormones in the body, are the same chemicals that influence estrogen metabolism. Of course, fat tissue secretes estrogen, and that feedback loop could be changing young girls' hormonal milieu. In other words, obesity plus exposure to EDCs leads to problems. So limiting obesogens and taming obesity itself are critical, which the Mediterranean approach to eating can accomplish.

For more on the Mediterranean diet, go to the Mayo Clinic's Web site at mayoclinic.org and search for "Mediterranean diet" or check out oldwayspt.org, a nonprofit food and nutrition education organization that endorses it. If you're trying to help your young girl lose weight, have your health care practitioner make recommendations tailored for her body and health conditions.

Avoid the Big Three, Starting with Sugar

Steering clear of as much sugar, unhealthy fat, and salt as possible will do any body good, from the youngest children to the oldest adults. These three ingredients are ubiquitous and often found in combination, and we sometimes challenge our patients' parents to log how much of them their children are getting. This can be a very illuminating exercise for those who have no idea of just how much sugar, salt, and unhealthy fats their child is consuming at school and at home. In fact, focusing on cutting sugar intake alone can be transformative, and it's perhaps the main task you need to accomplish in improving overall dietary habits. Logging the amounts will help you identify hidden sources of these unhealthy ingredients. They don't show up just in classic junk foods, candy, sodas, fruit juices, fast foods, and the like. They can be stealth ingredients in whole-grain cereals and cereal bars, natural granola and energy bars, yogurts, fruit products like applesauce and canned fruit, prepared snacks, spaghetti sauce, flavored milk, muffins and "wholesome" baked goods, and even foods labeled "organic" or with other health claims (e.g., "all natural," "whole grain," "low fat"). The only way to know is to read labels. If a food has more than 10 grams of sugar per serving (and take note of the serving size!) or if sugar is one of the first two or three ingredients listed, then you know it's not as healthy as it might claim to be. Watch out for ingredients synonymous with sugar, such as corn syrup; dextrose; brown rice syrup; fructose; maltodextrin; and sucrose.

> **NEW PUBERTY FACT**
>
> The amount of sugar on food labels is measured in grams. But it's hard to know how much sugar we are consuming. Just remember this formula: 4 grams = 1 teaspoon. So if a cereal has 12 grams of sugar in a single serving—usually just ¾ of a cup—it has 3 teaspoons (1 full tablespoon!) of sugar.

Our colleague Robert Lustig, MD, is a pediatric endocrinologist and specialist on pediatric hormone disorders; he's also the leading expert in childhood obesity at the University of California, San Francisco School of Medicine. He is the author of *Fat Chance: Beating the Odds Against Sugar, Processed Food, Obesity, and Disease*. And he is sugar's worst enemy. More than 4½ million people have viewed his 90-minute 2009 lecture posted on YouTube called "Sugar: The Bitter Truth," in which he makes a compelling argument that sugar is a toxin or poison on a par with any other. According to Lustig, consuming too much sugar wreaks havoc on metabolism—regardless of weight—and feeds into the vicious cycle of obesity and hormonal challenges.

Lustig highlights not only the power of sugar, but also its prevalence. Thanks in large part to his rallying cry to reduce our consumption of sugar (although estimates vary, each one of us consumes about 130 to 150 pounds of it a year), the public is now more aware of sugar's pervasiveness, as well as that of its alter egos, like high-fructose corn syrup. And we agree with him: Limiting added-sugar consumption will go a long way toward cleaning up one's diet and significantly reduce the unhealthy effect it has on metabolism. It may also help to correct any hormonal issues sugar consumption has caused and return the body to a more balanced state.

While we realize that it's unrealistic to eliminate all forms of sugar, do your best to, first, become more aware of the whole family's—and especially your girl's—overall sugar consumption by learning what foods it hides in, and second, manage that consumption smartly. You'd be surprised by how much sugar you can cut from your diet if you just read labels and view things like fruit juices, sodas, and yummy sweet muffins, fruit roll-ups, and organic cereal bars as what they really are: treats that should be eaten in moderation.

And if you don't quite know where to begin, then start where it seems to be packing its greatest punch (and packing on the most pounds): beverages. Patricia Crawford, DrPH, University of California, Berkeley School of Public Health, has spent her career trying to decrease the incidence of childhood obesity. She studies the role of diet and nutrition in health outcomes and disease, especially with children. She asserts that the data linking obesity and diet are irrefutably strong—much stronger than that linking obesity and inactivity. Though she agrees that we need to continue to encourage more physical activity, which no doubt helps reduce the risk of obesity and counters some of the effects of high sugar consumption, she's found that the intake from sugary drinks alone correlates with the rise of obesity in the past 2 decades. And she's not alone in this line of thinking; several experts have argued that the dramatic shift in our BMIs has been due primarily to higher caloric intake, because physical activity has changed very little. "Twenty percent of all the pounds gained by the population over the last 40 years can be directly attributed to sugar-sweetened beverages," she says. "We treat it as if it's a food group."

We should point out that some scientists argue that physical inactivity has indeed been a huge factor in our increased waistlines, but Crawford echoes the general consensus among top researchers today: We drink much more sugar than ever before. Juices and juice boxes, sodas, sports drinks, fruit-infused "vitamin waters," juice bar concoctions, smoothies, and the like can pack a lot of sugar from both the fruit (minus the fiber) and added sugar. A 12-ounce glass of orange juice, for instance, is typically seen as a healthy choice and has become a staple in the American diet. But it contains 36 grams of sugar (and no fiber to slow down the processing of that sugar in the body, which hits the bloodstream quickly and triggers a surge of insulin). That's 9 teaspoons—3 tablespoons—of sugar, about the same found in a can of regular cola. What's more, many forget how much sugar is in those yummy coffee-shop drinks that come with domed tops and a dollup of whipped cream. Preteens and teens often drink these kinds of frothy

NEW PUBERTY FACT

Sugar can be sneaky—
One 12 ounce glass of
orange juice

= 36 grams of sugar

= 3 tablespoons of sugar

= 1 can of regular soda

confections daily. Focusing on reducing sugary beverages alone can result in dramatic positive benefits for health. Crawford offers a reasonable compromise: "Give kids real candy, if one must, not liquid candy." At least there is no denying that candy has sugar and calories. It is far too easy to down several sugar-loaded drinks a day under the false assumption that they hydrate the body.

What about artificial sweeteners? Don't be fooled. Turns out that the artificial sweeteners found in diet sodas and low-calorie juices and teas are not healthy substitutes. Although we haven't fully studied the effects of consuming high levels of artificial sweeteners, the current data show that they can be deceiving. "They don't reduce one's intake at the next meal and can interfere with satiety," Crawford says. "Satiety" is a fancy way of saying "feeling full" and satisfied, and these drinks interfere with it by keeping you from reaching it.

Further, sweetened beverages can prevent you from enjoying the flavors of unsweetened foods. If you get used to artificial sweeteners, which typically taste much sweeter than sugar, fruits and vegetables may not taste as sweet. Studies have proven that these artificial sugars can trigger overeating; the first one to show this came from Purdue University researchers who found that even though they don't contain calories, artificial sweeteners cause weight gain in animals. These researchers speculated that their intense sweetness tricks the brain into thinking that calories are on the way when they aren't. The body gets confused, slows metabolism, and ramps up appetite. And this imbalance in regulating calories leads to overeating.

A 2014 study from the Johns Hopkins School of Public Health further confirmed this phenomenon when it reported that overweight and obese people who drink diet beverages are likely to consume *more* calories from food than heavy people who consume sugary drinks. It's hypothesized that artificial sweeteners could change how the brain functions and could actually be encouraging the consumption of more calories to compensate for the lack of calories in the drink!

So now that you know the facts, let's turn to some practical strategies you can use to help you and your family avoid too much sugar, fat, and salt.

Drink More Water

In our practices, we ask children if they know what percentage of the human body is water. Most don't know, and they're shocked when we tell them it is approximately 60 percent. Then we explain that the thirst mechanism is their brain telling them they need to "fill up" with water, that we evolved during a time when water was the only liquid abundantly available. Sugary beverages were not available. For all of these reasons, most medical practitioners advocate that families simply move to water. You don't need to keep any flavored drinks, juices, sweet teas, or sodas around the house. The kids will likely get their fill of these "treats" outside the home.

Reduce Fast-Food Intake

Crawford also advocates reducing fast-food intake as much as possible: "On any given day, 30 to 40 percent of kids in the US are eating fast food." She also hopes to see kids being better taught about portion control and limiting screen time. Kids watch an average of more than 10 food-related ads daily, and 98 percent of those ads are for products that are high in fat, sugar, or salt. (Black children see 60 percent more calories advertised in fast-food commercials than white children.) Scientists increasingly document that fat-and-sugar combinations can have powerful effects on the brain, activating its dopamine pathway, which is turned on by pleasurable things and is implicated in addiction to alcohol or drugs. So imagine what this kind of exposure could be doing to our children. The more food ads they see, the more they want to eat, inevitably choosing unhealthy options that are convenient and ubiquitous.

Improve School Lunches

An additional challenge, as you can imagine, is changing how our schools prepare and serve meals, since our children are consuming a large portion of their calories at school and many schools' food choices are less than desirable. Crawford highlights a profound fact: "Today, we spend only 4 hours a year on food and nutrition education, yet kids get nearly 4 hours a week of media exposure telling them to eat foods and beverages high in sugars and fat." This needs to change. In 2011, popular chef Jamie Oliver famously tried to change the menu in Los Angeles's public school system as part of his Food Revolution mission to improve the way America eats. He targeted underprivileged communities but met with so much opposition and political red tape that he retreated. (And, contrary to what you might think, the opposition didn't come primarily from students or parents but from the school district, which resisted Oliver's encroaching on their territory.) This, too, needs to change.

Schools are a center of gravity for our kids in so many ways. Their lives revolve not only around family but also around school because that's where they spend most of their hours (and developing years). And it's the perfect place to instill good habits since it's a controlled environment. Some of the most poignant stories that came out of Oliver's show were about kids who had no idea what "healthy eating" meant, yet they went home to households in which at least one person was gravely ill with an obesity-related condition like diabetes or heart disease. (Some kids in West Virginia, where the first season was taped, had never seen a tomato.) Many of the kids he worked with one-on-one were also suffering from metabolic disorders, from diabetes to high blood pressure. No sooner did Oliver start teaching them about deceptive food marketing (cue the image of nasty pink slime in hamburger meat), cooking, and gardening than they began to change their habits and bring those new habits home. He also taught them about the power of community gardens and showed the kids how to grow fruits and vegetables. Studies show that when they know where their food comes from—especially fresh produce—kids are more likely to eat it and have a good relationship with these nutritious foods.

It will take time for our school districts to make the kinds of changes we'd all like to see, but at least each one of us can be doing our part on the household front. Marion Nestle, PhD, an acclaimed public health advocate and professor of nutrition and food studies at New York University, describes the challenge well in an interview for her latest book, *Eat, Drink, Vote: An Illustrated Guide to Food Politics*. She says:

> The job of the food industry is to produce products that will not only sell well, but will sell increasingly well over time, in order to produce growing returns to investors. Reconciliation requires companies either to sell less (impossible from a business standpoint) or make up the difference with sales of healthier products. Unfortunately, the so-called healthier products—and whether they really are is debatable—rarely sell as well. In practice, companies touch all bases at once: They put most marketing efforts into their core products, they proliferate new "better-for-you" products, and they seek new customers for their products among the vast populations of the developing world—where, no surprise, the prevalence of obesity is increasing, along with its related diseases.

As parents, teachers, and guardians of the next generation, we should be lobbying for school gardens and healthier options in cafeterias and vending machines. These changes can in turn help change what food companies manufacture. And activism doesn't have to mean protesting or picketing in public. Start by writing to your principal or local board of education and demand changes to school nutrition guidelines and lunch programs. Volunteer to run a parent-supported salad bar at your school. Ideas abound in activating change.

OPT FOR LOW-FAT, ORGANIC MILK AND DAIRY

Admittedly, the milk debate is tricky terrain. This is another area where the science hasn't spoken yet but everyone seems to have a strong (and different) opinion. Some experts claim that milk should be avoided and that even choosing organic milk doesn't help because cows whose milk is certified organic but that are treated with antibiotics for illnesses may not be taken out of the production herd (although USDA regulations say they are supposed to be). Moreover, we just don't know if hormones used to keep cows routinely pregnant, which may end up in regular milk, affect the human body or not. Other experts think we shouldn't worry so much about what's in the milk, organic or regular. Indeed, claims that regular milk is laced with pesticides from feed and may contain harmful levels of growth hormone and antibiotics can be grossly exaggerated. And all tanks of milk—whether filled with organic or regular milk—are supposed to be routinely tested to ensure there's absolutely no antibiotic content.

We believe, based on current data, that milk's pros outweigh the cons, but organic milk is preferable to limit your family's exposure to substances that might or might not influence normal human biology. Be sure to choose pasteurized milk, as going raw puts one at risk for ingestion of dangerous pathogens that the pasteurization process kills. (Note: When a baby reaches 1 year of age, she can start to drink regular whole cow's milk and can be switched to low-fat milk at age 2.) After all, milk provides a lot of nutrients that are otherwise lacking in the typical American diet, such as calcium and vitamin D. Eliminating milk entirely without replacing it with a nutritionally equivalent substitute, such as fortified soy or almond beverages, could have detrimental effects on bone health. And drinking milk is certainly preferable to drinking juices, sodas, or sports drinks.

We also recommend choosing low-fat organic dairy products (e.g., cheeses or yogurts). Of course, not every family can buy organic all the time. Don't beat yourself up over this; the science is much less definitive than some media stories would have you believe. As with so many of the decisions that need to be made in the interests of better health, every family will make different choices according to their preferences and financial means.

Our hope is that in the future, scientific data will inform how academic and government institutions regulate matters of health and that stricter policies will be enforced for food manufacturers and school administrators alike. Farm subsidies paying growers to produce corn and soy must end and eating healthfully must become cheaper. But until we get change from the top down, as a society we must work from the bottom up—starting with the individual choices we make for ourselves and our families. And this is true whether we're talking about matters of nutrition or any other aspect of life—from the kitchen to the playground to the bedroom.

GET ENOUGH SLEEP

Unfortunately, sleep gets short shrift in our society. But it's more influential in the health equation than most people think, especially for children. We are very strict when it comes to sleep in our respective homes. Julie's kids know that sleep trumps everything—even finishing homework, which can be done in the morning. Louise's kids cannot engage in any activities that lead to a late bedtime on a school night. Rules like these mean we as parents need to be strict with ourselves, and that we practice what we preach. But it's essential. Virtually every creature on the planet needs to sleep, especially mammals like us. During early development, sleep is actually the primary activity of the brain. The circadian rhythm known as the sleep–wake cycle is regulated by light and dark and develops after birth; this explains why newborns have irregular sleep patterns until their internal clock is set. A baby's rhythm begins to form at about 6 weeks of age, and by 6 months most infants have a regular sleep–wake cycle in place (this is when parents find relief from midnight feedings and can get a full night's sleep).

In the first 2 years of life, children spend more time asleep than awake. In fact, 40 percent of childhood is spent asleep, as sleep plays a major role in a child's mental and physical development. One 2013 UK study published in the American journal *Pediatrics* reported on children who had behavioral problems associated with irregular bedtimes. The study found that an irregular bedtime can disrupt the body's natural rhythm, triggering sleep deprivation that ultimately interferes with brain development and the ability to control certain behaviors. But once the kids established a more regular bedtime, their behavior showed clear improvement.

Most parents would agree that rearing children should involve as much consistency as possible, and this must apply to sleep routines, too. Although no two children are exactly alike in their sleep needs, if you want to encourage good behavior (and improve any unbecoming behavior), keeping the bedtime regular is essential. So what is so magical about sleep?

While it sounds cliché, we all need "beauty sleep," no matter what our age. Important restorative processes take place when we're asleep that just cannot happen during our wakeful hours, and they help keep us healthy. In the last 2 decades, sleep science has revealed astonishing insights into the power of sleep for humans of every age, and especially during our formative years. How well you sleep has an impact on your health directly and indirectly, affecting organs and systems at the cellular and molecular levels. Your ability to control your weight, fight off infections, innovate, learn new things, cope with stress, and even pull away from the dinner table before eating a second helping are all related to the quality of your sleep experience. Many adults today try to function on far less sleep than they need to be optimally healthy, and children and teens need a lot more sleep than adults—but many aren't banking it.

Contrary to how many people view sleep, the body doesn't go into idle mode during the night. This is actually when the body enters a state of high activity to some degree just so you can live another day. Clearly, a night or two of little shut-eye won't hurt you in the long run, but prolonged sleep deprivation over months or years carries serious risk factors. Among the many scientifically documented side effects of chronic poor sleep in adults are hypertension and cardiovascular disease, memory loss, weight gain and obesity, trouble with learning, a higher incidence of accidents (think of a sleep-deprived driver), and depression. How is this possible? And what does this mean for kids who are sleep deprived?

First, it helps to understand that our biological clocks, or circadian rhythms, are strongly tied to our sleep patterns. Our body's natural cycle of hormonal activity changes throughout the 24-hour day and revolves around our sleep habits, specifically with regard to the switch from daytime to nighttime. If you don't have a healthy day–night cycle (i.e., you're awake when the body doesn't want to be awake), it can create an imbalance of hormones that are associated with your appetite, metabolism, and immunity. The stress hormone cortisol, for example, should be at its highest level in the early morning and wane throughout the day. It bottoms out at night when melatonin levels rise for sleep. Melatonin is the hormone that gets pumped out by your pineal gland

> **NEW PUBERTY FACT**
>
> Many hormones related to healthy development are released overnight, so irregular, poor sleep can disrupt normal secretion patterns.

when the body senses it's dark outside. Once released, it tells your body to prepare for sleep, slowing down many functions and lowering both blood pressure and core body temperature. A higher melatonin level allows for better early sleep, which helps maintain a healthy level of growth hormone (GH), as well as the hormones that increase male and female sex hormones during puberty. The pituitary gland at the base of your brain *requires* sleep before it can release GH, which gets pumped out mostly during sleep. Within half an hour of a person falling asleep, high levels of GH start pulsing from the pituitary, and this happens a few times throughout the night. Kids produce more GH than adults so they can grow. A deficiency in kids is usually caused by a tumor or birth defect that adversely affects the pituitary gland's ability to manufacture and secrete it, but chronic sleep deprivation can lower the peak level of production in healthy kids when they are rapidly growing. Because GH is so tied to sleep, pediatricians like to tell new parents that their babies "grow longer" when they are asleep, though that's a bit of an exaggeration.

Everyone's circadian clock ticks at a different rate at various times in their life. If you have a teenager in the house, then you know they typically don't turn off the lights much before 11:00 at night, and they may need to be dynamited out of bed in the morning in time for school (and on weekends, they'll sleep in as late as they can). Adolescent sleep phase disorder, as it's known (or, more technically, Delayed Sleep Phase Syndrome), affects many teens. It means they don't feel sleepy until 2 hours after most adults have already passed their own body's bedtime. We doctors don't know the exact cause of this disorder, though it's common, affecting approximately 7 to 16 percent of adolescents, and it's probably just a normal part of their development. It isn't deliberate behavior, but some habits can worsen the condition (and further aggravate the effects of sleep deprivation).

Pubertal growth, in fact, chiefly occurs overnight, the most hormonally active time during the 24-hour day. In addition to GH, luteinizing hormone (LH) and follicle-stimulating hormone (FSH) are also secreted during the night. (In an adult female, LH stimulates ovulation and the development of the corpus luteum, a mass of cells that forms from an ovarian follicle after it releases a mature egg into the fallopian tube. FSH stimulates the release of an egg and production of a form of estrogen during the first half of the menstrual cycle.) If a child has irregular, abnormal sleep patterns, then she will have irregular, abnormal secretion of hormones that are critical to her growth and development.

Most parents who express concern about a child's weight don't think much about their child's sleep habits, and instead focus solely on dietary issues and exercise. But the two digestive hormones tied to sleep habits actually control feelings of hunger and appetite in everyone. Ghrelin is the body's "go eat" hormone; an empty stomach secretes it so your brain gets the message it's time to eat. When your stomach is full, on the other hand, fat cells release leptin, and your brain gets the message that you should stop eating.

Only in the last decade have we started to understand the effects of sleep deprivation on these two important hormones that regulate our eating behaviors and, in turn, our metabolism. One often-cited study showed that when people were allowed just 4 hours of sleep a night for 2 consecutive nights, leptin production dropped by 20 percent and ghrelin increased. Their hunger and appetite also soared by about 24 percent. But they didn't turn to classically healthy foods. Instead, they preferred lots of carbohydrate-rich products like salty, starchy snacks and sweets. From your own experience, surely you've had a bad night's sleep and found yourself gravitating toward carbs the next day. What's more, because we need sleep to metabolize glucose properly, sleep loss over time can impair the body's blood-sugar control and increase one's risk for diabetes. Granted, the studies on this so far have been on adults, but they likely reflect what's going on in our sleep-deprived kids, too.

We can go on and on about the value of sleep and the repercussions of not getting enough. The fact of the matter is that many of us, kids included, don't get the sleep we need. Bear in mind that our sleep habits as the adults are often mirrored by our children, who watch and model themselves on us. If you're sleep deprived, chances are your kids could be, too. In 2006, the National Sleep Foundation focused on teens and found that America's youth aren't getting the sleep they need, either. Interestingly, parents *think* their kids are getting enough sleep, but the kids know they're not. And in addition to teens having poor sleep habits (or bad "sleep hygiene"), caffeine and tech toys are as much sleep thieves in teens as they are in adults. The study also found that parents play a key role in helping their adolescent children get a good night's sleep. This, in turn, affects their moods, ability to learn, and problem-solving skills. And we have plenty of studies proving that problems can develop quickly in adolescents who get just a night or two of insufficient sleep. They are not only more prone to car accidents but also have problems performing in school and retaining information.

The average adult sleeps 6.9 hours on weeknights and 7.5 hours on weekends, or about 7 hours on average. Several epidemiological studies have demonstrated the connection between obesity and sleep in adults. One such study, from Columbia University in New York, used government data on 6,115 people to study the relationship between sleep patterns and obesity. Researchers found that those who slept a scant 2 to 4 hours a night were 73 percent more likely to be obese than those who got 7 to 9 hours.

The lesson: Prioritize sleep in your home. Modeling and teaching good sleep habits will not only help you ensure that everyone gets plenty of rest, but also manage adolescents' natural tendency to go to bed later and sleep in. Again, this is due to a circadian rhythm that's beating to a different tune than that of an adult, but unfortunately our society isn't built around a teenager's clock. A few high schools have changed their start times to accommodate this discrepancy, but in general, high schools start earlier than other schools. Many teens are the proverbial night owls living in an early-bird world.

NEW PUBERTY FACT

The younger you are, the more sleep you need. Adults need 7 to 9 hours and school-age kids (5 to 10 years old) need 10 to 11 hours.

This is how much sleep kids need according to the National Sleep Foundation:

- Newborns (0 to 2 months): 12 to 18 hours
- Infants (3 to 11 months): 14 to 15 hours
- Toddlers (1 to 3 years): 12 to 14 hours
- Preschoolers (3 to 5 years): 11 to 13 hours
- School-age children (5 to 10 years): 10 to 11 hours
- Teens (10 to 17): 8.5 to 9.25 hours

It's important that as parents we help our children practice good sleep hygiene, and this starts when they are babies. There's a reason why following regular, trusty bedtime routines with the very young—bathing, brushing teeth, reading books, etc.—can be so effective at preparing a child to go to bed and ensuring they get a good night's sleep. When they go through the same exact motions every night, starting at roughly the same time, their bodies get used to the routine and it promotes sensations of sleepiness. Few of us can go from a highly stimulating activity to instantly falling asleep, and the same is true for children and adolescents. They need the going-to-bed regimen to be a process that entails winding down, relaxing, and signaling the body that restful sleep is ahead. New research has indicated that setting up good sleep hygiene in childhood may be key to successful sleep in adolescence, and that the hormonal activities during the pubertal process may play less of a role in the quality of an adolescent's sleep than we thought. Bottom line: Teach kids how to get a good night's sleep when they're as young as possible so they will continue to have restful, restorative sleep during adolescence and beyond.

With all this in mind, let us offer some recommendations.

- Try to ensure your child goes to bed and wakes up at the same time 7 days a week, weekends included. Don't change the rules on weekends or holidays, because the body doesn't know the difference between Monday and Saturday.

- Have your child set aside at least 30 to 60 minutes before bedtime to unwind and prepare for sleep. During this time, she must avoid stimulating activities such as using a computer (or any other technological device) and doing homework. Sleep is more important than homework, because tired children are not good learners. You may want to set a stop time for homework, after which all screens are to be turned off. If your child has too much homework and cannot get it done by the cutoff time (despite good time management), then it's time to speak with her teachers. Be an advocate for your child. Sometimes teachers don't know how much homework their students are taking home nightly because they don't know what the other teachers are assigning.

- Reserve the child's bedroom for sleep only. Don't allow any electronics, TVs, cell phones, gadgets, or screens of any kind to be in the room (and if you do allow screens in the room for part of the day, set time limits). Recharge their batteries in another room. Model these behaviors by doing the same for your own bedroom. And keep the room clean, cool, and dark. If they are afraid of the dark, then use dim lighting.

- Be strict about using LED screens, the kind typically in computers and tablets, which emit a particular wavelength of light that disrupts the pineal gland's secretion of melatonin, the sleep hormone. Some studies have linked exposure to these lights to sleep disorders that, in turn, could be factoring into the onset of early puberty. So there's a difference between watching a program on a television screen and using a laptop or tablet (or other smart device). Have the electronic devices in your house go to bed half an hour or more before the children do—but not in a bedroom.

» If you live in a neighborhood where street noise can disrupt sleep, or if your home is small and your child goes to bed earlier than other members of the household, try using a white noise machine to stamp out ambient noise.

Just think: If you get your entire household to get a good night's sleep consistently, you'll have family members who are not only happier and healthier but also less cranky and prone to tears and tantrums. Yvonne Kelly, PhD, a professor of epidemiology at University College London, who led the UK study we described, stated it perfectly for *Medical News Today*: "Not having fixed bedtimes, accompanied by a constant sense of flux, induces a state of body and mind akin to jet lag and this matters for healthy development and daily functioning. We know that early child development has profound influences on health and well-being across the life course. It follows that disruptions to sleep, especially if they occur at key times in development, could have important lifelong impacts on health."

Enough said.

MOVE MORE AND MORE OFTEN

We trust that we don't have to spend too much time preaching the value of physical activity, for it's general wisdom now that being active is key to good health. It improves how every system in the body functions, helps normalize weight and maintain healthy levels of hormones, and supports emotional stability—in adults and kids alike. And, like sleep, we all need to get plenty of it, which is harder today than ever before due to the proliferation of technology and general life circumstances that keep us sedentary.

Most people don't realize how much physical activity we need. If we think about it from an evolutionary perspective, early humans were on the move a lot more than we are today. Our bodies were designed for constant low-level activity, with spurts of high-intensity movement. Our sedentary lives, whether we're sitting in school, in a car, at a computer, or with a tablet, do not match what is healthy for us.

Although Lawrence Kushi, whose expertise we tapped for the discussion on soy's effect on cancer risks in Chapter 3, is best known for his work on how food relates to health, he's quick to point out the importance of physical activity. He knows that the cure for childhood obesity isn't all about food and that we need to rethink how we design our neighborhoods. "If we're serious about tackling many of the issues around obesity and early puberty, we have to be serious about how we build our communities," he says. He praises leaders like Michael Bloomberg, who as mayor of New York City promoted programs and regulations to encourage more movement and less junk food. Bloomberg was the first leader in our country to ban trans fats from restaurants, and he pushed for more bicycle lanes to be installed, for bodega owners to reposition unhealthy snacks to make fruits more visible, and to limit the sizes of fountain soda cups. He also established the Center for Active Design, a nonprofit organization dedicated to promoting physical activity with built-space design changes, such as making stair use more visible and appealing.

The other place where we need to encourage physical activity is in our schools. Kris Madsen, MD, a pediatrician and associate professor at University of California, Berkeley, has conducted extensive studies into how we can combat childhood obesity by increasing physical activity. Parents can advocate that schools bring in programs like the nonprofit Playworks, which sends trained coaches into schools in low-income neighborhoods to make sure recess time is active and positive for all the kids. This approach is more feasible for them than changing their neighborhoods. Playworks playground coaches create safer spaces for physical activity by tamping down bullying and aggression, helping kids achieve better social–emotional outcomes, and getting kids who need encouragement to be active into the mix. They use games, bouncy balls, hula hoops, and jump ropes to engage and motivate kids to be active. (For more about Playworks, go to playworks.org.)

In addition to our communities and schools making changes to facilitate more movement, we as parents and guardians must encourage our children to move their bodies more, and more often. Kids who are already engaged in formal sports programs or who live in safe neighborhoods and enjoy outdoor play won't have any problems in this department. But so many kids today don't usually get the recommended daily 30 to 60 minutes of exercise. A bookworm or avid video gamer doesn't need to join a team sport at school or start playing tennis, though; she just needs to get her heart rate up and to break a sweat regularly by dancing in the living room to her favorite music, or power walking with mom or dad or a group of friends, or working out to a kid-friendly exercise video, or enjoying a playground that has lots of physically demanding structures for older kids to climb on. This isn't about joining a gym or using formal exercise equipment. It's just about getting a girl to find what kind of "play" she enjoys that gets her moving. Every girl will be different. Some love group play, while others prefer solo exercise. Help her figure out what she likes to do and then encourage more of it. She may not see herself as "athletic," but that needn't hinder her in being active. (Note: Wii Fit–style programs don't count! Video games that get kids moving are fun but should be considered bonus movement, not counted toward their daily goal.)

It also helps to talk to girls about the value of fitness from a health standpoint, emphasizing exercise's positive influence on overall health and physical growth. Talk about heart health and muscle strength, but don't bring up weight and, again, ditch the word "diet" entirely. Also mention how exercise helps their ability to learn new information and to feel happy.

Because girls can be very self-conscious about their developing bodies, help yours to keep exercising by making sure that she has comfortable athletic clothes and an appropriate sports bra when she is old enough to need one. There are lots of options today, and if your daughter is exceptionally uncomfortable talking about this with you, just buy some for her and leave them in her drawer. Additional tips:

- Set the example: Adults who lead sedentary lives don't make good role models. Even if you don't keep to a regular exercise routine yourself, get out with your kids and play with them. Help them explore what kinds of activities they enjoy and promote those. Start to channel their interests. Go for bike rides or hikes on the weekends. Plan vacations that include lots of fun outdoor activities. Limit the amount of couch-potato time they spend on days they don't have school.

- Change it up: While it's fine for a girl to excel in one particular sport, ensure that she doesn't play the same sport all year. This can set her up for injury. The explosion of teen sports medicine clinics around the nation is a testament to our single-sport-crazy culture. Just as it helps adults to mix up our routines and cross-train, it also helps our kids reduce their risk of injury and burnout and keep them interested. Engaging all the muscles is especially important as their bodies are developing.

- Don't overdo it: More than 15 to 20 hours of exercise a week is too much for a young girl. And if she's a runner, aim for less than 20 miles a week.

Many kids, especially girls, entering their preteen years start to think of themselves as unathletic if they are not great at playing organized sports. In our hypercompetitive culture, girls start dropping out at this age if they aren't superstars or on expensive club teams that require so much of parents, including time and money. Ball sports are overly emphasized, given all the other ways there are to be active. We see many girls who are great runners, swimmers, dancers—engaged in any number of physical activities—who think they aren't athletic because they don't play organized ball sports.

Here's an example of how being physically active can become difficult as a young girl grows: A 10-year-old starts thinking she's not athletic because she isn't a standout player in soccer, a game she's always loved. But as she gets older, the teams are getting more competitive, and she's no longer being picked for the best ones. Some of her friends are starting to do club soccer and others are just dropping out. Then, she starts to gain weight as a result of puberty and normal growth. If at this point she becomes much less active or drops out of sports altogether, she may gain even more weight, develop body-image issues, have her self-confidence falter, and lose motivation to be active and to see herself as athletic. Clearly, it's very much a snowball effect.

> **NEW PUBERTY FACT**
>
> Before puberty, boys and girls have about the same fat-to-muscle ratio. During puberty, however, boys' muscle tissue mass increases more quickly, than girls' fat tissue does. Boys will have one and a half times as much muscle as girls by the end of puberty, when the muscle-to-fat ratio will be 3 to 1 for boys and 5 to 4 for girls.

That's why it's critical for adults to encourage a girl like this to find activities she loves that get her moving. These can change over time as her interests and circumstances shift. It's not that hard to do. You just have to be creative and put some effort into it. The sooner, the better.

MONITOR WITHOUT HELICOPTERING

Perhaps nothing could be more challenging than trying to find the perfect balance between neglecting to watch closely over our children to ensure their safety and hovering or "helicoptering." Monitor too much and you can spoil the trust in your relationship and trigger frustration and resentment in a young girl who's trying to forge autonomy, independence, and trust. But on the flip side is letting her have too much independence and risk making unsafe choices. So let us offer some guidance in the spirit of striking that balance, which is a moving target during puberty and the entire adolescent process.

The most dangerous hours of the day for high-risk behavior are the ones between school dismissal in the afternoon and being home with family in the evening. This is especially true when parents work and are not home until dinnertime. During these hours, kids who are not properly monitored could, depending on their age and peer groups, encounter opportunities to engage in risky behaviors like drug or alcohol use, smoking, and sex. Girls who enter puberty early face an increased risk of partaking in these behaviors due to their more mature bodies, which may attract older friends and older boys. A girl may suddenly find herself in social settings where she has to make decisions her young brain isn't equipped to properly handle. Of course, not every girl who develops early will surrender to peer pressure and get involved with the "wrong crowd," but it's important for us to be aware of these risks and to do what we can to minimize the chances that the wrong choices will be made. Remember, too, that many people (including parents, teachers, and other adults) expect a girl who is further along in puberty to be more mature. And this can result in both positive and negative outcomes.

It's a good idea to stay tuned in to her circle of friends and know where she is when you're not around. When she's at home alone, check in with her frequently. Avoid letting her have friends over if you're not there (even if she wants to do homework with someone or needs to complete a group project). Older teenage siblings are often not the best monitors either. While they may be trustworthy when they're left on their own, their developmental stage can cause them to be self-focused and, therefore, unable to step outside of their own needs to closely monitor someone else's. In general, be cautious about overestimating a child's cognitive and social maturity just because they are more mature physically. They may be fully capable of making their own lunch or dinner or calling 911 in an emergency, but it still may be very difficult for them to say "no" to a peer who wants to come over when you're not home. In Chapter 8 we'll be covering the topic of building emotional closeness, which starts from day one of parenthood—not the day you realize she's blooming early and making friends with older boys. That way, by the time you have to monitor her more closely during puberty, you'll already have a solid relationship that will allow you to have those important conversations about what she might experience with puberty and how to navigate peer pressure.

While teaching a girl how to say "No, thanks" is helpful, an even better approach is to help her avoid these situations altogether. Limiting unmonitored time can help preteen and younger girls skirt trouble, but empowering older kids who are confident and centered to say no directly is essential. Talk with your girl about the friends she chooses and how they make her feel (e.g., respected, safe, or insecure). Stress that they should be good friends who have her back and respect her decisions. Do the friends share your perspective on things like smoking, for example? This, of course, really helps a child steer clear of trouble. Start talking early about what makes a good friend. Teach her that if she's dealing with peer pressure, a good friend will back off when she says something like "I don't feel like you are listening to me, and you are disrespecting my decision. Why do you keep asking when I already said no?" This is easier to do if a girl's friends respect the friendship and treat her well from the beginning.

As kids get older and people around them are experimenting, taking this direct approach can be really hard for some teens, especially those who don't have a good friend or wing person with them. We always recommend that at middle school dances, kids have a trusted buddy to rely on and watch out for each other. This is good practice for when they get older and social situations become more complex. Their peer group will determine how challenging it is to navigate these incidents. Julie's daughter and her friends communicate with each other at dances by raising one to three fingers: one finger signifies "I'm fine and having fun"; two fingers mean "I'm okay, but check back with me"; and three mean "Help, get me out of this situation."

To some degree, we can allow them to fabricate excuses or lie. For example, saying "I have to get up really early tomorrow" for some activity or another is a reason they can give to avoid an uncomfortable situation, or they can say "I have to stay in shape for track," or "There is alcoholism in my family," or "My uncle died from smoking." To say no to experimenting with drugs or alcohol, she can say "That makes me really sick and I think I'm allergic to it, because it runs in my family," or "No thanks, I quit," or "I tried it once and it didn't do anything for me, so no thanks."

One of the most reliable excuses for youngsters to use is to blame their parents, which is especially helpful for younger kids: "My mom is really crazy about the smell of smoke; it would be a *scene* if I smelled like smoke." Another one: "My mom would kill me if I let you in when she's not home and I can't risk it; I'd be banned from *Minecraft* forever."

You get the idea. Ideally, the goal is to talk to kids in advance about good practical strategies that go beyond a "just say no" mentality. In addition to giving her strategies for excusing herself from certain situations, explain to her the serious consequences that could come with some of the choices she might make, consequences that can last a lifetime. Be open and candid with her, but stay in your parental role. Far too often parents try to be "friends" with their children in the hope that it will make for better communication. But this can backfire.

Kids need superiors, rules, limits, and defined expectations. You can't give those if you're "friends" with your daughter. Susan Stiffelman is a popular family therapist and the author of *Parenting without*

Power Struggles. She offers a fantastic analogy for what lies at the heart of her teachings:

> If you're a passenger on a cruise ship, it's kind of cool if the Captain joins you for dinner. But his true value isn't as a social companion; you want and need him to be the guy who oversees the smooth sailing you signed up for, steering the ship through storms and around icebergs while you blithely sing your heart out at the karaoke bar. You want to be able to depend on the Captain, whether or not you like him or understand everything he's doing. It's a hierarchical relationship, with the Captain assuming his rightful role as the one in charge, and the passengers relaxing in the sense of safety that comes from knowing they can rely on someone to competently steer the ship through calm *and rough* waters. . . . Children need us to be the Captains of their ships.

Stiffelman makes a clear and important distinction between being in control versus being in charge. You want to focus more on the latter, as being in charge "means that we're capable of keeping our cool even when the seas are rough [and] when our children perceive us as steady and calm—regardless of their moods or behavior—they can relax, knowing they can rely on us to get them through the challenging moments in their lives." Picture yourself on that ship again, watching the captain running around in a panic shouting, "Oh no! I can't handle this!" If that were the case, you'd be very worried.

We couldn't agree more with Stiffelman's philosophy and approach, because it helps us to come *alongside* our kids as they mature rather than *at* them. More often than not, a child's misbehavior is an announcement that there's a problem. And the adults need to ask themselves what she must be feeling, thinking, or experiencing to make her behave like that.

It's hard sometimes to be the bad guy and play the captain, but it's imperative. Set limits and stick with them. This makes kids feel safe and secure even if they don't always thank you for it. Set consistent expectations and remind your child of them, as well as why you have them. And don't be emotional about it. Explain that this is how the family works, and while there's room for negotiation on some things, you are ultimately in charge of the rules and the penalties for transgressions. She will be mad at you occasionally, and that's okay. Contrary to what you might think, rules and limits help a girl feel protected. And remind her that it's fine for her to blame you if you say no to something and she has to find a way out of the situation. If her best friend wants to take her to a concert that you don't approve of, for instance, she can say, "My mom won't let me go." Then offer her alternatives to the concert, such as inviting a friend or two to share a night away (with parent chaperones) at an inexpensive local hotel that has a pool (look for great deals online) or going to a fun event or night out. If possible, establish a core group of parents of kids in your daughter's grade whose values and expectations align with yours. Then parents and kids can plan and share activities. The key is to be as involved as you can, even if that means coming up with alternatives to your 9-year-old reading the *Hunger Games* or going to a Lady Gaga concert.

One of the best ways to maintain a healthy parent–child relationship and assure your kids that you're keeping a close eye on them (from a safe distance) is to give them more responsibility. Kids need to take on responsibilities as they mature and grow older. Many preteen girls like to be parents' helpers and earn a little money by watching over younger kids while moms or dads are home. Start getting them engaged in community projects like bake sales or fund-raisers or projects that *they* conceive of to benefit an organization of their choice, like a local animal shelter or a children's charity. Let them start making their own lunches or at least add to their lunches in an independent way, such as by dropping a banana in the bag for a snack. Let them choose their own clothes. Begin to relinquish some of your constraints on their independence (within reason). Let them choose the instrument they want to learn to play. Give them special privileges that will help them feel special, older, and more responsible, like walking to the corner store to pick up something you need if it's safe for them to go alone. They also need a safe vehicle for channeling their energy and exploring their newfound sense of autonomy. Any number of things might attract them, such as volunteering to do community work or trying activities that thrill seekers enjoy, such as skateboarding or surfing. Or, they could write a letter to the school principal or even the president to advocate for something—whatever gets them excited.

Don't forget to give them choices as much as possible. Girls will naturally start to push away from their parents as they gain autonomy and search for their unique identity. If you offer choices to them, neither you nor your child will feel like you're always saying no and clamping down on them (and you'll avoid those power struggles). Create autonomy within clear limits that you set by, for example, saying that she must be back by a particular time or risk losing a special privilege. That will also show that you're flexible. After all, in the end, she will be her own person.

Because preteen girls can seem mature in one domain but not another, it can be hard to make decisions about what to allow and what to prohibit. They might be able to walk home from school on their own, but should they be home alone? These are the decisions that we parents have to make using the knowledge we have and, to some degree, our gut instincts. The same is true when it comes to deciding when to get them a cell phone, what kinds of parental controls are suitable on computers and televisions they use, and how much social media they're able to use. You might be keeping them off Facebook or Twitter, but are they using similar sites that have the same potential hazards, from exposure to graphic images and language to cyberbullying? Some parents are so unfamiliar with social media and the

Internet themselves that they are clueless about what their girls could be exposed to online. If you're among those behind the technology curve, get together with other parents at your daughter's school and bring in an expert who can teach you the ropes about social media sites and how to monitor and control them. Then you can establish rules about interacting online, like never giving out any personal information and immediately leaving a site if someone asks for your age, gender, e-mail address, or anything else that's personal (and make sure you clearly define what those things are). Social media sites are relatively easy to navigate, so it's worth the effort to learn just a little so you can follow your kids on platforms like Instagram and monitor who they follow. If you are not savvy, get an adult friend who can help you out. Then use what you've learned to teach your children how to use social media wisely; it's unlikely they're getting a lesson on this in school. "Follow" your child's social media profiles on these sites so you can stay tuned in to what they are posting, who their friends are, and what conversations are taking place. Again, be careful about relying on an older sibling to monitor your younger child's Internet presence; don't overestimate their judgment, skills, or maturity. But it's good for all children to know that you're all online and keeping a protective eye on one another. Some additional tips:

- Cell phones: Many kids today get these by the age of 12 for safety and logistical reasons. But be mindful of what they can do with those phones. It's best to purchase a plan that allows talking and texting, but no Internet access. Scientists don't yet know how cell phones affect a developing brain, so have them use earbuds to listen instead of the phone itself until we know more about the effects of holding devices next to one's ear.

- Beware of peer pressure on *you*: Just as kids are vulnerable to peer pressure, so are we as adults. Don't allow your daughter to do something you don't approve of just because her best friend's mother does. Everyone has different values and sets different rules. Be mindful of how your own shortcomings, susceptibilities, and sources of stress affect your judgment. We can't help our girls manage peer pressure and their own social stressors if we can't manage our own.

- Manage other stressors: Get help dealing with stressful things if you need it. Kids are uniquely dialed in to our stress, and asking for the help of a friend or counselor will both reduce your anxiety and show them a positive way to cope.

- Model good behavior: Put your phone away, especially when you should be engaging with your kid (not to mention when you are driving!). We can't tell you how many parents we see at the park staring at their phones for hours on end while their kids are playing. And then they wonder why their kids want phones at such early ages—they learn from their parents that they are the most fascinating objects around.

- Screen time: How much is enough? Less than 2 hours a day total for all screens, a standard recommendation endorsed by the American Academy of Pediatrics. Limit or forbid violent games.

- Stability and consistency are key: And these must come from the home. Julia Graber and Jay Belsky, whose work on the psychology of puberty was reviewed in Chapter 2, have both written extensively about the positive power a strong peer group can have, but they also underscore that the family remains a child's main point of contact, especially for young girls. You are the center of gravity that everything else in her life revolves around.

- Choose a K-through-8 school: If you can choose which school your girl attends, consider one that goes from kindergarten all

the way to grade 8 (as opposed to a school that enrolls kids in kindergarten through grade 5 or from 6th grade to 8th). Kids in
K-through-8 schools learn to have empathy with younger kids,
often through buddy systems that partner older and younger
kids, which helps older ones develop that sense of positive
responsibility we discussed earlier. Also, kids who grow up going
to a K-to-8 school establish strong relationships with teachers
they had in earlier grades whom they can visit with and talk to in
times of crisis. The children know that these teachers, and often
the principal, can provide trustworthy support. The parents at
K-to-8 schools are often more involved and volunteer more than
they do in middle schools. This means there are more adults
around, which can create a different and positive atmosphere. At
K-to-8 schools, the older kids generally feel more trusted and
responsible, which can inspire confidence and involvement in
them. For instance, running for student council may be less
intimidating at a K-to-8 school than at a large middle school. And
last, changing schools at 6th grade, during one of the most awkward developmental stages, can make kids more self-conscious
and uncertain. Of course, all kids are not the same, and some
really need the change of school, especially those who are confident and grounded and are seeking new experiences. For kids
who had trouble with a bully, were stereotyped, or weren't able to
live down an embarrassing episode at their K-to-5 school, the
switch to middle school presents a welcome chance to reinvent
themselves and start over. Talk to your child's teachers about
what school they think she might do best at, but in the end, look
to your own judgment, because you know your child the best.

Above all, remember that there's a lot of time for kids to grow up. They
don't have to do it all overnight or in a year once they hit puberty. Take
your time.

PREVENTION IS THE BEST MEDICINE

The late René Dubos, a French-born American microbiologist, environmentalist, and prolific author who won the 1969 Pulitzer Prize for *So Human an Animal,* wrote in his 1959 book *Mirage of Health*: "When the tide is receding from the beach it is easy to have the illusion that one can empty the ocean by removing water with a pail." How true that is. Eighteen years later, in 1977, Boston University researchers quoted Dubos when they wrote a seminal paper about what they saw as the real reason behind our astonishing jump in average life expectancy. At the turn of the 20th century, most people died in their late forties of infections like influenza and pneumonia. But by the 1970s, we were pushing 75 years young and eventually succumbing to chronic ailments strongly linked to aging, like heart disease and cancer. And here's the shocking conclusion that the researchers drew after they pored over health trends: The dramatic decline in our annual death rate wasn't due principally to better medical treatment. In fact, they calculated that more than a breathtaking 96 percent of the decline in mortality could be credited to *nonmedical factors* such as more prevalent affluence and literacy, and better housing and nutrition. They also noted that 92 percent of the progress had already been made by the middle of the 20th century, when modern medicine and health care spending started to take off.

While you'd think that better medicine, such as antibiotics and vaccines, would have had a huge impact in this increase in our longevity, it turns out that good health is likely more a result of social conditions and access to health-promoting goods and resources like community farmers' markets and recreational centers than anything else. And we can't ignore the fact that positive social conditions pave the way to healthful lifestyles. But they also lead people to behave in certain ways and establish the kinds of lifelong habits that ultimately fend off illness and infections.

Such realities are now, thankfully, being addressed by leaders like the Robert Wood Johnson Foundation's Commission to Build a Healthier America, which was formed in 2008 to identify other ways to improve the health of Americans beyond traditional health care. Their Time to Act campaign calls for less medicine and more prevention through education and building communities that promote healthy living. Head Start, a program of the US Department of Health and Human Services, was built on this premise as well.

We applaud such endeavors, and even though they may seem obvious to some degree, now we have the scientific proof that such strategies work. We know, for example, that poor education, substandard housing, poverty, living in disadvantaged neighborhoods, and exposure to significant adversity or excessive stress affect a number of health outcomes—including the timing of puberty. And we have a lot to combat: As reported by the Robert Wood Johnson Foundation, one-fifth of US children are living in poverty and half of African American children live in impoverished communities that lack job opportunities, quality housing, and access to health-promoting resources such as nutritious foods and recreational centers. Moreover, a third of our kids are overweight or obese, a fact that disproportionately affects people in low-income communities. These individuals are also more likely to endure greater exposure to chemicals that can further impact their health and alter the pubertal process.

Part of our mission in writing this book is to inspire people to think of ways they can contribute to disempowered communities. Obviously, we all have limitations on what we can and cannot change, and how much we can give back to others who may be in need. But there's a lot we can be doing at home and in our local communities to foster optimal health in our girls—and in everyone else, for that matter, adults included. This, in turn, will eventually impact our larger goals on a societal level, where growing income gaps continue to hamper efforts to combat the ills of poverty. These habits tie directly and indirectly into lowering all the risks associated with early puberty. They also relate directly (and indirectly) to the risk of suffering from pretty much any ailment. We realize it's a tad cliché to say that a lack of attention to lifestyle hazards—allowing a young girl to have a poor diet, be sedentary, regularly get too little sleep, be buffeted by family instability, etc.—has a hand in the overall health of a young girl growing up fast. We all know deep down that the choices we make every day play into our health, sometimes even regardless of what our underlying DNA predisposes us to. Eat too much and move too little, and you will gain weight; likewise, if you're living in a tumultuous household where hardship is frequently present and palpable, you will experience stress that can have adverse physical effects. But at no age does this have more influence than during the early years of a girl's life. We must start teaching the precepts of a healthy lifestyle long before she's noticing her body changing.

Indeed, "better medicine" starts at home.

CHAPTER SEVEN

"WHAT IS SHE THINKING?"

Inside the Brain of a Developing Girl

PARENTS WITH PUBESCENT CHILDREN SHARE many experiences in common, especially when it comes to feeling confused or alarmed by their girls' behavior. Consider the following laments:

My 9-year-old sometimes seems to act like she's a full-on teenager—talking back to me, stomping her feet, slamming doors, rolling her eyes, and saying "whatever" when I ask her to do something. What's going on in her head?

I can't stand it when my preteen, who started puberty early, uses a rude and nasty tone of voice with me and everything turns into an argument. Is this attitude normal?

My sweet girl started the 5th grade and suddenly turned into someone else. She no longer gets along with her younger siblings. In fact, it often seems like she provokes them. She's never been mean but it feels like she is now. Why? How did this happen?

I know that girls going through puberty are apt to say "I hate you" and not really mean it, but how concerned should I be when they say things like "I hate my life!" or "I wish I was dead"?

I try not to be too controlling over my daughter's life, especially now that she's going through puberty and seeks more independence, but she tends to make bad decisions. How long does this risk-taking behavior last? Where does it come from?

MANY PARENTS HAVE TOLD US that their elementary school–age girls are for the most part happy, cooperative, and intensely loving. You are the world to them. And they don't put up too much of a fight about wearing age-appropriate clothing and following household rules. Even when things go awry, they still crave your love and approval, and making up after an argument is usually pretty easy. Then something happens, seemingly overnight, once they hit puberty! Their attitudes and behaviors change. They start to challenge your authority and pay less attention to you; you are no longer their entire universe. Gone are the days when they did exactly as they were told, and their need to reconcile with you before they fall asleep at night seems to fly out the window. Sometimes you feel like conversations are filled with too much negotiation, nagging, and pleading, and you are losing your cool more than you ever thought possible. This kid you adored (and still adore) is getting under your skin on a daily basis. You wonder, *When did this all start? How did this happen? Is this normal? How long will it last? Did I do anything wrong?*

As Aristotle noted, "Youth are heated by Nature as drunken men by wine." Stereotypes of juveniles have proliferated throughout human history and been depicted in literature for centuries immemorial— they can be rebellious, lazy, irrational, egocentric, arrogant, disrespectful, irresponsible, emotional, and socially awkward. In actuality, adolescents—who are growing and changing rapidly—may get a bad rap because we adults may not be ready for this transition. So why, then, do these descriptors ring true sometimes? Because their immature brains make them act that way. But only in the last decade has science begun to really grasp from a neurobiological standpoint what makes the many changes in adolescence so noticeable and profound.

Now, if you have a 7- or 8-year-old girl who is showing signs of puberty (and you cannot stomach the word "adolescent" in reference to your daughter), then you're probably scratching your head and wondering how a chapter about the "teen" brain relates to you and your child. After all, much of the discussion about the behavior issues spawned by a developing brain revolves around teenagers in middle school and high school—not elementary school. Much of what we know today about the developing brain, however, isn't from studying just teenagers. Our understanding has come from studies involving young girls and boys from their toddler years up to their mid-twenties. And while it's true that most of the behaviors "stereotypical" of teenagers don't show up until a girl reaches 13 years old or beyond, an early-maturing girl will nonetheless experience brain changes that can indeed impact her mood and how she interacts with her family and her peers.

What is perhaps *most* important to know is that the bulk of these effects do not appear to be solely influenced by the brain itself; rather, they depend largely on a girl's social environment. The story of the pubescent brain no longer revolves around just anatomy and discrepancies in which areas mature faster or slower (or earlier or later) than others. There's a lot more going on. Neural connections taking place throughout the brain and within certain regions—all of which seem to be influenced by context—are at the heart of the real story. Which is why we adults must help create a positive social environment for growing girls to thrive and maneuver through shifting changes in behavior.

Let us be clear: In a lot of ways, children going through puberty do not embody the stereotypes that follow them. We may perceive them as defiant, discourteous, and intractable—and therefore frustrating—but typically they're just trying to be independent and autonomous. And to grow into thoughtful, productive adults, they must go through this period and we must do our best to accept and work with them during this phase. As you're about to find out, the developmental changes they experience may cause us to butt heads and misinterpret their signals, but that doesn't mean we can't find enough common ground to steer them in the right direction. Once you grasp what's really going on in a young person's head, you might be much more sympathetic and patient with them and, hopefully, more helpful as the adult figure in their life.

The information in this chapter will help you to appreciate what a girl's brain goes through and equip you to make the most of the time when she will be under the influence of her rapidly changing physiology. A wealth of new evidence shows that the hormonal events of puberty have sweeping effects on the brain's development and the behavior that results, but not in the ways people think when they picture a "hormone-crazed" youngster. These changes literally remodel the brain throughout adolescence and are believed to mold the perceptions, motivations, drives, decision making, and behavior of an individual, shaping maturation and independence. Even if a girl's still years away from the vast neural changes and peer influences we'll be describing, it helps to be prepared. The more you know today, the easier it will be to adjust to the changes as they happen and to be more sensitive to—not fight with—the tribulations of adolescence.

Of course, research on the adolescent brain is still in its infancy; we didn't know much about the relationship between puberty and neural development until recently. But we're close to getting answers with some really exciting research that's currently underway. The advent of functional magnetic resonance imaging, or fMRI, which records the brain in action and pinpoints which regions are involved in performing various mental tasks, has revolutionized the study of the brain. This technology has not only helped us literally see how the brain responds to certain stimuli but also revealed networks that are involved in all manner of thought processes, from recognizing faces to savoring a slice of birthday cake to feeling excluded when friends don't invite us along. In addition to giving you a quick summary of the long-established science, we're going to present you with information about the cutting-edge studies that haven't yet been covered by the mainstream press.

BRAIN ANATOMY 101

The human brain is a remarkable organ. Its size in comparison to the rest of our body is one of the most important features distinguishing us from other mammals. The brain of an elephant, for example, makes up $\frac{1}{550}$ of the elephant's total weight. Our brain is $\frac{1}{40}$ of our weight. But the feature that most sets us apart from all other species is our amazing ability to think in ways that reach far beyond mere survival. Fish, amphibians, reptiles, and birds, for instance, are assumed not to do much "thinking," at least in the way we conceive of it. But all animals concern themselves with the everyday business of eating, sleeping, reproducing, and surviving—these are "automatic" instinctual processes under the control of what's called the reptilian brain, which drives much of our behavior (perhaps more than we'd like to admit). As you've learned, the hypothalamus and pituitary—among the most ancient glands in our bodies, having evolved in mammals before humans split from the great apes—are at the center of the pubertal process.

But additional regions in our brains have evolved that allow us to do so much more than other mammals, including experience "growing up" in a unique way. As adults, we are better able than our children are to think with purpose and intent, control our impulses, form language, plan our future, pass judgment, experience and express deeply felt emotions, hold moral convictions, communicate our intentions, respond to nuanced social cues, and analyze information and stimuli in an exceptionally sophisticated fashion. Today, modern technology is allowing us a look at how our brain actually does all these things. For much of history, we didn't even know what a brain was. Aristotle wins points for his witty remark about youth, but he was dead wrong about

---

THE FACTS OF THE (BRAIN) MATTER

The new science of the brain has laid to rest many old myths and compelled us to redefine certain terms and reposition a few perspectives. As previously noted, we now have a very expanded view of "adolescence," which arguably stretches all the way from the preteen years through the early to mid-twenties, when the brain is still polishing off its development. This extended period of adolescence is largely the result of the shifting of social norms: It takes longer today than in generations past to grow up and become an independent, productive adult in our society. (Some have reframed this period as "emerging" adulthood from the age of 18 to about 25 years old.) Other factors contributing to the new definition of adolescence include the higher cost of living and the scarcity of job options for inexperienced young people. So the image of Generation Y-ers being plain lazy and having a poor work ethic is pure myth for the most part. In fact, even though many bash the millennials who are still living at home in their twenties, new research shows that there are upsides: closer connections within families and between youths and their aging parents, and more positive emotional support.

---

the brain; believe it or not, he saw it as a sort of refrigerator that cooled off the fiery heart.

But now, in addition to knowing that the brain is far from a refrigerator (or glob of phlegm, another ancient theory), we know that each part of the brain serves a defined purpose, and that these parts all link together to function in a coordinated manner. That last part is key to our new understanding of the brain. When we were in middle school, the brain was thought to be segmented by function—one area was for abstract thought, another for coloring within the lines, and so on. Perhaps you learned about Phineas Gage, one of the most famous survivors of a serious brain injury. His unfortunate accident illuminated so much about the inner workings of the brain at a time before we had advanced techniques to measure, test, and examine brain functions. A quick recap: In 1848, the 25-year-old Gage was working on the construction of a railroad in Cavendish, Vermont. One day, while he was packing explosive powder into a hole using a large iron rod measuring 43 inches long and $1\frac{1}{4}$ inches in diameter, the powder detonated. The rod shot upward into his face, penetrating Gage's left cheek, traveling all the way through his head (and brain) and out the top. His left eye was blinded, but he didn't die, and possibly didn't even lose consciousness, telling the doctor who first attended to him, "Here is business enough for you."

Gage's personality, however, did not survive the blow intact. According to some accounts, he went from being a model gentleman to a mean, violent, unreliable person. The curious case of Phineas Gage was the first to demonstrate a link between trauma to certain regions of the brain and personality change. He died at age 36 after experiencing a series of seizures, and he's been written about in the medical literature ever since.

Although documentation of Gage's accident gave us a glimpse of the brain's complexity, it took more than another century for us to understand that the brain's stunning capacity isn't simply due to its individual anatomical compartments. It's the circuitry and communication *between those sections* that make up our complicated responses and behaviors. Many areas of the brain develop (and, at the other end of the spectrum, deteriorate) at different rates and in different stages of our lives. For this reason, an adult solves problems differently than a child does. Likewise, an 80-year-old might struggle with motor skills such as walking and coordination while the teenager is a track-and-field star with perfect vision. We also know that brain architecture can change based on the social, cultural, and economic environments that children grow up in and in response to environmental factors like injury.

One question often debated in scientific circles is the following: Why do we humans take so long to mature relative to other species? We still don't know the answer. And it seems that the transition to adult roles in our society is taking even longer for youth today (a paradoxical change, considering the earlier physical maturation that's taking place). The slow pace of our development clearly has evolutionary costs: It demands more time and effort from parents and increases the offspring's risk of dying before reproducing. The predominant theory addressing this conundrum relates it to the complexity of our brains: A big and elaborate brain takes a lot of time to mature, and in humans a great majority of that development occurs after birth. What's more, the fact that we're socially advanced animals also influences our maturational time line. As we achieved ecological dominance, we began to compete almost exclusively within our species for resources, which compelled us to manage social relations adeptly and create alliances. Evolutionary forces thus favored the humans who were most adept at cooperation. Evolutionary biologist Richard Alexander, PhD, has characterized this remarkable phenomenon as a cognitive "arms race" within the species. The upshot is that we turned out to be much smarter than we needed to be to just hunt and gather successfully.

The Science of Building a Brain

On average, the brain reaches its maximum size in girls at about 11½ years of age (14½ on average for boys). By the age of 6, it is 95 percent of its maximum size. It triples in size in the first year of life, after which the rate of physical growth slows as we learn and "pack" more into our roughly 3-pound brains. What continues to develop, allowing this tremendous ability to process more and more information, is the complexity of the networks of neurons (brain cells) as they go through a process of "pruning," which we'll describe shortly. This helps explain why brain size is not necessarily directly correlated with intelligence. Science has increasingly shown that those neural connections are really important for a variety of complex abilities, including regulating emotions and making decisions.

NEW PUBERTY FACT

A developing brain during puberty and adolescence is very pliable or "plastic"— it's undergoing massive changes and can be uniquely vulnerable to its environment.

It used to be that we thought each person was born with a limited number of brain cells, for instance, and that even though a few more developed during early childhood, that was it. As adults, we were on a downward slope of continual brain-cell death. But as it turns out, we are not born with a finite number of neurons. We grow new neurons throughout our entire lives, a process called neurogenesis. That allows us to fortify our existing brain circuits and to create entirely new and intricate ones. However, there seem to be critical periods within which these processes are most malleable or "plastic," and the pubertal transition to adolescence is believed to be one of them.

Although scientists had long before demonstrated neurogenesis in various other animals, it wasn't until the 1990s that they began focusing exclusively on trying to show neurogenesis in adult humans. In 1998, the journal *Nature Medicine* published a report from a group led by Swedish neurologist Peter Eriksson, PhD, in which he demonstrated that the adult human brain could generate new cells. The authors hypothesized that an area of the brain known as the hippocampus (which plays a vital role in emotion and in the consolidation of memories) could generate neurons throughout life. And indeed, they were right: We all continue to experience development, at least in certain areas of our brains, as we age. This lent support to the concept called neuroplasticity (or brain plasticity), and the idea that there are unique periods when the brain is exceptionally plastic in special ways (e.g., during early life, when language develops). This concept of neuroplasticity replaced the old idea of the brain as a physiologically static organ. Now we know that the brain changes over time due to changes in the environment and behavior, and even to injury. This field has clearly helped pave the way for us to better understand the developing brain in adolescence.

Wire, Fire, Cut

Let's take a closer look at how the brain physically develops in order to shed light on how it affects the behavior of a young person, from thinking processes to controlling emotions.* Most everyone has heard about "gray matter," named for its distinctive color. It's a type of neural tissue in the brain and spinal cord that passes along sensory input, gathering information from the nerves of the entire body and ensuring its delivery to the correct destination. How fast that information is transmitted depends on the white matter, a type of neural tissue that looks white because the cells are coated in insulating layers called myelin sheaths that form to protect and speed up those neural transmissions.

---

* Much of the material about the developing brain in this section was synthesized from materials published by the National Institutes of Health. Go to nimh.nih.gov/health and search for *The Teen Brain: Still Under Construction,* or see the Recommended Reading section at the back of the book for details and further resources.

"Gray matter" is a synonym for intelligence, and for good reason: Individuals with genius-level IQs or unique skills tend to have a higher volume of gray matter in the specific areas of their brains that correlate with their ability. Combined, the gray and white matter form the central processing unit of the brain.

More specifically, gray matter is comprised of brain cells (neurons), the nerve fibers that project from them, and support cells. Synapses connect brain cells to form networks. They are the paths over which neurons speak to one another. Early in life, as the brain is growing, there is a large increase in the number of synapses followed by massive trimming or "pruning" as the brain matures. This "wire, fire, cut" activity is the essence of how the brain develops during puberty, keeping the connections that are used the most and discarding the unused ones (giving credence to the expression "use it or lose it"). We are all born with more synapses than we have as adults. Those synapses multiply rapidly in the first 2 years of life, so by the time we're toddlers, we have about twice as many synapses as adults. In fact, toddlerhood is one of the most active periods of reorganization in the brain; this is when an impressive buildup of neural connections happens, after which pruning begins to allow the strongest and best connections to function more effectively. Unfortunately, the "wire, fire, cut" process doesn't always translate into positive outcomes for a developing child, such as when she is exposed to abuse, chronic violence, or poverty. By the same token, however, if a young girl is learning to play the piano, engaging in sports, learning a new language, or studying hard, those are the connections that are more likely to become hardwired. If she's sitting on the couch watching TV or playing video games, those are the cells and connections that are going to be reinforced.

We scientists don't yet know all the details about this fluctuation in gray matter volume, but we do think that it's part of the brain's normal development and helps it become as efficient as possible. While genes likely play a role in the decline in synapses, some of the most astonishing research of late has highlighted the power of experience—how one's environment can profoundly influence the pruning process. It's the old nature versus nurture phenomenon in action. Synapses that are "exercised" by experience become stronger, while others get weaker and are eventually trimmed away.

Until recently, scientists focused heavily on brain matter as it first grows and then is winnowed away during the first 5 or 6 years of life. It was believed that most, if not all, of the significant and dynamic changes in brain organization and development took place before adolescence. After all, the brain reaches its full adult size by puberty. Put another way, we used to think that the adolescent brain was already developed and functioned like an adult brain. But we know better now (and as any parent or middle school teacher will tell you from their own experiences, this makes logical sense).

Evidence that a tremendous amount of change is going on in the maturing brain has come from studies in which scientists performed brain scans on the same children at multiple times as they grew up. The scans, typically using MRI, have revealed unexpectedly late changes occurring in the outer layer, or cortex, of the brain. This is where the processes of complex thought take place. Generally speaking, the more evolved the mammal is, the larger the cerebral cortex; the larger the cortex, the more developed the brain function. A human brain, for instance, has lots of folds and creases on the outside—that's the cerebral cortex—and, of course, the more folds there are, the greater the cerebral cortex's surface area, which translates into more advanced capabilities. It is this part of the brain—and more specifically, an area in the very front called the prefrontal cortex—that gives us our higher reasoning skills: the ability to think analytically and logically, to problem solve, to plan for the future, and to think abstractly. It also allows us to express our unique personality and manage our emotional impulses, which are chiefly controlled by the limbic part of the brain that lies below the cortex. This is what's called top-down brain functioning, meaning that the outer, more sophisticated cerebral brain regulates the more primitive, instinctual parts underneath it.

During childhood, the volume of gray matter in the cortex first increases and then decreases. This is a normal and necessary part of maturation. Although we don't yet know exactly why there's this change in volume, we do know that this is what pushes the time line of brain maturation into adolescence and young adulthood. According to brain scans, the rate of gray matter growth by the early twenties slows to become more like that of adults.

One particularly active area of study has been the cerebral cortex's frontal lobe. A longitudinal study by Jay Giedd, MD, and his colleagues at the National Institute of Mental Health has used MRI to scan the brains of healthy girls and boys beginning at the age of 3 and continuing until they reach 18 and beyond. Over the past 20 years, his lab has amassed more than 3,000 MRI scans, a colossal undertaking. Giedd is credited with discovering that just before puberty, the frontal lobe undergoes a second wave of reorganization and growth that results in millions of new synapses. This is eventually followed by a massive pruning of these connections that doesn't end until early adulthood.

Another important discovery that helps make sense of the pubescent brain is that different parts of the cortex mature at different rates. The first areas to mature are those that perform more basic functions, such as processing sensory information and controlling movement. The sections of the cortex that are responsible for the kinds of "top-down" control typical of adult behavior, such as planning ahead and controlling impulses, are among the last to mature. (That's why pre-teens drive us crazy with their need for independence combined with their clear lack of careful planning skills; as strategic, mindful, careful adults, we see the potentially dangerous flaws in their logic.) We know this from tracking how those newly created neurons become myelinated, or coated with myelin (the insulation that speeds up the electrical transmission of information). Compared to neurons that have none, myelin increases the speed at which transmission occurs by up to 100 times.

Myelin becomes established first in the more primitive areas of the brain, then gradually expands to the areas of higher-level functioning. It makes sense for certain neuronal connections that are critical to basic functions and survival to mature first. So, during the transition from childhood to the teen years, the number of connections increases, and those connections speed up. The degree of increased connectivity determines how well different parts of the brain operate together. Current research is showing that the complexity of this vast, interconnected network is what permits the growth of intellectual capacities such as reading ability and memory.

Not surprisingly, myelination happens *last* in the frontal lobe, which is the seat of those higher-order, "executive" functions we take being able to perform for granted as mature adults (i.e., planning, reasoning, passing judgment, and controlling impulses). When UCLA's Arthur Toga, PhD, and his colleagues compared scans of young adults ages 23 to 30 with those of teens ages 12 to 16, they looked for signs of myelin that would imply more mature, efficient connections. As expected, the frontal lobes of the young adults showed more myelination than the teens'. An individual's brain isn't done with its myelination process until probably the age of 30 or perhaps later. (Time-lapse animations produced by Toga's team that show the children's brains changing as they grow reveal that a wave of white matter growth begins in early childhood at the front of the brain, moves toward the back, and then subsides after puberty. From ages 6 to 13, noticeable transformations can be seen in areas

THE PREFRONTAL CORTEX'S CHIEF DUTIES

These functions are still "under construction" during the teen years.

- Control impulses
- Organize multiple tasks
- Set goals and priorities
- Practice self-control
- Empathize with others
- Make sound judgments
- Strategize and problem solve

- Control emotions
- Plan ahead
- Behave appropriately based on events
- Stop an activity upon completion
- Have insight

connecting brain regions associated with language development and understanding spatial relations. This growth drops off sharply after age 12, coinciding with the end of a critical period for learning languages.)

Suffice it to say, the restructuring of neural connections during adolescence has dramatic effects. The frontal lobe, the area right behind the forehead, is often referred to as the CEO of the brain. It is here that executive decisions are made and behavior is directed based on ethical and moral values. For this reason, it's been dubbed in neuroscientific circles as "the area of sober second thought." If this particular part of the brain becomes damaged somehow, say by injury, at any age, you probably will know what you're supposed to do but not be able to strategize how to do it. You might also have difficulty imagining the future consequences of your actions. And you're likely to be more uninhibited and impulsive. Sound familiar? Welcome to the preteen and teen brain! No wonder teens have difficulty controlling their emotions and risky behaviors, particularly in emotionally laden or emotionally stimulating situations: The circuitry they need for this control is still immature. And so are they.

Of course, these characteristics governed by the prefrontal cortex are what most preteens lack. These functions are very much "under construction" during puberty, which is why children at that stage aren't ready to be in charge of themselves just yet. Their brains lack the capacity for reasoned thinking under emotionally laden conditions and the kind of advanced functioning and problem solving they'll have as adults. Their brains simply haven't finished being pruned and polished.

We've noticed that once parents understand the basics of brain development, they can better understand why their girls are having trouble making good choices, diffusing even the most emotional family situations. Parents often have high expectations for their developing daughters, and because their girls deliver in many ways (doing well in school, being respectful to teachers and committed to sports, having good friends, or whatever), they sometimes assume that they are more cognitively and emotionally developed than they really are.

It helps to also realize that there is a continuum among youths even during this time of rapid growth and development. Try not to read what we've just outlined and think, *Oh no, my kid is really bad at some of these things, worse than her peers* and then wonder if she has a major, diagnosable problem. While in some cases there could be an underlying medical problem, especially if she has an additional condition such as attention deficit/hyperactivity disorder, for the most part the girl is just maturing at her own rate. As her brain matures, these capabilities will eventually catch up and there's nothing to be worried about. However, if you in fact see an important critical gap, then consider taking her to be assessed by a professional. The brain is incredibly pliable when it's developing, so it's important that intervention occurs early.

THE HAZARD ZONE

The changes taking place in the brain of a pubertal girl explain the paradox that she might be at her peak in terms of physical health, strength, and mental capacity, yet at a hazardous age in terms of behavior.

According to Ronald Dahl, MD, an expert in adolescent brain development and decision making at the University of California, Berkeley:

> Adolescence presents a striking paradox with respect to overall health statistics. This developmental period is marked by rapid increases in physical and mental capabilities. By adolescence, individuals have matured beyond the frailties of childhood but have not yet begun any of the declines of adult aging. Compared to young children, adolescents are stronger, bigger, and faster, and are achieving maturational improvements in reaction time, reasoning abilities, immune function, and the capacity to withstand cold, heat, injury, and physical stress. In almost every measurable domain, this is *a developmental period of strength and resilience.*
>
> Yet, despite these robust maturational improvements in several domains, overall [death and disease] rates *increase* 200% over the same interval of time. This doubling in rates of death and disability from the period of early school age into late adolescence and early adulthood is not the result of cancer, heart disease, or mysterious infections. Rather, the major sources of death and disability in adolescence are related to *difficulties in the control of behavior and emotions.*

Indeed, the top three causes of death among adolescents are accidents, homicide, and suicide; accidents account for nearly half of all teen deaths, with motor vehicle accidents being the most prevalent.

What's more, a second paradox exists: By any scientific measure, most adolescents have developed better reasoning capabilities and decision-making skills than younger children. And they are much better than children at the mental processes that underpin making logical and responsible choices. At the same time, despite these cognitive improvements, adolescents appear to be more prone to emotionally influenced behavior that disregards the risks and consequences. Work by Bonnie Halpern-Felsher, PhD, University of California at San Francisco, shows that adolescents actually understand and often even *over-estimate* the risks associated with "risky" acts, such as smoking and sex, but they still engage in these behaviors, often with intention. So they may be more strategic than we think in that regard. But in their work, Halpern-Felsher and others are now accounting for the fact that some behaviors have immediate benefits but longer-term risks that youths don't think about as much. Every behavior has risks and benefits. Smoking marijuana, for example, can lead to feeling included and bonding with friends—benefits that are immediate and powerful. The long-term risks associated with using marijuana, however, are distant and less tangible. So in the moment, thinking about the more immediate benefits is going to overpower considering the long-term risks of a behavior.

Getting peer and social acceptance can be immensely motivating for a pubertal girl who's trying to survive middle school, and when that's combined with her rising drive for risk or sexual desire, you're left with a volatile mixture. Halpern-Felsher notes, "While an adolescent can list the health consequences of smoking, including risk of heart attack and lung cancer, an adolescent might not think these outcomes will happen to them because they believe they have more control over these health outcomes or [that they] can quit smoking easily before they become at risk for health consequences—notably lacking an understanding of addiction. Furthermore, adolescents often put different weights on risks and benefits than do adults. For example, an adolescent girl might be far more concerned with making her boyfriend happy and securing their relation-

> **NEW PUBERTY FACT**
>
> Early developers can act like teenagers due to the changes taking place in their bodies and the potent interplay between the brain and activated hormones.

ship than about getting an STD and, therefore, choose to have unprotected sex, whereas an adult often puts more weight on health rather than social concerns."

Experiments show that youths are far more likely to make risky decisions (such as speeding up to make it through an intersection on a yellow light in a virtual driving task) when there are peers in the car than when they are driving alone. Research conducted in 2005 by Laurence Steinberg, the expert in adolescent development at Temple University mentioned in Chapter 2, showed that having friends in the car *doubled* risk-taking by youngsters but had no effect on adults' behavior.

The real-life results of this produce numbers that are quite chilling: Rates of death by injury (which includes car accidents) between the ages of 15 to 19 are about six times that of the rates between ages 10 and 14. In response, some states have instituted new restrictions on who can be in the car with a young driver, and when. Clearly, the most hazardous time is the later stages of puberty, but girls who enter puberty early might enter that high-hazard zone sooner than peers whose puberty begins a few years later. While they may not be driving just yet, they could easily find themselves among older peers who drive dangerously. But don't panic: Childhood experiences, genes, and the environment in which a young girl reaches puberty and adolescence all influence her behavior. And you, as a caring supervising adult who teaches and supports her along the way, will also impact her behavior. Never forget that you play a very important part, whether you are a parent, teacher, or medical professional, as your girl becomes increasingly independent; research has confirmed it!

So, as you've learned, there are reasons why adolescents are sometimes more emotional. We know that the emotional center in the brain matures before the frontal lobe and that the connections between the two are still under construction during adolescence. This often leads to emotion holding sway over rational processing, producing the seemingly irrational and overly emotional reactions of adolescents. The culprit here is the amygdala, a small, primitive part of the brain that reacts to fear and anger and can direct the responses we make to those feelings. It also responds to danger before other parts of the brain have had a chance to catch up, before experience can modify the response by weighing the risks and benefits. When preteens behave irrationally and we ask them, "What were you thinking?" they may struggle to answer because in many cases they weren't thinking reflectively, they were reacting impulsively or emotionally.

All of this research shows that in the adolescent brain, the parts involved in emotional responses are in the ON mode (and arguably more active than in adults), but the brain's circuitry for controlling emotions and impulses is still maturing. The imbalance leads to a tendency to act on impulse and without regard for risk and to seek novelty. Steinberg offers a useful analogy: Adolescents are like cars with powerful engines and weak brakes. The brakes strengthen over time, as the brain connections are fortified.

Teens also lack experience, which additionally challenges their decision-making ability in emotionally arousing situations. As parents, we can tell them about our own or others' reckless behavior and the negative repercussions, but that's often not very effective in teens who haven't experienced something themselves. So how can we "give" teens experience while sparing them from having to go through negative consequences? Role-playing is one way, but because it's usually done in the classroom (when kids are taught to "just say no" to peers about drugs), it doesn't simulate the strongly charged situations in which kids really make these decisions. But new technology could offer virtual ways to do a better job, for example, by using video games. (In the next chapter, we'll be giving you practical and actionable ideas for teaching children how to make good decisions. It all depends on the emotional bonds you establish in the relationship.)

Until your girl's brain reaches maturity, the decisions she makes in emotionally stimulating situations, particularly those involving peer acceptance, may be driven more by emotions than reason. Parents will see their kids making good, conscientious decisions in less-emotional situations ("cold" cognition settings) but behaving irrationally in others ("hot" cognition settings, like middle school dances). Kids might have the best intentions but succumb to their feelings when their brain rewards them for it. Welcome to the developing teen brain.

HORMONAL IMPACTS ON THE BRAIN

Recent evidence indicates that the hormonal changes that occur during puberty are responsible for structural reorganization and plasticity in the brain and that this effect is somewhat independent of chronological age. As you've probably seen in your own home or classroom, early developers can act like teenagers even though they're preteens. The reward-related centers and the dopamine pathways in the brain seem to be particularly responsive to these increasing hormone levels—hence the increase in risk taking before the neural pathways to assist with emotion regulation, impulse control, and so on have developed. Researchers also think that some regions of the brain might undergo more anatomical change than others and the changes might even differ between the sexes; for example, during puberty the amygdala, which gives rise to fear and anger, grows more in males than females, whereas in females, the greatest growth occurs in the hippocampus, a center for memory. As discussed earlier, the adolescent brain is also coping with hormone-driven changes in sleep regulation that contribute to the teen tendency to stay up late at night. Although this is just part of the brain's developmental process, it does have consequences in a society that isn't set up to accommodate it.

And, despite the terror that it strikes in the hearts of most parents, the adolescent hormonal milieu also increases sexual attraction and desire (unfortunately, this often begins before the "brakes" are at full power and able to manage them). This is just part of the brain's and body's maturational processes. Keep in mind, though, that early-developing girls of 8 or 9 years old aren't necessarily experiencing strong sexual desires—that doesn't come until later.

DESPITE HORMONES, CONTEXT MATTERS

Reproductive hormones—largely triggered by the brain—shape social behavior. However, Birdie Shirtcliff, the researcher we met in Chapter 2 who studies stress physiology in teens, underscores how much influence context—environmental factors—has on the brain's neuronal development and the body's hormonal changes. Take testosterone: "One of the biggest myths out there is the idea that testosterone turns you into a big jerk and that it only matters for boys," she says. But both boys and girls make testosterone, though girls have much lower levels on average than boys do. Their levels can fluctuate rapidly, exerting a huge impact on their behavior. Some of the variation is due to genes, but some is driven by environment—girls experiencing conflict in their social circles and family life have more testosterone swings, for example. "The conflict causes the testosterone variation, not the other way around," Shirtcliff clarifies.

In certain contexts, too, testosterone has many benefits: "Testosterone increases your motivation and narrows your focus to achieve a certain goal. So if [a pubescent girl has] a good positive goal, then

---

SURPRISING BENEFITS OF THE BIG THREE HORMONES

Testosterone: Helps with motivation to achieve goals

Cortisol: Helps with making friends and navigating social situations

Oxytocin: Helps with forming bonds and trusting others, including peers, parents, and other adults

---

testosterone or other hormones can help [her] work toward the goal." Although we tend to look negatively upon the influence of hormones in a girl's maturing body, they in fact provide more than the single benefit of sexual maturation. In Shirtcliff's words, "Kids will go through puberty, which isn't inherently good or bad. And hormones will be released—[that's] not good or bad."

Cortisol also gets a bad rap, she adds. Although cortisol is purportedly released when you feel typical, everyday stress, in truth it is only released in situations that are unpredictable or when you are physically ill. It's also released under certain types of psychological stress that are common in a teenager's life, particularly those that are heavily laden with social implications, or especially socially ambiguous, judgmental, or "evaluative" situations in which a girl doesn't know whether people like her and might be evaluating her. That pretty much defines social life for developing girls in middle school and junior high. Cortisol helpfully cues them to be alert in these situations. As Shirtcliff says, "Social interactions are important physiologically and neurologically. The hormone cortisol tells you to pay attention to this, to focus in on it. This is key, because this is how you make a friend."

So rather than cortisol being a "stress hormone" that has only negative effects, it also plays a positive role in enabling a pubertal girl to be social, to make friends, and even sears these uniquely intense social interactions and the emotions they elicit in her memory. Shirtcliff says that's useful because "this is important for survival and contentment; these social connections are critical." In one of her studies, girls with higher cortisol levels were shown to have more friends—which is to say, cortisol is a girl's best friend for *making* friends.

The hormone oxytocin—the famous "bonding hormone"—also serves in both positive and negative ways, depending on the context. We tend to think of oxytocin as a glue that brings us closer to others and makes us feel good. Like testosterone and cortisol, when oxytocin is associated with a positive social experience, it's highly motivating. But if it's released in response to a negative experience, such as being rejected by someone, it can have negative effects.

According to Shirtcliff, "You bond when you need someone. So when someone has your back in a stressful or challenging situation, then your brain releases this chemical and your brain tells you to keep this person close. It's a very intense reward, as salient as cocaine and more long lasting than that transient high. Just *thinking* about that person can make you release this hormone. But the downside is that [it can cause you to] reject other people." And that isn't always a good thing. Think about a preteen girl who is finally getting attention from the most popular girl in school. She instantly blows off her best friend since early childhood (despite her friend's obvious disappointment) to eat lunch with the "in" group.

As we continue to study the brain and how developmental changes, teen behavior, and health are related, we still have a lot of questions, among them: How do experiences, the environment, and genetics all interact to influence the maturing brain and future cognitive abilities and behavior? In other words, how much does what a young girl experiences mold her brain and affect the rest of her life, including her risk for substance abuse and addictions later on? And why do symptoms of many mental disorders first appear in adolescence?

Scientists who are studying brain development from infancy to adulthood are trying to answer the last question. Many mental health problems are now thought to be developmental in nature, meaning that they arise because something goes awry in how the brain develops. In the future, we hope we will be able to identify when and for what reasons these problems occur so we can do what we can to prevent them or lessen their impact.

CHANGE AND OPPORTUNITY ARE CONSTANTS IN A PUBESCENT BRAIN

The National Institute of Mental Health's (NIMH) insightful publication *The Teen Brain: Still Under Construction* puts it best when it states:

> It is not surprising that the behavior of adolescents would be a study in change, since the brain itself is changing in such striking ways. Scientists emphasize that the fact that the teen brain is in transition doesn't mean it is somehow not up to par. It is different from both a child's and an adult's in ways that may equip youth to make the transition from dependence to independence. The capacity for learning at this age, an expanding social life, and a taste for exploration and limit testing may all, to some extent, be reflections of age-related biology.

We couldn't agree more.

But for us as parents and adults trying to steer our pubertal children onto the right path and avoid serious injury to themselves, the hard part is being patient and somewhat tolerant of their largely "normal" behavior. A provocative article for *New York* magazine by Jennifer Senior in early 2014 actually spoke about this topic, and the headline said it all: "The Collateral Damage of a Teenager: What Adolescence Does to Adolescents Is Nowhere Near as Brutal as What It Does to Their Parents." It was excerpted from her book *All Joy and No Fun: The Paradox of Modern Parenthood,* in which she chronicles the trials and tribulations of adolescents' *parents*—not the adolescents themselves. And she raises a challenging question: "Is it possible that adolescence is most difficult—and sometimes a crisis—not for teenagers as much as for the adults who raise them? That adolescence has a bigger impact on adults than it does on kids?"

Indeed, this is ripe for discussion. Senior cites some illuminating points made by Laurence Steinberg: "It doesn't seem to me like adolescence is a difficult time for the kids," he says. "Most adolescents seem to be going through life in a very pleasant haze." To which Senior has a useful addition: "Which isn't to say that most adolescents don't suffer occasionally or that some don't struggle terribly. They do. But they also go through other intense experiences: crushes, flirtations with risk, experiments with personal identity. It's the parents who are left to absorb these changes and to adjust as their children pull away from them."

To that end, we'll add that it's also the parents who are left to help manage a young girl's path through the weeds of puberty that can be filled with pitfalls. Even though she may be naturally driven to engage in inherently risky behaviors, that doesn't mean she can't satisfy that natural urge by experimenting with relatively less risky acts and sports that are still a source of thrills. Examples of this run the gamut, which makes finding an activity attuned to a girl's liking all the easier. Encourage her to try exciting but safe sports. She could take surfing lessons or go snowboarding, freestyle skiing, or mountain biking. She could perform dance or theater, take on a cause that is meaningful to her, or step out of her childhood comfort zone in any number of healthy, safe ways. Other ideas include encouraging a girl to run for student council or get involved in community-based activities that advocate for change in their schools or help underserved families. She can, for instance, serve dinner at Thanksgiving at a local organization. Small risk-taking steps in safe contexts may be plenty for some kids while others will seek out bigger challenges.

It's important to note that as guardians of our daughters' well-beings, we should worry more about whether they are engaged in healthy behaviors with age-appropriate peers and less about whether they are "cool" and socially precocious. In 2014, an illuminating 11-year study came out that revealed the importance of learning to manage peer relationships in adolescence. How one deals with the competing demands of feeling connected with friends—being accepted and liked—but simultaneously maintaining autonomy to resist negative peer influences plays strongly into long-term outcomes, such as whether an individual struggles with relationships later on in life and even with substance abuse and criminal behavior. What was most surprising about the study was that it illustrated how "pseudomature" behavior—the term the *New York Times* used to describe individuals who act older than they really are during adolescence (but who aren't really mature)—can in fact be a better predictor of problems with alcohol and drugs later in life than levels of substance abuse in early adolescence. Why the downward spiral? The researchers, led by psychology professor Joseph P. Allen at the University of Virginia, suspect that while these kids are chasing popularity they may be missing an important developmental stage—one where you learn to balance those competing demands and develop social skills that allow you to feel confident in your choices even if they won't gain you greater social status. If a girl is leading the social parade in early adolescence, she's more likely to gravitate toward older teenagers who might not be the best role models and whose influences might be difficult to resist. Parents sometimes unintentionally reinforce these trajectories when they send messages to their kids that it's important to be "popular." So bear this in mind the next time you're trying to reinforce qualities that help a child withstand peer pressure. Being the most popular kid in early adolescence may not always be a good thing! As articulated in the study, "Adolescents who established themselves as both desirable companions and as autonomous vis-à-vis [resisting] peers were rated as most successful by their parents at age 23."

Protecting teenagers while they're evolving into adults biologically and aching for autonomy can be exhausting for parents. The home can be a place of perpetual tension, with everyone vying for power to some degree. Sometimes parents can't agree about whether a child is an adolescent or a grown-up; other times the parents agree but the child does not. This situation, in turn, generates stress that can ultimately impact the parents the most.

The good news is that we can turn a girl's vulnerabilities into opportunities at every step along the way, and as the next chapter explains, step 1 happens long before you're in a screaming match with your teenage daughter. Yes, a girl going through puberty is under the influence of numerous changes physically, hormonally, neurologically, and socially, but she is also under the influence of the relationship you've been sharing since birth. Meaning, the ties that really bind us in our parent–child roles have less to do with hormones and brain chemistry than with how we build emotional closeness.

CHAPTER EIGHT

DON'T HAVE "THE TALK," START THE CONVERSATION

Building Emotional Closeness

PERHAPS THE MOST CHALLENGING ASPECT of parenthood isn't the exhausting logistics of keeping up with the ongoing daily demands—feeding, supervising, escorting, helping, nurturing, responding to needs, and so on—it's the task of building emotional closeness when a child is young and nourishing a healthy relationship through all the ups and downs of physical, emotional, and sexual maturation. And this undertaking requires considerably more energy, time, patience, and commitment than any other task of parenthood. From the day you first snuggle with your infant to the last conversation you have with your young adult before she moves out of the home, maintaining a psychological connection with a growing child is essential. Consider the following scenarios—perhaps you can identify with one of them.

As a teacher who works with 4th-graders every day,
I am bombarded by questions from parents whose daughters
are entering puberty early. One question that I increasingly

get is why their girls seem to turn off the moment they head home. Animated and engaged in the classroom, these girls give their parents the silent treatment. Is this part of going through puberty early? What can I do to help parents reconnect with their girls?

My daughter has really been blowing up since she started puberty, and I feel like she's most angry at me all the time. Nothing I can say or do is right, so I've stopped saying anything. We used to be really close and now I just feel distant from her. My friends tell me that she'll come around in her twenties and we'll be friends then, but I can't imagine just letting her deal on her own until then. How do I support her without getting my head bitten off?

My 6-year-old daughter isn't showing any signs of going through puberty yet, but I want to broach the subject with her so we're both prepared. And I'd like to avert many of the risks associated with early puberty if she in fact goes through it before her peers. Where do I begin?

ATTACHMENT IS AT THE ROOT of emotional closeness. A large body of research on parent–child attachment shows that deep and enduring emotional bonds are essential. The most primal need a child has is attachment. The now-famous attachment theory was originally developed by the late John Bowlby, a British psychiatrist at a London pediatric psychology clinic during the 1930s, where he treated many emotionally disturbed children and started to think about how a child's relationship with her mother affected her social, emotional, and cognitive development. In the early 1950s, when he was heading up the Tavistock Clinic in London, he worked with James Robertson, a psychiatric social worker, to make sense of the severe distress he witnessed in infants who had been separated from their parents. Bowlby had noticed that infants would go to extraordinary lengths (e.g., crying, clinging, frantically searching) to prevent or end their separation from a parent. When Bowlby was first publishing papers on his ideas, psychoanalytic theory—then the prevailing paradigm for psychological treatment—viewed these behaviors as the child's immature psyche attempting to defend itself against the emotional pain caused by separation. But Bowlby saw the same behavior in the young of a wide variety of mammals, not just in humans, suggesting that it offered an evolutionary advantage for survival. In his 1969 seminal book *Attachment,* he defined it as a "lasting psychological connectedness between human beings."

In addition to Bowlby, several other pioneers in the field helped to illuminate the power of attachment, proving that it's the cornerstone of parenting. Margaret Ainsworth, PhD, a developmental psychologist who was once part of Bowlby's research team at the Tavistock Clinic, conducted experiments that showed that for attached children, mothers serve as a secure base as they go off to explore the world bit by bit. And the classic experiments of Harry Harlow, PhD, in America during the 1950s also reinforced the theory. Harlow's experiments are now considered cruel, but they yielded important information about how an infant handles being raised with varying degrees of security. Harlow raised baby rhesus monkeys in four different ways: in total isolation from both mothers and peers; without their mothers but with peers; with their mothers but no peers; and in a normal family group. The monkeys raised in total isolation displayed very disturbed behavior and depression, whereas those raised in incomplete social groups showed varying degrees of sociability, and those raised as normal easily learned to play and socialize. Some baby monkeys raised without their mothers were given two maternal surrogates, one made of wire and the other of wood covered with soft cloth. The infants chose to cuddle with the cloth dummy, seeming to find it more comforting, and went to the wire dummy only to feed when it was the only one equipped with a bottle. The babies raised with dummy mothers showed clear signs of psychological distress and maladaptive behavior into adulthood. This was foundational research showing how important contact with a parent figure is to infant psychological and social development.

In humans, as you can probably guess, attachment begins at birth and develops in stages during infancy. Some parents may find it relatively easy to build a connection with a young child, but if the relationship begins to break down for some reason, it's vital that steps be taken to restore that all-important connection. And of course, how difficult it is to reconnect when things go awry (like when you hit a serious rough patch with your adolescent) depends on how strong that core connection is from the start. All effective efforts to shape a child's behavior originate from safe and secure attachment.

So how can you fulfill this monumental duty to establish and maintain a secure bond with an early-developing girl without hovering or "helicoptering"? How can you guard against inadequately meeting your child's emotional needs? What are the secrets to laying an emotional foundation strong enough that talking about and preparing her for puberty are as comfortable as any of the other conversations you'll have along the way?

Helping you accomplish that is our goal in this chapter. Puberty can be a confusing, anxious time for both children and parents, one that requires parents to take on new roles they may not feel prepared for. Quite often, we hear from parents that *their* parents never told them anything about puberty, or in the best cases, relatively little. And in preceding generations, adolescents were basically on their own. So, we are breaking new ground here. We may be the first generation to actually *want* to talk to our kids about their pubertal development. And doing so is much easier than you might think if you are equipped with the right information, adequate encouragement, and the correct vocabulary for having healthy conversations that keep you from going down roads that can fuel resistance. Both parent and child need to feel empowered, and the tools we provide in this chapter—accompanied by examples and sample dialogue—will facilitate those seemingly elusive goals.

Now that you've gained a wealth of knowledge about early puberty—the facts, the challenges, and plenty of practical tips to help reduce the risks associated with the early onset of this very important stage in your girl's life—it's time to address what's arguably the most important ingredient in helping a young girl set the right tone for life, emotional closeness. In fact, it's ground zero. It's forging the kind of relationship with her that will provide her with a foundation for the trials she will inevitably face, whether they are issues with her body's changes or social struggles with peers. The relationship you nourish today will be with her for life, and its quality can even help her to establish loving relationships with close friends, future romantic partners, and, someday, her spouse. While it may be hard for you today to think about a young girl's relationship prospects decades from now, it's inevitable that the experiences she has with her parents and other influential adults in her early life will unquestionably play into how she relates to platonic friends, dates, and romantic partners, and whom she chooses as a mate later in life.

Puberty frequently provokes anxiety not just in parents but also in other adults who work with girls who are maturing early. Teachers, coaches, and even medical professionals often feel helpless when it comes to the emotional and relational changes that puberty brings. We can immediately start catastrophizing—thinking that the worst can and will happen. We can feel a sense of powerlessness that our girls are at the mercy of stressors, environmental factors, and peer pressures, and there's not much we can do to help. Despite the fact that puberty is very much a normal process, we may still struggle with helping our children deal with it while we are also handling our own challenges in life.

We want to suggest that sometimes this fear and helplessness may be due to your own experiences during puberty. A generation ago, few parents talked about this transition with their developing daughters, and fewer still felt comfortable doing so. But puberty needn't stir such emotional, sometimes irrational thoughts. If you have the right tools to navigate this path with your girl from Day 1, everything will be okay. For parents, Day 1, as you just learned, was the day she was born and you first held her in your arms. For professionals who work with early-blooming girls and for parents who adopted their daughters, if you hope to establish nurturing relationships with them, Day 1 was the day you first encountered a girl, regardless of her chronological age. According to Jay Belsky, whose work has focused largely on parent-child relations during infancy and the early childhood years, the relative security of the infant–mother bond can factor mightily into the daughter's pubertal timing. Belsky's research has also shown that starting day care at an early age doesn't necessarily undermine attachment so long as the infant is well cared for and has a secure attachment with her mother.

NEW PUBERTY FACT

The strength of the infant-mother bond can influence when a girl goes through puberty.

Belsky is known for his experiments that show an early childhood experienced in an unstable environment is among the reasons girls mature early. In a study on development in early childhood sponsored by the National Institute of Child Health and Human Development, Belsky and his colleagues looked at the data collected on 373 white females. The girls were followed starting at birth until they were

15 years old. At 15 months, the security of each girl's attachment to her mother was evaluated in a university laboratory using the standard technique of separating and then reuniting the baby and mother. Babies who expressed appreciation for their mother's return (i.e., smiling, vocalizing, or reaching for her) were considered to be secure, while those who avoided their mother or could not be comforted after she returned were considered insecure. The status of each girl's pubertal development was evaluated at annual physical exams starting when she was 9½ years of age.

As the researchers predicted, the girls who were insecure as babies entered puberty sooner—by about 2 to 4 months—than girls who were secure as babies. The girls who started puberty earlier also got their first period earlier than those who were secure infants, ending their puberty process sooner.

When asked to explain his results, Belsky turns to the evolutionary biology perspective: "Nature just wants you to reproduce. Thus, under those conditions in which the future appears precarious, where I might not even survive long enough to breed tomorrow, then I should mature earlier so I can mate earlier before that precarious future might get me."

Clearly, attachment is more than just physical proximity. And it extends far beyond those infant years. It's also a verbal relationship that starts early and evolves over time. Through our physical and emotional connections, we provide that "psychological nutrient," to use Belsky's term. We act as a buffer for what a child experiences. The closeness forms in early childhood, evolves as a girl matures into a woman, and ultimately becomes the emotional core a girl needs to feel loved, safe, watched over, and cared for—for a lifetime. The sooner you start this verbal relationship, the better you'll be able to create trust and a secure foundation for the relationship. And that will help you feel and actually be more in control from a parental perspective, even when she pushes you away emotionally and slams her bedroom door on you. You'd be surprised by how much having that emotional closeness with a girl can do to disarm or limit the most significant and potentially harmful peer and social influences, which often aren't under your control. As Julia Graber says, "Start early in terms of building good, strong, high-quality [warm and supportive] family relationships. Structure, clear expectations, consistency, and teaching a girl how to control her emotions through your own modeling are all protective."

At the end of the day, if you've established a strong bond with a girl and she views you (even if she doesn't always like you) as someone she trusts who is consistent and honest, then she will try to make good decisions. When she fails, she'll be more likely to share her concerns with you. As Robert Hiatt reminds us, "Parents have the capacity to change the environment. Despite social class and the neighborhoods in which a family lives, parents can influence the nature of a girl's broader social environment, the psychological stresses she faces, the potentially harmful chemicals to which she is exposed, and healthy lifestyle factors like good nutrition and physical exercise. The things that make girls healthy are probably the same things that will influence them to develop later in terms of puberty, which is a good thing." This is consistent with Belsky's notion of the psychological nutrients that the parent provides.

We'll add that so much power comes precisely from this ongoing conversation between parents and daughters. It comes from guiding and informing a developing girl about what makes her body and mind healthy, about the importance of things like physical activity and eating healthful, nutritious foods, about what makes a good friendship, and about the potential consequences of making poor choices. You can make sure she is raised in a safe, healthy physical and emotional environment. And to help her learn how to decide wisely for herself out in the real world, you can start with the conversation.

THE CONVERSATION: AN ONGOING DIALOGUE

This isn't about having a single "talk"; it's about maintaining an ongoing conversation that goes through phases and begins long before you address the birds and the bees. This is where many parents and adults get it wrong. If you think you have to save all of your information for an hour-long lecture before bedtime or during a long drive someday, think again. And please don't assume that her sex ed class at school will cover everything.

Unfortunately, sex ed programs are generally offered far too late in a child's physical development, whether she's blooming early or not. It is *not* "puberty ed." The curriculum typically begins in 5th grade or so, when an early bloomer is already beyond the first stages of hormonal changes that have kicked off breast and pubic hair growth. Topics like body-image issues, the pubertal process, and intercourse get lumped together as if they are experienced all at once. Sex and puberty often are discussed jointly, when perhaps girls would be better served by a health education class about puberty and their bodies that would be followed, several years later, by sex ed. (The median number of hours of any form of sex ed across the United States is 17.2 hours, with 3.1 of that in elementary school, 6 in middle school, and 8.1 in high school. But the majority of sex ed happens between 7th and 12th grades—long after an early-maturing girl has likely thought about sex.)

As for the classes' content, suffice it to say that most sex ed programs are in desperate need of a makeover. At the heart of the deficiency is that they don't deal with the social aspects of the pubertal transition, which set the stage for all future relationships, whether they're platonic or romantic. And very few (if any) address issues of emotional strength and empowerment, which we know are critical for girls to be able to weather the effects of the sexualized media on body image and self-esteem as they develop.

We hope that this changes in the future, because girls (and boys) should learn about their bodies and how they will change during puberty long before they hear anything about sex. In some parts of the country, the necessary change is already underway. Norman Constantine, PhD, of the Public Health Institute in Berkeley, California, an expert in sex ed implementation in that state, is currently conducting a large evaluation of a sex ed program in Los Angeles schools. In a 2013 contribution to an academic work, he and his colleagues boldly called out the goal and the problem.

> Sexuality education can be an important tool in helping adolescents navigate the biological, cognitive, and social transitions that transform how they look, think, feel, and interact with others. However, most formal sexuality education does not have such a wide-ranging agenda. In many countries and communities, the concept of sexuality education is highly polarizing and political. In these contexts, the policies that undergird and fund sexuality education programs often reflect the interests and concerns of organized pressure groups. This can result in programs that are restricted in content as well as their purposes, which may include fostering a preference for sex within marriage; discouraging premarital sex, teen pregnancy, or teen childbearing; lowering youths' risks of becoming infected with HIV or another sexually transmitted infection; or helping youth avoid sexually coercive behavior.

But Constantine sees some light from his perch in California, citing the state's groundbreaking educational standards that have been a model to other states in mandating minimum requirements for any sexuality education taught in public schools (and later expanded to include any sex ed programs supported by state or state-administered funds). The code demands that the education be age appropriate, medically accurate, and cover all FDA-approved contraception and STD protection methods. This is good news, though time will tell how and when California's leadership will land in other states. But until such standards are widespread throughout the country, it's imperative that we adults take control of the conversation outside of formal education to supplement what our kids learn in school.

This continuous dialogue should span the range of subjects, from the ones that relate directly to the physical to even the spiritual and emotional. If a girl knows that she can come to you for help and advice and that you will be consistent in your parenting, she won't open up just about her worries, concerns, and curiosities related to puberty. She will rely on you for all sorts of guidance and counseling as she learns to make good decisions for herself. If you aren't a girl's parent but rather a parental figure in some other capacity, you, too, can help determine not only her experience during puberty and adolescence but also help shape her developing belief systems, values, goals, and eventually her success in life. This is particularly true for those in the lives of girls whose mothers are for some reason unavailable for those traditional "mom" talks—even if you're dad or another father figure.

So with that in mind, let us set out 10 principles to help you achieve a mutually enriching, positive relationship with the girl in your life. The simple tips and encouraging words you'll find will pull together all you've learned to help you act for the benefit of the girl in your life.

Principle #1: Be Patient, Don't Panic, and Start Small

You are in charge. And it's okay to feel anxious or even petrified about your child going through puberty (though we hope this book has comforted you!). There's much you can do to ensure that your daughter navigates puberty successfully, even if she's experiencing it early and begins to be heavily influenced by her peers. Although you may feel like it's all happening too fast, maturation is actually a slow process, so there's time to develop this conversation in a way that feels natural to both of you. The responsibilities you give your girl and the expectations you have for her behavior need to be in tune with her age.

It's incredibly important for bonding with your child that you give her your undivided attention on a fairly regular basis. You'll really be able to engage her in conversation that way. The conversations you have when she's just beginning puberty will help you develop emotional closeness. Over time, you'll naturally graduate to deeper conversations as she begins to tell you more about things going on in her life. It's vital that you take the time to really *listen,* and that is getting harder and harder today with all the family demands and schedules. Ask yourself, when was the last time you had some downtime together? Conversations between parents and pubertal children happen primarily during downtime, when everyone is relaxed and it's easier to make space for talking. Leave all the electronic devices at home and take a walk or a drive together.

If body odor is what first alerts you to the need to start talking with her about puberty, then use that as your launchpad. As you explain how to use soap and a washcloth to bathe more thoroughly under her arms, you can simply say, "This is what's starting to happen, your body is about to go through some changes." Then mention a few things she can expect in the near future (e.g., pubic hair, changes in her breasts). Parents should understand that deodorant isn't medically necessary (nor is shaving, using a tampon, or in most cases wearing a bra; these are all cultural choices). It's perfectly fine for a girl to take her time before starting to use commercial products like deodorant. Just good old soap and water will go a long way toward keeping her clean and smelling fresh until she's ready to graduate to using deodorant. And when she does, go for an unscented natural deodorant, not an antiperspirant (for ideas, go to ewg.org). As puberty progresses, you can discuss new physical changes in a neutral manner, whether she starts with pubic hair or breast development.

But don't overload her with information she doesn't need yet. Be careful not to cover too many topics at one sitting to avoid instilling fear or rushing into subjects she's not ready for. Answer the question that is being asked, and offer a little glimpse into the near future if you like, but don't cover the next several years. When women think about puberty, they often think about their periods and sex and forget about the early days, long before these were concerns and the questions in their heads were much simpler.

If talking about body odor is enough of a start for you, then that's fine. Most kids will have body odor first anyhow, and it's an excellent starting point for opening that line of communication about body issues. You won't be going from teaching her how to wash under the arms to showing her how to shave her legs and use a tampon in a single day. Because pubertal changes happen over time, *you, too,* have time to address the topics she wants to know about. Obviously, it helps to be in a situation where you won't be interrupted, and you have privacy and space. Dive in as far as you can go (that's appropriate), and be brave. But also be patient. You'll have years to work through all the issues in conversation.

Above all, make sure you're comfortable. Children are uniquely cued in to our anxieties; it's as if they are equipped with special radar that detects when we are uneasy or nervous. They sometimes seem to read our emotions no matter how hard we try to hide them. Don't approach them with anxiety and edginess, because it will get in the way of the conversation and could stall future ones. Be prepared for what they might tell you. If you seem hurt or upset with them, they might not tell you the next time. Remember, the hormonal changes a pubescent child is going through leave most of them prone to moodiness. Emotions are very strong at this time in her life, but her cognitive capacity is still immature and struggling with those emotions. Her heightened levels of hormones might also cause her to react strongly, particularly in situations that are stressful or stimulating.

By the time your girl starts puberty, even if it's early, you will have spent so much time over the years solving problems for her that your first reaction is to try to solve them all. Now, when social issues are starting to or soon will arise—having conflicts with peers, being excluded from a clique, being made fun of, falling victim to a bully—as the adult, you'll have to decide when you should just listen and when you need to intervene.

NEW PUBERTY FACT

As adults, we tend to want to problem solve for children when it's best just to listen to them.

But we tend to be much better problem solvers than listeners, so that's what we need to be working on ourselves: becoming better listeners. Sometimes it's best to resist the urge to solve a problem for a girl. She is becoming a more complex thinker, and now is the time to prepare her for thinking on her own as an adult. These are moments of opportunity to build emotional closeness.

Generally, at this age it's more important to listen to and help a child feel understood than to solve her problems for her. What is in fact *most* helpful is to let them know we hear them, we support them, and we are here to help them solve their own problems. So when your daughter is upset, don't try to fix it for her immediately. Show her you understand by listening, asking questions, and reflecting her emotions. As parents, we want to heal and fix—and that's natural. But to build connection, we need to listen first and make sure we understand. And then, we need to problem solve together. This is a shift in our perspective that will encourage her to share more as she gets older. Stay calm, don't overreact, don't interrupt, and first, listen.

Watch out: If you're too rushed to listen properly or you start solving the problem for her when that's not what she wants—even if you feel like your beloved child can't handle the problem and you badly want to make it right—you'll either be signaling that it's too much for you and she will shut down or letting her know that you aren't listening to her. Sometimes parents (any adults, really) don't actually understand what their child is telling them before they jump in to make it right. If you overreact, then you might not seem like a safe person to share with. The next time your child could use some help, she may go elsewhere or, more likely, just keep it to herself.

And if you ever find yourself uncertain of the answer to a really important question about puberty or relationships, don't panic. Just say something like "That's an excellent question. I'm not sure what the answer is. Let's look it up." (See the resources section starting on page 231 for where to find great info.) Or if it's about what to do in a sticky peer situation, you can say, "Hmm, I'm not sure. There are probably a couple ways to approach this. What do you think some of them are?" Let her respond, and then ask, "What do you think would happen if you did that?" Weigh the consequences together, then ask her, "What's another idea?" and so on. Eventually, the two of you will figure out a solution that she can try. Sometimes that might be to actively pursue a resolution with someone, or it might be that she just needed to emotionally process what happened and will decide it isn't something worth pursuing.

Also be aware that as adults, we sometimes make the proverbial mountain out of a molehill. We'll hear our daughter lament something terrible that happened that day between her and a friend, only to find that the problem was resolved by the next day, before you talked to the other parent, contemplated reaching out to the principal, and e-mailed the teacher.

Take a breath, be patient, and don't forget to listen before you act.

Principle #2: Don't Procrastinate

Life gets busy. Life gets *so* busy that we can find ourselves using its "busy-ness" to put off uncomfortable but crucial conversations. How easy it is to tell ourselves that conversations about puberty can wait until tomorrow. And we can forget to schedule or take one-on-one time with our kids before they start experiencing difficult issues, such as peer and self-esteem issues that should have been buffered by a conversation long ago. It really is vital that you make time for these opportunities, no matter what. Don't assume that the perfect moment will organically (perhaps magically) present itself. Take advantage of long car rides and opportunities that come up when you least expect them, such as after the two of you have watched a movie that included some suggestive themes.

Don't buy into the myth that says you should wait for your child to start asking questions or bringing things up. That simply doesn't work when a girl is going through puberty early. An early-maturing girl needs to be educated in an age-appropriate way about what's going on with her changing body, before many of her later-developing peers need to know. Parents need to be courageous in this realm and introduce developmentally appropriate topics regardless of how uncomfortable it feels. (We do offer some "get out of jail free" cards, though; see Principle # 7.)

Principle #3: Find Activities You Both Enjoy and Let Her Choose

We've mentioned this before, but it's key in laying the foundation for this evolving conversation. You both will likely find yourselves much more able to open up about sensitive topics and personal details when you're engaged in an activity that you both enjoy and you aren't necessarily looking one another in the eye. She probably will also feel much more comfortable about it if you haven't asked her to tell you about her life. And that's the holy grail, for we'd much prefer that our girls freely share what's going on in their lives and what worries or stresses them out rather than having to pry it out of them. When your kid discloses something voluntarily, that's a magical moment. Have your radar antenna up for these moments so you can tune in no matter how busy you are when they pop up.

Plenty of activities can provide a pathway to this conversation: Hiking, doing a mother–daughter book club, taking sewing lessons together, cooking, baking cookies, ice-skating at a local rink, kicking a soccer ball around, getting a mani–pedi together, shopping at the mall, playing a game of checkers or cards, having a picnic in the backyard or at a local park, going to a movie, or volunteering at the local animal shelter are just a few ideas. These activities are key to building a relationship that lets you have comfortable conversations, though it might be that nothing serious comes up for years. You'll be ready whenever it's time.

Let her choose what she'd like to do with you. When you empower a girl to make choices, the trust between you deepens. You also nurture the multiple facets of her personality, allowing her to tap into her interests and strengthen various aspects of her life. Whatever her proclivities, do things together that will further these strengths and help her build confidence. It helps to find things you both really like to do rather than faking it. If you do, she'll sniff you out. Find those common interests and then make time for them!

Here's a question for you: Can shopping for a bra be considered an activity that you suggest because you think it's time? It depends. Again, this is where offering choices is important. Consider the story of Keri, an 8-year-old who refuses to wear a bra even though she is developing breasts early and it's becoming obvious through her thin cotton T-shirts. Her mom, Victoria, is really concerned about how Keri will be perceived by teachers and other parents. She feels that her daughter's refusal to wear a bra reflects poorly on her as a mother. What should Victoria do?

First of all, Victoria needs to let go of the idea that what her child does is a direct reflection on her. Holding on to that idea will be a source of misery for her (and her daughter) throughout the pubertal years, so it's best to ditch that hang-up early on lest it prompt anxiety in Mom and power struggles later.

Second, none of Keri's classmates may be wearing a bra (or at least none of her close friends), so Keri may fear being "called out" on it by the boys or perceived as different. Also, she may think wearing a bra is uncomfortable. When girls first begin to develop, some are more comfortable wearing a camisole or a tank top under a T-shirt. Victoria could try to find out why Keri doesn't want to wear a bra, but Keri may not be able to express her reasons (see Principle #5). And this is when providing her with options and letting her choose is enormously helpful.

Stocking up on tank tops (some of which have little shelf bras) that she likes can be a great option, as is buying shirts that are a bit thicker. Keri may not like the look or feel of a traditional bra but be open to a sports bra or crop bra, which falls between a tank top and

BRAS AND PADS: NOT ALWAYS A FUN CONVERSATION, BUT IT CAN BUILD EMOTIONAL CLOSENESS

Options in bras, like in sanitary products and deodorants, are now plentiful for young girls. The fact that halter or crop bras are available for early-developing and for active younger girls is a welcome advancement in our society, and certainly empowering for girls. The more choices they have, the more empowered girls feel, and the more comfortable they are with their decisions. In a sense, parents today are far luckier than our parents were when product options were limited for young girls, and particularly for early developers.

Similarly, the technology of sanitary products (e.g., tampons and pads) has changed dramatically in our lifetime. These products are much more absorbent, yet discreet and comfortable (and "junior" sizes are now available to fit young girls' bodies better). When we were girls, playing sports or swimming during your period was a lot harder than it is today, but things are different now, and this helps reinforce for our girls that there's really nothing they have to stop doing just because their bodies are changing and they're experiencing things like breast growth and periods. They will be more self-conscious of their bodies during puberty, but thankfully there is an abundance of comfortable clothing and sanitary products today for them to use that will help allay their discomfort.

That said, don't assume a girl will know how to use a pad, or even know what to do if she begins her first period when she isn't at home.

bra. Again, let her choose what kind she likes. She can keep them in her drawer until she's ready. By providing lots of options and not forcing her, Victoria can show her daughter that she understands her feelings and honors her choice. She signals to her daughter that wearing a bra is a choice but not a necessity and also that her decision might change (as it often does for girls), so she can choose to wear one when (or if) she is ready someday.

Demonstrate what to do long before she gets her period, and tell her she can tie a jacket around her waist if her period comes unexpectedly and stains her clothes. She can carry a pad along with an extra pair of underwear in a small cosmetics bag at the bottom of her backpack. Show her where to find pads at school, too. If the bathrooms aren't equipped with sanitary supplies (or if there's nowhere to dispose of them), talk to the school nurse or someone in the front office. Let her know that most adult women have at least one funny story about getting a period unexpectedly.

The same goes for shopping for that first bra. If her friends aren't wearing bras yet, she may not even realize that a bra might make her more comfortable. All girls develop differently; some experience fast breast growth that can be unsettling, while others develop very slowly, which can be equally as unnerving. Be mindful of how she relates to and feels about her changing body. Tell her that not all breasts look the same as they grow and mature, and that she shouldn't compare herself to her girlfriends or worry that she's odd. Likewise, in a growing girl, each breast may look different, making her feel lopsided. Reassure her that this is normal.

Share your own stories with your girl to help her open up. All of this will build closeness between you as you demystify the experience that nearly every human female on the planet goes through!

Victoria followed these guidelines and Keri started wearing tank tops under her shirts. She did this for a year before she started wearing sports bras in 4th grade, when several girls her age began wearing bras. Eventually, she opted for a "real" bra, but that wasn't until well into middle school. She confessed to her mother that when they first had their conversation about bras at age 8, she thought all bras were like the type her mother wore and she found those "embarrassing."

Principle #4: Be Careful with Your Questions

Avoid asking questions that invite monosyllabic responses, like "How was school today?" Instead, engage her in a real conversation that encourages her to describe her day and express her feelings, like "What was the best thing that happened today?" Follow up with "What was the hardest?" Or borrow the phrases that the Obamas use with their girls: "What was the rose of your day?" "What was the thorn?" Keep in mind that her school day could be long over by the time you're asking about it over dinner at 6:00 or 7:00 p.m. A child's sense of time and the structure of her day are different from ours. Sometimes, it's not until they are lying in bed and we are saying good night that our daughters actually reflect on their day. Try to make sure she goes to bed early enough that these moments when you can talk aren't rushed. You can even start a ritual of talking about a couple of things that each of you was grateful for in the day. The most amazing things sometimes come to the surface during this quiet, restful time before sleep.

Principle #5: Teach Them Emotional Language

As adults, we tend to forget that at our girls' age, we, too, lacked a large vocabulary we could use to express ourselves authentically, to get our points across to others, to ask for what we needed or wanted, and to convey our emotions verbally so we could be heard. In fact, some of us are still learning the right words! Children—especially young ones—will likely need help early on to allow them to express emotions in conversation. Provide them with the language they need to effectively communicate.

Among the emotion words that can help them describe difficult or complicated issues are *frustrated, excited, confused, irritable, stuck, anxious, worried, scared, angry, unsafe, suspicious, curious, rejected, isolated, left out,* and *lonely.* Teaching them how to label complex emotions that might encompass several distinct emotions at the same time will help them become better communicators in general. Encourage them to vividly express themselves with sentences like these.

- Did that make you feel left out and isolated? Or were you comfortable with that situation?

- How did that make you feel? Angry and confused?

- Do you feel frustrated? Stuck? Or do you feel like you need help handling this?

- It's okay to feel scared or anxious about it.

- Do those older boys make you feel unsafe or weird in any way?

Questions like these can also help you learn more about what's going on in her life and keep you from making assumptions about how she feels. It's easy to jump to conclusions if you don't ask. You might feel confused or anxious or angry about what your child shares with you, but it's important that you ask her how she feels and not assume that your emotions are her emotions. This can guide you through conversations about things like what makes a friendship good and what kinds of treatment aren't okay from friends.

Talks like this bolster the self-esteem she'll be able to draw upon later, when she begins dating and having romantic relationships. Friendships are the proving grounds for how we expect to be treated. Be frank about the fact that she's a beautiful, growing girl who will naturally attract boys and may find herself in situations that make her feel uncomfortable. Equip her with language she can use to say no or get herself out of a tricky situation, such as when friends try to get her to experiment with drugs or alcohol at a party or an older boy tries to woo her. A 10-year-old girl can look so mature that boys may show interest in her. Let her know that if that happens, she can deter him by blaming you with something like "My parents say I'm too young to date." If a boy is flirting with her, suggest that she just roll her eyes and toss her head in a dismissive manner. Eye rolls annoy us adults, but they have strategic uses with peers!

It's important to explain that emotions lead to thoughts, actions, and behaviors. One of life's most critical skills is to be able to stop and take stock of your emotions before acting. Tell her that her first reaction to an emotion, even if it's strong and hard to ignore, could lead her to do something she might later wish she hadn't. Remind her that actions have consequences. Keep in mind, however, that a child often isn't as attuned to the realness of consequences (recall from Chapter 6 that her storehouse of experiences is still small), which is why she needs us to teach and warn her. She will no doubt make mistakes and jump into action once in a while (and learn from those mistakes), but hopefully your guidance can keep her from making costly mistakes that threaten her life and health. You can help her learn how to consider the possible consequences of her actions just by using the following questions.

- Well, if you did that, what do you think the consequences would be?

- What do you think would happen?

- What's another approach you could try?

- If that happened, how would you feel? How would others feel?

- What do you think is the best thing to do?

Help her think through possible solutions and what the consequences of those solutions could be. You will be building emotional closeness as you talk.

Emotions also lead to thoughts that exacerbate emotions. One of the main principles of the cognitive-behavioral school of thought is that feelings of inadequacy, for example, can lead to negative, distorted thoughts, which make her feel even worse about herself and do things that are unhealthy or unproductive. Take the example of Sandra, a 7-year-old early developer who was teased at school about running slower than the other kids in phys ed (PE) class. (PE and recess, by the way, offer abundant opportunities for bullying and teasing.) So her emotions—shame, exclusion, and sadness—led her to think, *I'm not an athlete, I'm fat. I suck at PE, and I'm a bad person.* These thoughts of course made her feel worse, discouraged her from trying in PE lest she be ridiculed, and caused her to withdraw from physical activity even outside of PE. Sandra's mom was devastated. Her daughter had always played and run outside and loved to be active. What's challenging is that being younger might cause an early developer to have an even harder time putting together the facts and her emotions in a clear way.

Sandra's mom helped her understand that running fast is not the only definition of "athletic." There were other ways Sandra loved to be active and engaged. She helped change Sandra's way of responding by helping her change her thoughts. And in reality, it was only one bully who was teasing her, and he said mean things to lots of kids. Sandra wasn't fat, either, she was just built differently than the other kids in the class, and her mother talked with her about how people come in all shapes and sizes. Sandra also found a more confident friend in PE who ran at about the same speed she did, and together they would tell the bully to back off (social support is very helpful). Sandra's mom also fed her thoughts to keep in her mind to replace the negative, self-defeating ones. Some examples:

- I am a slow and steady runner, and I can run farther than a lot of other kids.

- It's really not important how fast I run as long as I love doing it.

- My body is unique and part of my heritage. I have an athletic, healthy build.

- He's teasing me because he's unhappy with himself. It's not about me, it's about him.

The conversation between mother and daughter was revived whenever Sandra went to that negative place in her head. Eventually, Sandra was able to change her own thoughts and, in turn, her feelings. In this case,

Sandra's mom also talked to the school and the PE teacher about the boy who was bullying her and others, but only after letting Sandra know that she was going to do this and why she felt it was important.

If you ever find yourself troubled or confused by something your child says to you, realize that she could just be having a very hard time expressing her feelings. Remember, a child's vocabulary isn't as large as an adult's, and she isn't adept yet at using words to show her thoughts and feelings. Children need to develop this skill over time with our help. Patience is key!

Principle #6: Beware of Befriending

As we noted earlier in the book, parents who aim to befriend their children are in for a rude awakening when their beloveds hit puberty. There's a difference between providing "scaffolding" (more on this word in a moment) and nurturance for a child and befriending her—a difference that can determine whether you cruise painlessly through this journey or struggle mightily. Being your child's friend is not the same as taking on a role that allows you to help steer the ship and guide her in the right direction.

"Scaffolding" is a term used in psychological circles, especially as it relates to teaching children and helping them learn. Similar to erecting scaffolding when a structure is being built and then slowly removing it as the structure is completed, "to scaffold" means to provide external support to help a child learn something she wouldn't be able to without your support because her developing brain is not yet mature enough. Scaffolding techniques are age-appropriate methods a teacher or parent uses to guide the learner to a greater understanding and mastery of the task. It is key to learning and growing. This requires having consistent expectations and setting limits. You can't provide scaffolding for a child if you're acting like her peer. There must be a hierarchy in place that sends a clear message to a child about who is in charge. Remember, even when they don't act like they want it, children need to feel that they can count on us. If you don't take on your role as the authority, you will feel powerless and may even resort to threats, bribes, emotional coercion, or even pleas to get them to behave in the way you'd like them to. As Susan Stiffelman reminds us, "Love your child in the way [she] most needs it: by being the calm, confident Captain of the ship as your child navigates the sometimes smooth, sometimes rough, waters of growing up." When you operate under this defined separation of power, you're able to come alongside your child rather than at her, and she will feel like you are her ally and advocate. Put simply, children don't need the adult caretakers and supervisors in their lives to also be their friends.

However, that doesn't mean you're always right. Adults also make mistakes in their relationships with children. It's important to know when to admit you were wrong and to apologize in a sincere and honest way. This models taking responsibility and can actually deepen the relationship.

Principle #7: When in Doubt, Use Books or Workshop Programs

We understand that for some parents, it can be just too tough to talk about certain topics that make almost everyone uncomfortable or even queasy, particularly if you're not a trained professional or have had little experience with the topic. If you don't communicate with children all day long or work as a medical professional, then it might be challenging, for example, to come home one day and broach the subject of human anatomy using words like "vagina," "pubic hair," "breasts," and "discharge" (if you're blushing as you read this, then you're probably whom we're talking to!). There are some excellent resources out there that help make this conversation much easier on both parents and kids from the age of 8. For girls, we love *The Care and Keeping of You* series from American Girl, as well as *It's So Amazing* and *It's Perfectly Normal* by Robie H. Harris and Michael

Emberley. When the time is right, read these books to your girl and talk about the subject matter. Let her ask questions. And whenever you find yourself in a bind for a good answer, don't be afraid to turn to books like these for advice, facts, and ideas on addressing difficult topics.

Or, if you need some guidance first, start a book club with other caregivers. Read some of the books we've recommended and discuss them. Please beware of sharing too much personal information about your own struggles with your daughter or confidential information she has shared with you—a key aspect of having her view your relationship as a safe and honest one is to keep what she tells you to yourself; someone else might not keep this information confidential. But with friends, you can talk in generalities, and you can certainly share your own feelings about parenting. After reading the books and discussing them, you might be ready to launch into a conversation with your daughter about puberty.

If having these first conversations one-on-one is too much for you, another option is to host a "puberty party," a potluck lunch or dinner for your daughter's girlfriends and their mothers, and steer the talk toward puberty. (You might want to call it a "health workshop" rather than a "puberty party," lest you embarrass the girls.) You can start with just basic anatomy, health, and hygiene. Let a parent who is more comfortable with the subject and language—perhaps a nurse, physician, teacher, counselor, or health educator—be the leader so that everyone can be comfortable, too. Share the information and the giggles. The adults can relay information and tell stories about their own experiences with puberty. Inject as much humor as possible. Humor is like a secret sauce for successfully discussing any serious topic.

Julie Metzger, RN, and Rob Lehman, MD, developed a wonderful workshop program called Heart to Heart: A Seminar on Growing Up for Parents and Kids that's offered in Seattle and now also at Stanford University's Lucile Packard Children's Hospital in Palo Alto, California. In it, they take the agony out of many parents' attempts to discuss puberty with their kids, from talking about all the physical changes to social issues and sexuality. There are also books for the program that enable them to share the information with children and their parents nationwide (e.g., *Will Puberty Last My Whole Life?*). Programs like this are beginning to crop up throughout the country, so you might want to check out your local Girl Scout troop or a nearby university's course catalog. Metzger and Lehman also offer their book and classes through their company in the greater Seattle area. For more information, go to greatconversations.com.

Principle #8: Don't Forget Dad

There might be some conversations that involve just a woman and a girl, like those on sensitive topics like body issues, buying a bra, and preparing for a first period, but that doesn't mean fathers and father figures should take a backseat throughout puberty—particularly if Dad is a single father or the family has two dads. To the contrary, they must stay involved and add to the conversation when they can. After all, we know that father–daughter relationships factor mightily into a girl's pubescent experience and what behavior she'll be at risk for later, particularly in terms of sexual behavior. Some men feel uncomfortable when their daughters start to develop, causing them to pull away emotionally. It's critical for dads to fight that impulse and find ways to remain emotionally close with their girls.

According to Bruce Ellis, whom we first met in Chapter 2 and who has studied the role of fathers in parenting and puberty, "Warm and cohesive relationships with parents—including fathers—forecast later puberty." He goes on to add that once girls have started puberty, major stressors may add to the risks associated with early puberty and make pubertal changes a lot more daunting. Stressors include such things as moving, transitioning to a middle school, and divorce, which happens frequently during this time in a girl's life. Ellis underscores the importance of not only creating the most stable and loving relationship possible before puberty to limit and combat stressors but also nurturing and supporting the relationship with the father's involvement throughout puberty. According to Ellis, "Fathers have a particular and unique influence on girls' development."

Many researchers, including Ellis, are interested in the pheromonal regulation of puberty—how a father's scent, which is caused by chemicals the body releases—can influence the pubertal process. This is virtually impossible to study in humans. We know, however, that a girl's exposure to unrelated adult males has been shown to accelerate puberty, whereas having a close relationship with her biological father before puberty delays its onset and may even slow the process itself. This is an exciting area of research that has been explored in animal studies, but linking it to humans is tricky.

Dads might not be invited to those puberty parties, but they should engage their daughters in one-on-one activities to increase and maintain that all-important emotional closeness, just as mothers should. This is when having (or developing) a shared hobby comes in handy. Our own girls get plenty of daddy time in shared activities. One of our husbands likes to cook, while the other loves to surf in the frigid northern California waters. By finding something special for the two of them, they have a unique time to bond. Girls may not want to talk about breasts and pubic hair with dads, but fathers can certainly provide the male perspective regarding what boys are going through at the same time. And for families where there's no biological father, there's likely a father figure around who can step in and fill that role. He might be a close family friend, an uncle, or a grandfather. He just needs to be someone a girl trusts who can be a lifelong source of guidance, warmth, and attention.

Principle #9: Have Empathy and Follow Your Gut Feelings

Children learn by example. We can't stress this enough. If you're living a healthy lifestyle and doing the kinds of things that make you healthy and happy, then chances are they will, too.

Lorah Dorn, PhD, is a psychologist, pediatric nurse practitioner, and professor of nursing and pediatrics at Pennsylvania State University and a respected researcher on adolescent behavior and puberty. Several of her major papers published in high-profile medical journals have been related to the biological transitions that adolescents inevitably make. "Parents are afraid of puberty," she says. "We need to nip that in the bud. Parents need to understand this transition better. How can we get adults to better think about and understand puberty?" She offers a useful analogy for putting ourselves in our girls' shoes: As an adult, consider the prospect of moving into a new house, starting a new job, finding your way around a new community, and making new friends while still maintaining old ones—all at the same time. Consider how you might function under that degree of strain. And add to that the expectation that you are supposed to please everyone around you. Tough shoes to fill? This is like what we expect of girls as they navigate puberty. They are going through events that are equally as challenging as those. "Expectations are out of line," Dorn says. She thinks the adults need to put things into better perspective and try to find more empathy for their girls. She also calls out—quite rightly—that the combination of puberty and parents who are scared to death of this transition is a tough one. We, the adults and caretakers of these rapidly changing girls, must shift our attitudes about puberty. Put simply, we need to take the fear out of puberty.

Her insights into how we can reframe the whole notion of puberty in our heads are invaluable. Dorn asserts, "Puberty is probably a great opportunity for making health and development better. It's a time when kids' cognition is enhanced, so they are developing the capability to understand messages better; kids are eager to learn at this time—and learn from parents and older people, often indirectly. But you also have to balance it with the emotional regulation aspect of development that is occurring at this same time. As such, it's a really good time to intervene, as there are so many years to live more healthfully. It can impact their future before really problematic health behaviors set in. Your child may not adhere to your messages right away or even let you know they heard them, but trust that they've been received loud and clear."

This last point is critical. While we may think that our parenting efforts may not even be received, they are likely getting absorbed and will indeed have an impact in the child's behavior and decision making now and in the future. Dorn adds, "Most parents need to trust their gut about what their kids are doing or what they suspect they might be doing. Remember that you are the parent and not their best friend. You need to let them know what is acceptable and not." Dorn also reminds us that even for medical professionals, the subject of puberty can be challenging. That means kids may not get the attention they need in this arena at the doctor's office, and you can't just rely on your pediatrician or nurse practitioner to handle all the hard conversations. You also can't assume that if real problems, such as body-image issues, eating disorders, or early signs of depression, start to present themselves, the doctor will be able to diagnose them quickly if there are no obvious early warning signs, because health care visits are often short. Doctors need your help, because you know your girl best. For this reason alone, it's vital to have a strong bond with your child. With that bond in place, it will be much easier and more intuitive to notice when your child is not acting "like herself" and to trust your gut instinct about what's going on with her. Some signs of trouble are slipping grades when she's always done well or major changes in whom she's friends with. Approaching your daughter when you suspect there's a problem to discuss will also be much easier. And, if you're really concerned, taking her to see a professional is a great way to get a handle on any developing problems before they become serious. We are always surprised by parents who feel like they shouldn't think about seeing a therapist or making an appointment with a school counselor until there are real problems. Prevention is the best medicine. Short-term therapy can be an opportunity for assessment and coaching to get you, your daughter, and your family on track.

Principle #10: Be Realistic As You Look Ahead

You can have all the knowledge and practical tools you need to help a girl go through puberty but still feel like you come up short once in a while. Yes, there will be times when it feels like your child is acting like a relatively mature being, but there also will be moments when you are immensely frustrated and maybe even angry at events that are occurring during this unique time period. For instance, as practitioners, we hear regularly about two things some daughters start doing that really drive their parents crazy during early puberty: eye rolling and using an unpleasant tone of voice. These types of behavioral changes take supreme patience and confidence to manage. There are two important concepts we hope you take with you. One is to have faith in the positive power of puberty, and the other is to be mindful of what you can and cannot control.

Just because it's a time that can be characterized by added conflict doesn't mean that it's inherently "bad" or negative. Puberty is an extraordinary time of growth and development—for both parent and child! We all emerge from this period a little wiser, more patient, and definitely better equipped to handle any challenge life throws at us.

Laurence Steinberg has made it his mission to dispel the myth that at puberty family relationships tank inevitably. Even though there can be a constant tug-of-war as kids try to have more autonomy, be treated like they are more mature, and have more control over their lives, that doesn't necessarily mean relationships need to take a downward spiral. As with many of the experts we interviewed, Steinberg doesn't buy into what he calls "the myth of the querulous teen." Steinberg summarizes the research in the field in his popular textbook *Adolescence* when he writes that "The hormonal changes of puberty have only a modest direct effect on adolescent behavior; rebellion during adolescence is atypical, not normal." In fact, most current research suggests that social and familial environments play a much larger role in how an early developing girl functions emotionally and behaviorally than we previously thought.

This is something we all need to keep in mind, especially when the bonds with our kids feel tenuous or challenged in some way.

The second concept is all about being open-minded about the kind of person your child is becoming—or not. In other words, keep your expectations in check. Although we adults are helping to shepherd our girls to adulthood, we cannot fully control the people they are becoming.

Finally, we'd like to add that you're not the one ultimately responsible for their success or even happiness in life. As long as you're doing the best you can with what you've got today, then you get an A in parenthood.

"BUT EVERYONE ELSE IS DOING IT, SO WHY CAN'T I?"

We saved addressing this question for last. It's one that virtually every girl will utter at some point, and the answer allows us to sum up several of the points made in this chapter. Even the strongest relationship between a parent or guardian and a girl won't escape this question, or some variation on it. It won't be free of moments when she rolls her eyes, uses a harsh tone of voice, and complains that you're being mean and unlike "everyone else's parents."

In 2013, bestselling author Bruce Feiler (*The Secrets of Happy*

Families) wrote a piece for the *New York Times* about "the line between sweet and skimpy." He writes: "The issue of appropriate clothing for girls has been the subject of increasing academic and popular scrutiny, fed by skimpy panties printed with 'wink wink' or skinny leggings that say 'cute butt sweat pants.' In 2007, Wal-Mart bowed to parental pressure and pulled pairs of pink girls' underwear off its shelves because they were printed with the words 'Who needs credit cards . . .' on the front and 'When you've got Santa' on the back."

We know it's hard to combat the marketing power of companies selling sexually suggestive products to your girls. And it's harder still to see young girls wearing clothing that's clearly inappropriate for their age. But the challenge lies in managing the competing demands of a girl's desire to be trendy and protecting her from sexual innuendo (which she may not even be aware of). So how can a parent let early-maturing girls have the freedom they deserve but still set guidelines that adhere to the family's values?

When you tell her no, you explain to her that your family does things differently and that every family is different. You don't need to get into the details of how or why certain clothing is sexual, because your girl might not be ready for that part of the conversation. You can frame the explanation in terms of safety. Talk about how other people might view her if she wears that clothing (again, not getting into sexual topics). Try "We have rules in this family, and this is just one of them. Every family has different rules. That's how life works. I'm sorry if it upsets you, but this is the way we do things. The rules are to keep you safe."

Most important, don't get emotional with her if she blows up. If she has a tantrum when you say no, let her calm down before reengaging in the conversation. Remind yourself that children's emotions can easily get the better of them, so don't be hard on them when they can't manage their feelings, however strong they seem to be!

This approach also works for "Mom, I want a smartphone"—or tablet, or whatever—"because EVERYONE has one." Find out who really does (ask their friends' parents directly) and then pull out the tactic above.

Above all, whether you're dealing with a well-behaved angel today and a girl who seems possessed tomorrow, nurturing that bond is all about being consistent, sticking to your guns, repeating your expectations without getting emotional, picking your battles, and not getting into power struggles. Here's a mantra to say to yourself:

Stay brave.

Stay in charge.

Stay patient.

Stay present.

Stay consistent.

Stay open and loving.

ACKNOWLEDGMENTS

WHEN PEOPLE SAY THAT WRITING a book takes a small village of excellent human beings, they are speaking the truth. Putting this one together was no different, and we were lucky to be in the company of many talented, bright, and energetic fellow villagers who helped us navigate our path to publication. We owe everyone we've ever worked with through the years a heartfelt thank-you, especially the girls and their parents who've been the inspiration for this book. The unwavering support of our families, friends, and colleagues has also given us indispensable guidance, insights, and feedback to arrive at these pages. *The New Puberty* is as much yours as it is ours.

Collectively, we'd like to express our gratitude to the many extraordinary people who participated in this project from start to finish. To those who provided their knowledge and offered comments, and to the experts who allowed us to quote their remarks and sage contributions, we thank you.

To our indefatigable agent, Bonnie Solow, who went beyond the call of duty and orchestrated so much of our creative energy when we were just beginning to talk about writing a book but didn't know if we could actually do it! This book was a figment of our imagination until she provided the road map and took us by the hand so it could become reality. She is in many ways the midwife of this book, and we couldn't have done it without her invaluable leadership and support. Thanks to Bonnie, we met our writer, Kristin Loberg, who committed our thoughts, voices, and ideas to the page; seeing her translate complicated scientific concepts into understandable language was a powerful process to watch.

To the tenacious team at Rodale, our publishing stewards who made this all come to fruition. Thanks especially to: Mary Ann Naples, who championed this book from the beginning as a mother of two young daughters; Kristin Kiser, also a mom of a young girl; and Alex Postman, whose editorial genius and insights as a mother herself made for the best book possible. Thanks also to Marilyn Hauptly, Carol Angstadt, Amy King, Mollie Grewe, Yelena Nesbit, and Aly Mostel. And special thanks to Majed Abolfazli, Jody Holman Webster, and Patrick Yore for working their magic with our photos and Web site.

To everyone in CYGNET and BCERP: Larry Kushi, Bob Hiatt, Gayle Windham, Kaya Balke, Noushie Mirabedi, Cecile Laurent, Mary Wolff, Susan Teitelbaum, Maida Galvez, Frank Biro, Janice Barlow, and Susan Pinney. Also to Marcia Herman-Giddens, Ken Cook, Pat Crawford, Brenda Eskenazi, Kim Harley, Birdie Shirtcliff, Paul Kaplowitz, and Zero Breast Cancer. And to our friends who put up with endless discussions about titles, subtitles, cover ideas—you were our original target audience and you know who you are!

And now, to a few more individuals that each of us would like to call out:

From Louise:

I have to start with thanking my endocrine teachers, the mother and fathers of pediatric endocrinology at the University of California,

San Francisco: Selna Kaplan, Melvin Grumbach, and Felix Conte, as well as mentors Stephen Gitelman and Stephen Rosenthal. At Kaiser Permanente San Francisco, I had unyielding support from my chiefs, Dewey Woo and Robert Mithun, as well as from many staff members, including Joe Fragola, and all my colleagues and friends.

To my family—my parents for your continuous encouragement, and especially my husband, for never doubting this project from day 1, and for providing the practical support at home that allowed me to do this. Thanks for all the meals, wordsmithing, and love. And finally, our children, who put up with endless times when I sat typing away in the living room and never seemed to mind. Yes, kids, Mommy's book is done!

From Julie:

I have been incredibly fortunate to have outstanding and caring mentors, without whom I would never have become the scientist, teacher, and writer that I am today. Heartfelt thanks to Nancy Gonzales, Mark Roosa, Jeanne Tschann, and Nancy Adler. I am also indebted to the wonderful clinicians at the University of California, San Francisco's New Generation Health Center, who always helped keep the research real and are deeply dedicated to the youth they serve: Andrea Raider, Debby Davidson, and Tina Raine.

Finally, to my friends and family who watched my kids, cooked food for me, took over the carpools, and made this book possible. To my parents, whose support for my endeavors has always been unwavering. To my kids, Reese and Aidan, who constantly amazed me throughout this process with their humor and endless supply of love and hugs. Finally, to my husband, Rich, who encouraged me to write this book before it was even a nugget of an idea.

SELECTED REFERENCES

THE FOLLOWING IS A PARTIAL LIST of books, scientific papers, and online destinations that you may find helpful in learning more about the ideas and concepts expressed in this book. We've organized this list by chapter, noting the sources we've called upon aside from those people and publications adequately identified in the text. This is by no means an exhaustive list, but it will get you started in gaining a better understanding of the new puberty and the current science behind strategies to address it. These materials can also open other doors for further research and inquiry. For access to more studies and a list of references updated on an ongoing basis, please visit thenewpuberty.com. If you do not see a reference listed here that was mentioned in the book, please refer to the Web site, where an updated list is found.

Introduction

National Institutes of Health: nih.gov

F.M. Biro, et al., "Pubertal Assessment Method and Baseline Characteristics in a Mixed Longitudinal Study of Girls," *Pediatrics* 126, no. 3 (2010): e583–e590. doi: 10.1542/peds.2009-3079.

M.E. Herman-Giddens, et al., "Secondary Sexual Characteristics and Menses in Young Girls Seen in Office Practice: A Study from the Pediatric Research in Office Settings Network," *Pediatrics* 99, no. 4 (1997): 505–12.

Cohort of Young Girls' Nutrition, Environment, and Transitions Study: cygnetstudy.com

Breast Cancer and the Environment Research Program: bcerp.org

F.M. Biro, et al., "Onset of Breast Development in a Longitudinal Cohort," *Pediatrics* 132, no. 6 (2013): 1019–27. doi: 10.1542/peds.2012-3773.

M.E. Herman-Giddens, et al., "Secondary Sexual Characteristics in Boys: Data from the Pediatric Research in Office Settings Network," *Pediatrics* 130, no. 5 (Nov 2012): e1058–e1068. doi: 10.1542/peds.2011-3291.

Chapter 1

B. Weber, "Dr. James M. Tanner, an Expert in How Children Grow, Is Dead at 90," *New York Times*, August 23, 2010.

J.M. Tanner and W.A. Marshall, "Variations in Pattern of Pubertal Changes in Girls," *Archives of Disease in Childhood* 235, no. 44 (1969): 291–303.

F.M. Biro, et al., "Pubertal Assessment Method and Baseline Characteristics in a Mixed Longitudinal Study of Girls," *Pediatrics* 126, no. 3 (2010): e583–e590.

L. Aksglaede, et al., "Recent Decline in Age at Breast Development: The Copenhagen Puberty Study," *Pediatrics* 123, no. 5 (2009): e932–e939. doi: 10.1542/peds.2008-2491.

A.S. Parent, et al., "The Timing of Normal Puberty and the Age Limits of Sexual Precocity: Variations around the World, Secular Trends, and Changes after Migration," *Endocrine Reviews* 24, no. 5 (2003): 668–93.

Centers for Disease Control and Prevention, Childhood Obesity Facts, February 27, 2014, cdc.gov/healthyyouth/obesity/facts.htm.

E. Terasawa, et al., "Body Weight Impact on Puberty: Effects of High-Calorie Diet on Puberty Onset in Female Rhesus Monkeys," *Endocrinology* 153, no. 4 (2012): 1696–1705. doi: 10.1210/en.2011-1970.

L. Beil, "Early Arrival: Premature Puberty among Girls Poses Scientific Puzzle," *Science News* November 16, 2012. sciencenews.org/article/early-arrival.

A. Shrestha, et al., "Obesity and Age at Menarche," *Fertility and Sterility* 95, no. 8 (2011): 2732–34. doi: 10.1016/j.fertnstert.2011.02.020.

K.K. Davison, E.J. Susman, and L.L. Birch, "Percent Body Fat at Age 5 Predicts Earlier Pubertal Development among Girls at Age 9," *Pediatrics* 111, no. 4, Pt 1 (2003): 815–21.

J.M. Lee, et al., "Weight Status in Young Girls and the Onset of Puberty," *Pediatrics* 119, no. 3 (2007): e624–e630. doi: 10.1542/peds.2006-2188.

Environmental Working Group, *Pollution in Minority Newborns: BPA and Other Cord Blood Pollutants,* November 23, 2009, ewg.org/research /minority-cord-blood-report/bpa-and-other-cord-blood-pollutants.

World Health Organization and United Nations Environment Program, *State of the Science of Endocrine Disrupting Chemicals–2012,* Geneva, Switzerland: World Health Organization Press, 2013. who.int/ceh/publications /endocrine/en.

B.J. Ellis and M.J. Essex, "Family Environments, Adrenarche, and Sexual Maturation: A Longitudinal Test of a Life History Model," *Child Development* 78, no. 6 (2007): 1799–1817.

S.K. Cesario and L.A. Hughes, "Precocious Puberty: A Comprehensive Review of Literature," *Journal of Obstetric, Gynecologic, and Neonatal Nursing* 36, no. 3 (2007): 263–74.

R. Morello-Frosch, et al., "Understanding the Cumulative Impacts of Inequalities in Environmental Health: Implications for Policy," *Health Affairs* 30, no. 5 (2011): 879–87. doi: 10.1377/hlthaff.2011.0153.

M.S. Wolff, et al., "Investigation of Relationships between Urinary Biomarkers of Phytoestrogens, Phthalates, and Phenols and Pubertal Stages in Girls," *Environmental Health Perspectives* 118, no. 7 (2010): 1039–46. doi: 10.1289/ ehp.0901690.

A. Bergman, et al., "The Impact of Endocrine Disruption: A Consensus Statement on the State of the Science," *Environmental Health Perspectives* 121, no. 4 (2013): A104–A106. doi: 10.1289/ehp.1205448.

T.J. Woodruff, T.A. Burke, and L. Zeise, "The Need for Better Public Health Decisions on Chemicals Released into our Environment," *Health Affairs* 30, no. 5 (2011): 957–67. doi: 10.1377/hlthaff.2011.0194.

T.J. Woodruff, "Bridging Epidemiology and Model Organisms to Increase Understanding of Endocrine Disrupting Chemicals and Human Health Effects," *Journal of Steroid Biochemistry and Molecular Biology* 127, no. 1–2 (2011): 108–17. doi: 10.1016/j.jsbmb.2010.11.007.

T.J. Woodruff, A.R. Zota, and J.M. Schwartz, "Environmental Chemicals in Pregnant Women in the United States: NHANES 2003-2004," *Environmental Health Perspectives* 119, no. 6 (2011): 878–85. doi: 10.1289/ ehp.1002727.

B.J. Ellis and J. Garber, "Psychosocial Antecedents of Variation in Girls' Pubertal Timing: Maternal Depression, Stepfather Presence, and Marital and Family Stress," *Child Development* 71, no. 2 (2000): 485–501.

A.A. D'Aloisio, "Prenatal and Infant Exposures and Age at Menarche," *Epidemiology* 24, no. 2 (2013): 277–84. doi: 10.1097/EDE.0b013e31828062b7.

D.E. Buttke, K. Sircar, and C. Martin, "Exposures to Endocrine-Disrupting Chemicals and Age of Menarche in Adolescent Girls in NHANES (2003-2008)," *Environmental Health Perspectives* 120, no. 11 (2012): 1613–18. doi: 10.1289/ehp.1104748.

K.G. Anderson, H. Kaplan, and J. Lancaster, "Paternal Care by Genetic Fathers and Stepfathers I: Reports from Albuquerque," *Evolution and Human Behavior* 431 (1999): 405–31.

K.G. Anderson, et al., "Paternal Care by Genetic Fathers and Stepfathers II: Reports by Xhosa High School Students," *Evolution and Human Behavior* 451 (1999): 433–51.

E. Stice, K. Presnell, and S.K. Bearman, "Relation of Early Menarche to Depression, Eating Disorders, Substance Abuse, and Comorbid Psychopathology among Adolescent Girls," *Developmental Psychology* 37 (2001): 608–19.

M. Fisher, W.D. Rosenfeld, and R.D. Burk, "Cervicovaginal Human Papillomavirus Infection in Suburban Adolescents and Young Adults," *Journal of Pediatrics* 119 (1991): 821–25.

T.H. Lam, et al., "Timing of Pubertal Maturation and Heterosexual Behavior among Hong Kong Chinese Adolescents," *Archives of Sexual Behavior* 31 (2002): 359–66.

J. Belsky, R.M. Houts, and R.M.P. Fearon, "Infant Attachment Security and Timing of Puberty: Testing an Evolutionary Hypothesis," *Psychological Science* 21 (2010): 1195–1201.

J. Belsky, et al., "The Development of Reproductive Strategy in Females: Early Maternal Harshness → Earlier Menarche → Increased Sexual Risk Taking," *Developmental Psychology* 46 (2010): 120–28.

J. Belsky, "Childhood Experience and the Development of Reproductive Strategies," *Psicothema* 22 (2010): 28–34.

J. Belsky, "War, Trauma and Children's Development: Observations from a Modern Evolutionary Perspective," *International Journal of Behavioral Development* 32 (2008): 260–71.

Chapter 2

K. Tamakoshi, "Early Age at Menarche Associated with Increased All-Cause Mortality," *European Journal of Epidemiology* 26, no. 10 (2011): 771–78. doi: 10.1007/s10654-011-9623-0.

B.K. Jacobsen, I. Heuch, and G. Kvåle, "Association of Low Age at Menarche with Increased All-Cause Mortality: A 37-Year Follow-Up of 61,319 Norwegian Women," *American Journal of Epidemiology* 166, no. 12 (2007): 1431–37.

J.S. Fuqua, "Treatment and Outcomes of Precocious Puberty: An Update," *Journal of Clinical Endocrinology and Metabolism* 98, no. 6 (2013): 2198–2207. doi: 10.1210/jc.2013-1024.

J.L. Marino, et al., "Age at Menarche and Age at First Sexual Intercourse: A Prospective Cohort Study," *Pediatrics* 132, no. 6 (2013): 1028–36. doi: 10.1542/peds.2012-3634.

E.C. Walvoord, "The Timing of Puberty: Is It Changing? Does it Matter?" *Journal of Adolescent Health* 47, No. 5 (2010): 433–39.

J. Mendle, E. Turkheimer, and R.E. Emery, "Detrimental Psychological Outcomes Associated with Early Pubertal Timing in Adolescent Girls," *Developmental Review* 27, no. 2 (2007): 151–71.

F.M. Biro, P. Khoury, and J.A. Morrison, "Influence of Obesity on Timing of Puberty," *International Journal of Andrology* 29, no. 1 (2006): 272–77.

F.M. Biro, "Secular Trends in Menarche," *Journal of Pediatrics* 147, no. 6 (2005): 725–26.

F.M. Biro and L.D. Dorn, "Puberty and Adolescent Sexuality," *Pediatric Annals* 34, no. 10 (2005): 777–84.

Breast Cancer Fund, *Advocate's Guide: The Falling Age of Puberty in U.S. Girls,* n.d. breastcancerfund.org/assets/pdfs/publications/falling-age-of-puberty -adv-guide.pdf.

J.R. Speakman, "Evolutionary Perspectives on the Obesity Epidemic: Adaptive, Maladaptive, and Neutral Viewpoints," *Annual Review of Nutrition* 33 (2013): 289–317. doi: 10.1146/annurev-nutr-071811-150711.

Chapter 3

L. Aksglaede, et al., "Recent Decline in Age at Breast Development: The Copenhagen Puberty Study," *Pediatrics* 123, no. 5 (2009): e932–e939. doi: 10.1542/peds.2008-2491.

L. Aksglaede, et al., "Age at Puberty and the Emerging Obesity Epidemic," *PLoS One* 4, no. 12 (2009): e8450. doi: 10.1371/journal.pone.0008450.

P.B. Kaplowitz, et al., "Earlier Onset of Puberty in Girls: Relation to Increased Body Mass Index and Race," *Pediatrics* 108, no. 2 (2001): 347–53.

J.M. Lee, et al., "Weight Status in Young Girls and the Onset of Puberty," *Pediatrics* 119, no. 3 (2007): e624–e630.

J. Deardorff, et al., "Maternal Pre-Pregnancy BMI, Gestational Weight Gain, and Age at Menarche in Daughters," *Maternal and Child Health Journal* 17, no. 8 (2013): 1391–98. doi: 10.1007/s10995-012-1139-z.

L.R. Shull and P.R. Cheeke, "Effects of Synthetic and Natural Toxicants on Livestock," *Journal of Animal Science* 57, no. 2 (1983): 330–54.

I. Colón, et al., "Identification of Phthalate Esters in the Serum of Young Puerto Rican Girls with Premature Breast Development," *Environmental Health Perspectives* 108, no. 9 (2000): 895–900.

D.L. Davis, et al., "Medical Hypothesis: Xenoestrogens as Preventable Causes of Breast Cancer," *Environmental Health Perspectives* 101, no. 5 (1993): 372–77.

National Institute of Environmental Health Sciences, *Endocrine Disrupters*, May 2010. niehs.nih.gov/health/materials/endocrine_disruptors_508.pdf.

J.D. Meeker and K.K. Ferguson, "Relationship between Urinary Phthalate and Bisphenol A Concentrations and Serum Thyroid Measures in U.S. Adults and Adolescents from NHANES 2007-08," *Environmental Health Perspectives* 119, no. 10 (2011): 1396–1402. doi: 10.1289/ehp.1103582.

University of Michigan, "Large Human Study Links Phthalates, BPA and Thyroid Hormone Levels," *Science Daily*, July 11, 2011. sciencedaily.com /releases/2011/07/110711131614.htm.

B. Ellis, et al., "Quality of Early Family Relationships and the Timing and Tempo of Puberty: Effects Depend on Biological Sensitivity to Context," *Development and Psychopathology* 23, no. 1 (2011): 85–99. doi: 10.1017/ S0954579410000660.

J. Deardorff, et al., "Father Absence, Body Mass Index, and Pubertal Timing in Girls: Differential Effects by Family Income and Ethnicity," *Journal of Adolescent Health* 48, no. 5 (2011): 441–47. doi: 10.1016/j. jadohealth.2010.07.032.

F.M. Biro, et al., "Onset of Breast Development in a Longitudinal Cohort," *Pediatrics* 132, no. 6 (2013): 1019–27. doi: 10.1542/peds.2012-3773.

M. Meaney, et al., "Maternal Programming of Sexual Behavior and Hypothalamic-Pituitary-Gonadal Function in the Female Rat," *PLoS One* 3, no. 5 (2008): e2210. doi: 10.1371/journal.pone.0002210.

J.M. Tither and B.J. Ellis, "Impact of Fathers on Daughters' Age at Menarche: A Genetically and Environmentally Controlled Sibling Study," *Developmental Psychology* 44, no. 5 (2008): 1409–20. doi: 10.1037/a0013065.

G. Teilmann, et al., "Increased Risk of Precocious Puberty in Internationally Adopted Children in Denmark," *Pediatrics* 118, no. 2 (2006): e391–e399.

C. Mucignat-Caretta, A. Caretta, and A. Cavaggioni, "Acceleration of Puberty Onset in Female Mice by Male Urinary Proteins," *Journal of Physiology* 486, no. 2 (1995): 517–22.

US Department of Health and Human Services, Centers for Disease Control and Prevention, and National Center for Environmental Health, *Fourth National Report on Human Exposure to Environmental Chemicals: 2009*. n.d. cdc.gov /exposurereport/pdf/FourthReport_ExecutiveSummary.pdf.

H.M. Blanck, et al., "Age at Menarche and Tanner Stage in Girls Exposed in Utero and Postnatally to Polybrominated Biphenyl," *Epidemiology* 11, no. 6 (2000): 641–47.

C. Cajochen, et al., "Evening Exposure to a Light-Emitting Diodes (LED)-Backlit Computer Screen Affects Circadian Physiology and Cognitive Performance," *Journal of Applied Physiology* 110, no. 5 (2011): 1432–38.

B. Wood, et al., "Light Level and Duration of Exposure Determine the Impact of Self-Luminous Tablets on Melatonin Suppression," *Applied Ergonomics* 44, no. 2 (2013): 237–40.

Chapter 4

G.M. Fara, et al., "Epidemic of Breast Enlargement in an Italian School," *Lancet* 314, no. 8137 (1979): 295–97.

D.M. Sanghavi, "Factors Linked to a Risk of Early Puberty—Health and Science—International Herald Tribune," *New York Times*, October 18, 2006.

D.M. Sanghavi, "Preschool Puberty, and a Search for the Causes," *New York Times*, October 17, 2006.

O. Humblet, et al., "Dioxin and Polychlorinated Biphenyl Concentrations in Mother's Serum and the Timing of Pubertal Onset in Sons," *Epidemiology* 22, no. 6 (2011): 827–35. doi: 10.1097/EDE.0b013e318230b0d1.

D.V. Henley, et al., "Prepubertal Gynecomastia Linked to Lavender and Tea Tree Oils," *New England Journal of Medicine* 356, no. 5 (2007): 479–85.

Chapter 5

Much of this chapter relied on our interviews with experts and data from public resources such as the Centers for Disease Control and Prevention (cdc.gov), the Environmental Protection Agency (epa.gov), the National Institutes of Health (nih.gov), and the World Health Organization (who.int). Several of the studies mentioned in the chapter were previously cited. Below are additional sites and resources to check out.

M. Cone and Environmental Health News, "Should DDT Be Used to Combat Malaria?" *Scientific American,* May 4, 2009. scientificamerican.com/article/ddt-use-to-combat-malaria.

TEDX: The Endocrine Disruption Exchange: endocrinedisruption.org.

Center for Environmental Research and Children's Health (CERCH)—UC Berkeley: epa.gov/ncer/childrenscenters/centers/berkeley_chamacos.html.

S. Goodman, "Tests Find More Than 200 Chemicals in Newborn Umbilical Cord Blood," *Scientific American,* December 2, 2009. scientificamerican.com/article/newborn-babies-chemicals-exposure-bpa.

L.N. Vandenberg, et al., "Urinary, Circulating, and Tissue Biomonitoring Studies Indicate Widespread Exposure to Bisphenol A," *Environmental Health Perspectives* 118, no. 8 (2010): 1055–70. doi: 10.1289/ehp.0901716.

M.N. Bates, et al., "Workgroup Report: Biomonitoring Study Design, Interpretation, and Communication—Lessons Learned and Path Forward," *Environmental Health Perspectives* 113, no. 11 (2005): 1615–21.

Environmental Protection Agency, "Biomonitoring: An Exposure Science Tool," n.d. epa.gov/heasd/research/biomonitoring.html.

Environmental Health News: environmentalhealthnews.org.

Saint Louis University, "Children Eat More Fruits and Vegetables If They Are Homegrown," *Science Daily,* April 19, 2007. sciencedaily.com/releases/2007/04/070418163652.htm.

Chapter 6

J.B. McKinlay and S.M. McKinlay, "The Questionable Contribution of Medical Measures to the Decline of Mortality in the United States in the Twentieth Century," *Milbank Memorial Fund Quarterly: Health and Society* 55, no. 3 (1977): 405–28.

Robert Wood Johnson Foundation Commission to Build a Healthier America: rwjf.org.

R. Estruch, et al., "Primary Prevention of Cardiovascular Disease with a Mediterranean Diet," *New England Journal of Medicine* 368, no. 14 (2013): 1279–90. doi: 10.1056/NEJMoa1200303.

R.H. Lustig, *Fat Chance: Beating the Odds against Sugar, Processed Food, Obesity, and Disease* (New York: Hudson Street, 2012).

P.B. Crawford and K.L. Webb, "Unraveling the Paradox of Concurrent Food Insecurity and Obesity," *American Journal of Preventive Medicine* 40, no. 2 (2011): 274–75.

P.B. Crawford and W. Gosliner, "State-Level Policies Can Help Reduce Consumption of Sugar-Sweetened Beverages in Schools," *Journal of Pediatrics* 161, no. 3 (2012): 566–67.

S.E. Swithers, "Artificial Sweeteners Produce the Counterintuitive Effect of Inducing Metabolic Derangements," *Trends in Endocrinology and Metabolism* 24, no. 9 (2013): 431–41. doi: 10.1016/j.tem.2013.05.005.

S.N. Bleich, et al., "Diet-Beverage Consumption and Caloric Intake among US Adults, Overall and by Body Weight," *American Journal of Public Health* 104, no. 3 (2014): e72–e78. doi: 10.2105/AJPH.2013.301556.

Prevention Institute, "The Facts on Junk Food Marketing and Kids," n.d. preventioninstitute.org/focus-areas/supporting-healthy-food-a-activity /supporting-healthy-food-and-activity-environments-advocacy/get -involved-were-not-buying-it/735-were-not-buying-it-the-facts-on-junk -food-marketing-and-kids.html.

Marion Nestle, *Eat Drink Vote: An Illustrated Guide to Food Politics* (New York: Rodale, 2013).

Y. Kelly, J. Kelly, and A. Sacker, "Changes in Bedtime Schedules and Behavioral Difficulties in 7 Year Old Children," *Pediatrics* 132, no. 5 (2013): e1184–e1193. doi: 10.1542/peds.2013-1906.

National Sleep Foundation: sleepfoundation.org.

C.E. Landhuis, et al., "Childhood Sleep Time and Long-Term Risk for Obesity: A 32-Year Prospective Birth Cohort Study," *Pediatrics* 122, no. 5 (2008): 955–60. doi: 10.1542/peds.2007-3521.

M.P. St-Onge, et al., "Sleep Restriction Increases the Neuronal Response to Unhealthy Food in Normal-Weight Individuals," *International Journal of Obesity* 38, no. 3 (2014): 411–16. doi: 10.1038/ijo.2013.114.

B. Weber, "Irregular Bedtimes Linked to Kids' Behavioral Problems," *MedicalNews Today,* October 14, 2013. medicalnewstoday.com /articles/267366.php.

K. Madsen, et al., "The Feasibility of a Physical Activity Referral Network for Pediatric Obesity," *Childhood Obesity* 10, no. 2 (2014): 169–74.

K.A. Madsen, et al., "Physical Activity Opportunities Associated with Fitness and Weight Status among Adolescents in Low-Income Communities," *Archives of Pediatrics and Adolescent Medicine* 163, no. 11 (2009): 1014–21. doi: 10.1001/archpediatrics.2009.181.

Susan Stiffelman, *Parenting without Power Struggles* (New York: Atria, 2012).

Chapter 7

In crafting this chapter, we partly relied on published materials by the NIH's National Institute of Mental Health, specifically *The Teen Brain: Still Under Construction* (NIH Publication No. 11-4929, 2011, nimh.nih.gov/health /publications/the-teen-brain-still-under-construction/). Below are additional sites and resources to check out.

D.F. Bjorklund, *Why Youth Is Not Wasted on the Young: Immaturity in Human Development* (New York: Blackwell, 2007).

M. Flinn, D. Geary, and C. Ward, "Ecological Dominance, Social Competition, and Coalitionary Arms Races: Why Humans Evolved Extraordinary Intelligence," *Evolution and Human Behavior* 26 (2005): 10–46.

P.S. Eriksson, et al., "Neurogenesis in the Adult Human Hippocampus," *Nature Medicine* 4, no. 11 (November 1998): 1313–17.

Pat Wolfe, "The Adolescent Brain: A Work in Progress," patwolfe.com/2011/09/ the-adolescent-brain-a-work-in-progress/

D.R. Weinberger, Brita Elvevåg, and Jay Giedd, "The Adolescent Brain: A Work in Progress," publication for the National Campaign to Prevent Teen Pregnancy, June 2005.

Jay Giedd, et al., "How Does Your Cortex Grow?" *Journal of Neuroscience* 31, no. 19 (2011): 7174–77. doi: 10.1523/JNEUROSCI.0054-11.2011.

Jay Giedd, et al., "Prenatal Growth in Humans and Postnatal Brain Maturation into Late Adolescence," *Proceedings of the National Academy of Sciences* 109, no. 28 (2012): 11366–71. doi: 10.1073/pnas.1203350109.

A. Toga, et al., "Mapping Continued Brain Growth and Gray Matter Density Reduction in Dorsal Frontal Cortex: Inverse Relationships during Postadolescent Brain Maturation," *Journal of Neuroscience* 21, no. 22 (2001): 8819–29.

R. Dahl, "Adolescent Brain Development: A Period of Vulnerabilities and Opportunities: Keynote Address," *Annals of the New York Academy of Sciences* 1021 (2004): 1–22. pmbcii.psy.cmu.edu/dahl/Dahl_Adolescent _brain_development.pdf.

B. Halpern-Felsher, et al., "Adolescents' Perceived Risk of Dying,"
    Journal of Adolescent Health 46, no. 3 (2010): 265–69. doi: 10.1016/j.
    jadohealth.2009.06.026.

B. Halpern-Felsher, et al., "Perceptions of Smoking-Related Risks and Benefits
    as Predictors of Adolescent Smoking Initiation," *American Journal of Public
    Health* 99, no. 3 (2009): 487–92. doi: 10.2105/AJPH.2008.137679.

B. Halpern-Felsher, et al., "The Development of Reproductive Strategy in
    Females: Early Maternal Harshness → Earlier Menarche → Increased
    Sexual Risk Taking," *Developmental Psychology* 46, no. 1 (2010): 120–28. doi:
    10.1037/a0015549.

M. Gardner and L. Steinberg, "Peer Influence on Risk Taking, Risk Preference,
    and Risky Decision Making in Adolescence and Adulthood: An Experimental
    Study," *Developmental Psychology* 41, no. 4 (2005): 625–35.

W.D. Killgore and D.A. Yurgelun-Todd, "Sex-Related Developmental Differences
    in the Lateralized Activation of the Prefrontal Cortex and Amygdala during
    Perception of Facial Affect," *Perceptual and Motor Skills* 99, no. 2 (2004):
    371–91.

J. Senior, "The Collateral Damage of a Teenager," *New York,* January 12, 2014.
    nymag.com/news/features/adolescence-2014-1.

S.J. Blakemore, S. Burnett, and R.E. Dahl, "The Role of Puberty in the Developing
    Adolescent Brain," *Human Brain Mapping* 31, no. 6 (2010): 926–33. doi:
    10.1002/hbm.21052.

Chapter 8

J. Zucker, "The Birth of Attachment Theory," *This Emotional Life* [blog]. pbs.org
    /thisemotionallife/blogs/birth-attachment-theory.

J. Bowlby, *Attachment* (New York: Basic Books, 2nd ed., 1983).

J. Belsky, R.M. Houts, and R.M.P. Fearon, "Infant Attachment Security and the
    Timing of Puberty: Testing an Evolutionary Hypothesis," *Psychological
    Science* 21, no. 9 (2010): 1195–1201. doi: 10.1177/0956797610379867.

L.D. Dorn, et al., "Influence of Treatment for Disruptive Behavior
    Disorders on Adrenal and Gonadal Hormones in Youth," *Journal of
    Clinical Child and Adolescent Psychology* 40, no. 4 (2011): 562–71. doi:
    10.1080/15374416.2011.581614.

B. Feiler, "The Line between Sweet and Skimpy," *New York Times,* May 10, 2013.

RECOMMENDED READING AND ADDITIONAL RESOURCES

THE FOLLOWING LIST OF WEB sites, books, and programs will help you gather more information regarding puberty and relevant health topics. Many of these resources were also mentioned in the text, but we thought you would find a comprehensive guide useful. And remember to visit thenewpuberty.com for our most updated list of resources.

For more about our ongoing research, and, in particular, the Breast Cancer and the Environmental Research Program (BCERP):

- BCERP.org

- cygnetstudy.com

For more on environmental toxins and safe products to buy:

- Environmental Working Group: ewg.org

- Toxic Matters from UCSF's Program on Reproductive Health and the Environment: prhe.ucsf.edu/prhe/toxicmatters.html

- Healthy Child Healthy World: healthychild.org

- NIH Household Products Database: hpd.nlm.nih.gov

- Children's Environmental Health Center at Mount Sinai Hospital in New York: at mountsinai.org, search for "Children's Environmental Health Center"

- Zero Breast Cancer Organization: zerobreastcancer.org /get-informed/resources

- National Institute of Environmental Health Sciences Kids' Page: cdc.gov/nceh/kids

- Center for Environmental Health: ceh.org

- US Environmental Protection Agency: epa.gov/children

For more on safe and healthy eating:

- Federal food safety information: foodsafety.gov

- Monterey Bay Aquarium's Seafood Watch: seafoodwatch.org

- The Mayo Clinic (mayoclinic.org) offers information about the Mediterranean approach to eating if you search for "Mediterranean diet" on the site.

- "Oldways" (oldwayspt.org) is a nonprofit food and nutrition education organization with more information on this approach to eating.

- The Food and Drug Administration's "Read the Label Youth Outreach Campaign" is an initiative to teach children ages 9 to 13 to use the Nutrition Facts Label on food and beverage packages to make healthy choices. You can access lots of information and videos at: 1.usa.gov/UuXyU5. The site includes kid-friendly videos to share with the family.

- The Environmental Working Group (ewg.org) maintains comprehensive lists of "dirty" foods to avoid and those that are relatively clean of synthetic chemical exposure. In addition to general information on safe and healthy eating, the EWG provides guides for buying the best foods for you and your family.

For more on making healthy lifestyle choices:

- For girls ages 10 to 16 to learn about health, growing up, and issues they may face: girlshealth.gov
- Health information for kids and teens: kidshealth.org
- Boston Children's Hospital Center for Young Women's Health: youngwomenshealth.org
- America's Move to Raise a Healthier Generation of Kids: letsmove.gov
- Harnessing the power of play so kids can thrive: playworks.org
- The National Sleep Foundation: sleepfoundation.org
- The Centers for Disease Control and Prevention includes information on child development, positive parenting tips, and free resources: cdc.gov/ncbddd/childdevelopment/index.html

For trustworthy health information:

The Internet can be a highly resourceful place to gain information but it also can be a dangerous place to navigate if you're not visiting trusted Web sites that present quality data and evidence-based advice from top institutions. We recommend the following sites:

- The National Institutes of Health: nih.gov
- The National Institutes of Health, NIH Office of Research on Women's Health: Women's Health Resources—Women's Health Resources from NIH: womenshealthresources.nlm.nih.gov/about.html
- The National Institute of Child Health and Human Development (NICHD): nichd.nih.gov/health
- The Centers for Disease Control and Prevention: cdc.gov
- The Mayo Clinic: mayoclinic.org
- The Cleveland Clinic Health Information Center: http://my.cleveland clinic.org

- The American Academy of Pediatrics: healthychildren.org

- The American Academy of Family Physicians: familydoctor.org

- The American Academy of Child & Adolescent Psychiatry–Resources for Families: aacap.org (click on Families & Youth)

- The Office of Disease Prevention and Health Promotion: heathfinder.gov

- US Department of Health and Human Services, Office on Women's Health: http://womenshealth.gov

- US Food and Drug Administration (for Women Consumers): fda.gov/ForConsumers/byAudience/ForWomen/default.htm

- The American Heart Association: americanheart.org

- The American Cancer Society: cancer.org

- National Cancer Institute: cancer.gov

- The American Diabetes Association: diabetes.org

- Substance Abuse and Mental Health Services Administration (SAMHSA): samhsa.gov/

- The National Library of Medicine: MedlinePlus.gov

- WebMD: webmd.com

- MedicineNet: medicinenet.com

- Family Doctor: familydoctor.org

- Net Wellness: netwellness.org

- eMedicine Health: emedicinehealth.com/

- Healthy Women: healthywomen.org

- Kids Health: kidshealth.org

- Teen Health: nlm.nih.gov/medlineplus/teenhealth.html

- Dr. Greene: drgreene.com

For access to citations for biomedical literature, visit: PubMed.gov

For your girls' library:

- *Will Puberty Last My Whole Life?* by Julie Metzger and Rob Lehman (Sasquatch Books, 2012)

- *It's Perfectly Normal: Changing Bodies, Growing Up, Sex, and Sexual Health* by Robie H. Harris (Candlewick Press, 2014)

- *It's So Amazing! A Book about Eggs, Sperm, Birth, Babies and Families* by Robie H. Harris (Candlewick Press, 2014)

- *Sex, Puberty and All That Stuff: A Guide to Growing Up* by Jacqui Bailey (Barron's Educational Series, 2004)

- *"What's Happening to Me?" A Guide to Puberty* by Peter Mayle (Lyle Stewart, 2000)

- *My Body, My Self for Girls* by Lynda and Area Madaras (Newmarket Press, 2007)

- *Period: A Girl's Guide to Menstruation with a Parents' Guide* by JoAnn Loulan et al. (Volcano Press, 2008)

- *The Care and Keeping of You: The Body Book for Younger Girls* by Valorie Schaefer (American Girl Library, 2012)

- *The Care and Keeping of You 2: The Body Book for Older Girls* by Cara Natterson (American Girl Library, 2013)

- *The Feelings Book: The Care and Keeping of Your Emotions Paperback* by Dr. Lynda Madison (American Girl Library, 2013)

- *The Period Book: Everything You Don't Want to Ask (But Need to Know)* by Karen Gravelle, Jennifer Gravelle and Debbie Palen (Walker Publishing, 2006)

- *What's Happening to My Body? Book for Girls* by Lynda Madaras, Area Madaras and Simon Sullivan (Newmarket Press, 2007)

- *Puberty Girl* by Shushann Movsessian (Allen & Unwin Pty., Limited, 2005)

- *The Girls Body Book: Everything You Need to Know for Growing Up YOU* by Kelli Dunham (Applesauce Press, 2013)

- *Ready, Set, Grow!: A What's Happening to My Body? Book for Younger Girls* by Lynda Madaras (William Morrow Paperbacks, 2003)

For your library:

- *Wise Minded Parenting: 7 Essentials for Raising Successful Tweens + Teens* by Laura S. Kastner (Parent Map, 2013)

- *Girls Will Be Girls: Raising Confident and Courageous Daughters* by Joann Deak (Hyperion, 2003)

- *Raising an Emotionally Intelligent Child, the Heart of Parenting* by John Gottman, Ph.D. (Simon and Schuster, 1998)

- *Talk to Me First: Everything You Need to Know to Become Your Kids' "Go-To" Person about Sex* by Deborah Roffman (Da Capo Lifelong Books, 2012)

- *Why Do They Act That Way? A Survival Guide to the Adolescent Brain for You and Your Teen* (revised and updated) by Dr. David Walsh Ph.D. (Atria Books, 2014)

- Bookmark the National Institute of Health's Web site at nih.gov. There, you'll find access to a library of topics and can further access the NIH's Institute of Mental Health where you'll find brain-related information. This is where you can find articles and research papers, for instance, on understanding the developing brain from birth through adulthood.

Programs, seminars, and workshops:

- We are most familiar with the following two programs on the West Coast. You can likely find one near you just by researching online and asking for referrals from friends, educators, or your child's pediatrician. This is a rapidly changing area with new programs cropping up in many communities across the country.

Great conversations:

- Julie Giesy Metzger, a registered nurse, and Dr. Robert Lehman, a pediatrician and adolescent medicine specialist, founded this Seattle-based program to "improve the conversations on puberty, sex, decision-making, and growing up." They offer classes and presentations to families, teens, and professionals. Learn more and access their resources at greatconversations.com.

For girls and their mothers:

- A Heart-to-Heart Talk on Growing Up: Stanford University's Children's Hospital has adopted Metzger and Lehman's "Great Conversations" program and similarly offers classes and seminars on subjects regarding puberty (as with the Seattle-based programs, seminars covering boys are also available). These programs are year round in the Bay Area. Learn more at stanfordchildrens.org/en/classes/community/heart-to-heart.

For information about boys:

Although this book focuses on girls, we thought it would be helpful to include some resources that discuss boys and their experience of growing up today. We realize that many of you may not only be in the company of girls, but boys, too. Many of the Web sites and programs already mentioned devote space to the subject of boys, but here are some additional books to check out:

- *The Boys Body Book: Everything You Need to Know for Growing Up YOU* by Kelli Dunham and Steve Björkman (Applesauce Press, 2013)

- *The American Medical Association's Boy's Guide to Becoming a Teen* by the AMA, Kate Gruenwald Pfeifer, and Amy B. Middleman (Jossey-Bass, 2006)

- *What's Going on Down There?: Answers to Questions Boys Find Hard to Ask* by Karen Gravelle, Nick Castro, Chava Castro, Robert Leighton, and Walker & Co (Walker Childrens, 1998)

- *My Body, My Self for Boys: Revised Edition* by Lynda Madaras and Area Madaras (William Morrow, 2007)

- *What's Happening to My Body? Book for Boys* by Lynda Madaras and Area Madaras (William Morrow, 2007)

- *The Body Book for Boys* by Rebecca Paley, Grace Norwich, and Jonathan Mar (Scholastic, 2010)

INDEX

Underscored references indicate tables or boxed text.

239